Stop Paddling
& Start Rocking
the Boat

Stop Paddling & Start Rocking the Boat

BUSINESS LESSONS FROM THE SCHOOL OF HARD KNOCKS

LOU PRITCHETT

Authors Choice Press
New York Lincoln Shanghai

Stop Paddling & Start Rocking the Boat
BUSINESS LESSONS FROM THE SCHOOL OF HARD KNOCKS

Authors Choice Press
an imprint of iUniverse, Inc.

iUniverse books may be ordered through booksellers or by contacting:

iUniverse
2021 Pine Lake Road, Suite 100
Lincoln, NE 68512
www.iuniverse.com
1-800-Authors (1-800-288-4677)

Originally published by HarperCollins Publishers, Inc.

FIRST EDITION
Designed by Caitlin Daniels

ISBN: 978-0-595-44501-1

Printed in the United States of America

This book is for the three most important people in my life, my wife, Barbara Burnette Pritchett, and our two sons, Bradley Louis Pritchett and Robert Joseph Pritchett.

Contents

Acknowledgments

For those of you who ever tried to write a book, you know that it is never done single-handedly. In fact, when I first started on this book's manuscript in 1990, I had written fewer than a thousand words when I began to call old friends and colleagues asking for their input and remembrances.

One very special friend I must single out is George Billingsley. George and I have been friends for almost fifty years, starting in the '40s when we were Tenderfoot Boy Scouts together at Camp Currier, Mississippi. George is the person who not only introduced me to Sam Walton but was the person who stood ready to help me, Sam, Wal-Mart, and Procter & Gamble over any hurdles during the formative years. For almost fifty years, I have asked George for help, advice, counsel, and support. He has always delivered and never once let me down. George Billingsley is that rare friend most of us only read or dream about. Thank you, George, for being there for half a century.

Others were wonderful in their responses, and each time I talked or received a letter or fax from them, I jotted down the name. When I wrote the last line of this book, I had a list of thirty people who had been willing to think, share, and tolerate me for five years. For these very special thirty, I thank you most sincerely and I hope that your collective contributions will in some way help the reader to decide to *Stop Paddling and Start Rocking the Boat.*

Listed below are the magnificent thirty in alphabetical order:

Samir Ayache, Geneva, Switzerland
Rodney Bell, New York, New York
George Billingsley, Bentonville, Arkansas
Jim Bradshaw, Hilton Head, South Carolina
Bill E. Burk, Memphis, Tennessee
Bill Burns, Cincinnati, Ohio
Dan Cope, Boca Raton, Florida
Harry "Chigger" Danciger, Memphis, Tennessee
Soli Dastur, University Park, Florida
Gene Ellerbee, Dallas, Texas
Paul Graf, Los Angeles, California
Bob Hayden, Manila, Philippines
Doris Holzheimer, Cincinnati, Ohio
Bob and Joyice Jones, Tampa, Florida
Jack Llewellyn, Atlanta, Georgia
Frank Maguire, Memphis, Tennessee
Bert Manlapit, Manila, Philippines
Jim McWhorter, Huntsville, Alabama
Tom Muccio, Fayetteville, Arkansas
John Perry, Cincinnati, Ohio
Earl Pool, Cincinnati, Ohio
Tom Quinn, Morris Plains, New Jersey
Joe Reynolds, Spring, Texas
Ed Rider, Cincinnati, Ohio
Jack Ruppert, Cincinnati, Ohio
Ed Sweeney, Crossville, Tennessee
Mary Teahan, Buenos Aires, Argentina
Dave Waters, Pawley's Island, South Carolina
Larry Wilson, Minneapolis, Minnesota
A. M. Wood, Dallas, Texas

I also want to offer a very special thanks to the editors and staff at HarperCollins Publishers. I knew I had made the major leagues when I met Publisher Adrian Zackheim in Harper's Manhattan offices, and I listened to his advice on the wild and woolly book business. I knew after that meeting I was dealing with real professional talent. Of course, I cannot say enough about Kirsten Sandberg, who took the manuscript, worked her magic and made it come alive. My copy editor, Michael O'Neal, deserves a very special thanks for the wonderful job he did in polishing and enhancing the flow. To all HarperCollins staff—thanks for the confidence and belief that I could do it.

Additionally, I would be remiss if I failed to recognize and thank my speaking and book agents, Bill Leigh of the Leigh Bureau and his colleague Les Tuerk. These two not only insisted that I write the book but kept rekindling the flame when I was about to let it go out. I'm most appreciative of their support, confidence, and friendship.

Finally a megaton thank-you to my writer colleague and friend, Bob Pack of Bethesda, Maryland. Bob, a lawyer, an investigative reporter, and an accomplished author with a string of successful books to his name, including *Speaking Out with Larry Speaks*, is the kind of person that everyone attempting to write a book should have the opportunity to work with. I say this because Bob has the almost uncanny ability to ask questions that beget more questions and to probe so deeply into the recesses of your mind that he enables you to retrieve thoughts, events, and learning you had forgotten you ever knew. Bob also has the persistence to force you to keep writing and keep thinking long after you think you can do no more. Finally, Bob's talent and ability to take forty years of a person's experience and put it into sequential order is a mind boggler. I owe more to Bob Pack than I will ever be able to repay. As they say in the Philippines, I have *utang na loob* (a lifelong debt of gratitude) with Bob Pack.

Lou Pritchett
Hilton Head Island, South Carolina
October 1995

Note to Readers: Here's Your Wake-up Call!

In 1989 I informed my friend Sam Walton that I had decided to retire after thirty-six years at Procter & Gamble, where I had advanced from sales rep in Tupelo, Mississippi, to vice-president in charge of sales—as well as prophet without portfolio, speaking out as a lonely voice in the wilderness and trying to rouse Procter & Gamble from what I saw as its mood of complacency.

Working together during the last half of the 1980s, Sam and I had conceived and established a revolutionary partnering relationship between Procter & Gamble and Wal-Mart. Upon hearing my news, Sam said to me, "Lou, I hope you will continue to be out there, giving wake-up calls to America. Because we need it. If we fail to drive costs out of our systems, we're all going to wind up selling hamburgers to each other."

Shortly after I retired, I attended a social function on Hilton Head Island, South Carolina, where I live now. Another recently retired corporate officer started talking to me about our mutual experiences in business. He asked me when I would be returning to P&G's corporate headquarters for my "annual debriefing." Annual debriefing? What did he mean? He explained that his former employer sends every retired officer a plane ticket back to company headquarters each year during the first three years of retirement. During these sessions the retirees participate in focus groups. They discuss their insights into such issues as the economy, politics, domestic and global business changes, competitors, and how their products are viewed.

They also talk about their former company's current strategy, marketing plans, and management's handling of business.

I was stunned—what a marvelous idea! Why doesn't every company do this? Then reality set in: There simply is no institutional memory. Most institutions, especially in business, live for the day, the quarter, the year, and the blessing of almighty Wall Street. This obsession with the short term allows few, if any, of us to take time or make an effort to step back and consider our place and our company's place in the world, let alone capitalize on the rich resource of our experienced senior people while they are still employed or immediately after they retire.

The more I pondered this subject, the more I realized the tremendous waste in failing to capture this body of knowledge from longtime veteran employees. What a gold mine of learning, if we recorded and shared the experiences of everyone throughout the rank and file! Young people at the entry stage could be given the collective wisdom of their predecessors.

I realized that I might not reform corporate America all by myself, but I could at least take that critical first step by writing and offering my own personal business experiences to anyone who wanted to listen—and save themselves a lot of grief down the road. *Stop Paddling and Start Rocking the Boat* has been building up in me for many years. My files are jammed with memos I wrote as long ago as the late 1960s and early 1970s, outlines of my ideas for improving corporations and managers and employees and people in general.

What follows is your wake-up call, just like Sam Walton said.

Stop Paddling & Start Rocking the Boat

"In times of accelerated change, Lou Pritchett relates how and why we all need to rock the boat."
—J. D. Power III, President, J. D. Power and Associates

"Thirty minutes with Lou, and you are ready to go out and slay dragons, reorganize companies, and completely redefine the idea of working with customers. That's Lou Pritchett. . . . Lou is pointing the way to the future, to relationships that go beyond solving problems with products and services, that result in businesses coming together in more meaningful ways."
—Larry Wilson, author of *Stop Selling, Start Partnering*

1
Introduction:
Take It from the Old Soap Salesman

Doing It *with* Your Customers and Everyone Else,
Instead of Doing It *to* Them.

Once upon a time, let's say it was in the early 1950s, there was this hard-charging young Turk Procter & Gamble sales rep who would do anything to make the sale. Let's call him Lou Pritchett.

That take-no-prisoners, hardball-playing SOB had a lot of success. But after he evolved into someone whose philosophy became "A Love Affair with Your Customers," he had even more success—much, much more. I'm not talking about mouthing the word "love," which is often overused by today's "touchy-feely" self-styled "gurus." No, what I'm describing is a genuine love affair with your customers, with your suppliers, with your own employees. As the education of Lou Pritchett progressed—and it was learned on the job, in the School of Hard Knocks, rather than in any graduate school of business—I came to understand that the way to succeed in both business and in life is to do it *with* other people instead of doing it *to* others. As I became enlightened, I realized that instead of trying to win at all costs, instead of always looking out for Number One, instead of letting the end justify the means, you can make the people you come into contact with happy and still succeed. In fact, the happier you make them, the more you will succeed. And along the way I discovered that making other folks happy makes Lou Pritchett happy, too.

Yes, a love affair with the customer and with everyone else is what I discovered is important. And not just a love affair, but a *torrid* love affair. By love affair, I don't mean asking them for a date; I mean asking them to in effect marry you. It's called part-nering—partnering between sellers and buyers, partnering between manufacturers and suppliers, partnering between management and employees. Wherever I have found partnering practiced, the way it is between Wal-Mart and Procter & Gamble, that's where I have found success achieved. Let part-nering work for you, as it has for me. Let me teach you a corol-lary of partnering, which applies specifically to selling: Selling is marketing—marketing yourself as well as your products.

This book is about the education of a salesperson and a busi-nessperson named Lou Pritchett. How I got from where I was to where I am. How I went from being somewhat of an SOB to being a genuine people-person. How you can do the same. Because in the last half of the 1990s and into the twenty-first century, the one thing that will separate the top-performing businesses and businesspeople from all others will be their abil-ity to create and sustain genuine love affairs with their cus-tomers, their suppliers, and their fellow employees.

You Can Set Your Mind to Do Anything You Want, and I'm Going to Show You How.

During my career with one of the largest and most successful corporations in the world, Procter & Gamble, I was promoted nine times altogether, an average of once every four years. After each and every promotion, I would find a private corner—my car, my bedroom, the backyard—and stand by myself for a few min-utes and thank my lucky stars for the good fortune that had just befallen me. It was as though every time I had just about mastered my present job, P&G's powers that be somehow found out and immediately boosted me on up the ladder. I considered myself the luckiest fellow in the world to work for a company like that.

In those private, personal moments of triumph, I always reflected back to where I came from: a tiny house at 1528 Leland Street in the Cow Hollow section of south Memphis. "Wow," I would say to myself, "if only the boys could see me now!" And I thought about my years at little Memphis State College, and again exclaimed, "Wow, I wish the guys and girls could see me now!" I went through this same ritual every single time I was promoted. It was as if this was my good-luck mantra, and if I failed to do it, the promotions might stop.

I've been retired from Procter & Gamble since 1989, but hardly a week goes by that I still don't wonder in amazement how that skinny, average kid from south Memphis with little money, one who lost his father as a teenager and who went to the local college that was far from being on the cutting edge of education—how that kid wound up as a corporate officer of the nineteenth largest company in the *Fortune* 500.

How did I do it? I ask myself. My conclusion is that if I could do it, anyone can, provided they have the right influences, the right people in their corner, and, perhaps, the right advice.

This Is Lou Pritchett.

Allow me to begin by explaining to you what I am *not*. I am not a psychologist, or a behaviorist, or a human resource guru, or a personnel expert. Most of all, I am not a business school professor. In fact, I attended what was then a small state teachers school, Memphis State College, during the late 1940s and early 1950s. I'm definitely not qualified to tell you what you did or did not learn at the Harvard Business School or any other B-school, because I never took a single business school course. If I'm on the faculty of any school, you might say it's the School of Hard Knocks.

So, what—and who—am I, Lou Pritchett? I am a realist, a critic, a coach, and, most of all, a change agent. Since my retirement from P&G, I've traveled all over the United States, and, for that matter, around the world, speaking to *Fortune* 500 companies and other organizations about business, about management, and about sales. Sales was my specialty at Procter & Gamble, but for four years I was president and general manager of Procter's subsidiary in the Philippines, a business with revenues of over $100 million a year and a microcosm of the parent company. I have had the opportunity to absorb a wealth of knowledge about every aspect of business, especially management, in addition to sales.

I think, I hope, I believe, that sharing with you what I've learned over the course of the last forty odd years will help you and your company—whether you're the CEO or down at the bottom of the heap, whether your company is dominant in its field or just struggling for survival—to improve, to succeed, and to prosper.

Oh, by the way, please think of me as "Lou." My father was "Mr. Pritchett." A failing of many business executives is to demand that their employees address them as "Mister" and "Sir." I have always encouraged—make that required—everyone who worked for me to call me "Lou" instead of "Mr. Pritchett." Being on a first-name basis with your subordinates—as well as with those above you in the corporate structure—is another way of establishing that your company believes that all employees are created equal. Some of America's best companies, including Mars, the candy manufacturer, and Disney, have this policy. Yours should, too.

The things I talk about, I talk about from experience. I'm a man of practice, not theory. The way I always describe myself is as a guy who carried the bag, as The Old Soap Salesman. When CEOs introduce me before I give my talks, they say, "Well, here's a guy who actually carried a bag for thirty-six years; he really did it. Lou Pritchett is not an academician or a theoretician or a writer; he's a guy who has actually been out there in the trenches." That's right, I went from store to store—fifteen stores in a typical day—calling on customers and selling them soap and shortening and other Procter & Gamble products.

I enjoy being identified as an Old Soap Salesman because I know my limits, I know where I came from. People understand that I'm just a regular guy, an average guy, not a guy who's trying to show off, and absolutely not some pompous ass. A soap salesman is about as basic as you can get, but, at the same time, truthful and honest. I'm a classic example of a guy who started carrying the bag in the field, survived, and rose to become a corporate officer. I didn't do it through nepotism or favoritism but simply through what's always been so important in business—commitment to the job, focus, and hard work; plus, naturally, to some extent, just being in the right place at the right time. Believe me, there was no genius involved. I'm just an average guy like all the rest of you men and women, a guy who was able to demonstrate to the company that I had some talents that it needed, and a guy who has something to offer to other average people like myself. In other words, if Lou Pritchett can make it, so can you.

When I say that I'm average and that I always try to teach people that a common person with average intelligence can do almost anything that needs to be done if he or she has the right attitude, I may even be giving myself a little bit too much credit. In some ways, I was below average. When I was an ROTC officer in high school I was about four feet nine, before I grew to my current five feet, eleven inches; in fact, I was so short that I always had to keep my hand on my sword hilt to keep it from dragging on the ground. I knew that, physically, there was no way I could be the star of the football team, but I vowed, "I'm going to find something I can excel in." Military training was it. And, even though I was so short, I worked hard, made an all-out commitment, and wound up being chosen to lead our precision drill platoon as we marched down Main Street in Memphis in all the holiday parades.

When I joined Procter & Gamble straight out of Memphis State in 1953, those who had not gone to Ivy League colleges or to the Harvard Business School were a definite minority. And here I was, a guy from little Memphis State College, which cost $28 a quarter to attend. My whole attitude was that nothing is impossible if you're willing to pay the price. Paying the price means learning, learning, learning all the time, zeroing in on your weaknesses and trying to correct them, and, most important, capitalizing on your strengths. Use what you have, don't cry about what you don't have. I *never* felt sorry for myself or moaned that I was handicapped by my background or worried about not having an MBA. Instead, I concentrated on what I *do* have, which is an innate ability to get along with people, to communicate with people, to get people to do what I want them to do, and to get them to enjoy it in the process. That's why I feel you can do anything you set your mind to. When I took over Procter & Gamble's operations in the Philippines in 1981, I made up my mind that I was going to change the way that enterprise interacted with its customers. My experience in Manila, which I'll describe at some length later on, proved, as I've been arguing for most of my life, that one person *can* make a difference! I guarantee you, the barrier to what you can and cannot do is all self-imposed. It's like high jumping. If you put the bar at four feet or five feet and say to yourself, "I'll never clear it," chances are you'll never clear it. But I maintain that the guy who puts the pole at eight feet and says, "God damn it! I'm going to do this someway, somehow," he may never make it, but I guarantee you he'll jump higher than the guy who sets the pole at four feet. Most successes and failures in life depend on where you set the bar.

But most of us, unfortunately, put limitations on ourselves. Often, that makes us our own worst enemy. A lot of times you'll find that you can do even the things you think you can't do if you're able to open your mind and remove that negative.

Another reason I was successful is that from the day I started working until the day I retired from Procter & Gamble (and now in the lecturing and consulting work I do, as well) I have absolutely loved what I was doing. At P&G, I thought I was really helping my customers be better at their business. And, number two, I honestly believed I was helping the people who worked with me grow and become everything they could become. I knew that I was selling quality products and that I was with the crème de la crème of the corporate world, and I absolutely loved it for damn near forty years. As I like to say, I loved my work so much that every night I would come home and spike my briefcase on the living room floor, just like a guy spiking the ball after he scores a touchdown. I can tell you, I wore out a lot of briefcases doing that.

Most weekends, I used to go camping or waterskiing with my best friend, A. C. Rolen. Along about the middle of Sunday afternoon he'd say, "Uh-oh, it's time for Lou to start revving up!" Because I would start getting ready to go out there Monday morning and hit the street running. So one of my lessons is, do what I did—make your work be fun instead of a chore—and see how much pleasure you can have.

Be a Victor *over* the System—Not a Victim *of* the System.

During my last few years at Procter & Gamble, I continually asked my friend and mentor, Tom Laco, then the vice-chairman of the P&G board, "Why do so few of us see that the global marketing environment is changing at light speed, and why aren't we taking steps to change our very culture, let alone our organizational structure? Unless we do this, our successes during the twenty-first century will pale by comparison with our successes over the last fifty years of the twentieth." Neither Tom Laco nor I ever came up with a satisfactory answer.

During my first few years of retirement, the question, "If I had to live my business career all over again, what would I do differently?" kept surfacing. At that point I was averaging almost one speech a week to various *Fortune* 500 companies and experiencing very enthusiastic responses. More and more people in my audiences kept asking for copies of my remarks, or suggesting that I write a paper on my experiences and distribute it at the conclusion of my presentation. After discussing this with my wife, Barbara, and several close friends, I realized that simply addressing the issue of what I would have done differently might not be all that instructive in and of itself. All of us concluded that a lot more was involved. As a result of this input, I took a different tack. Instead of focusing on what I would have done differently, I vowed to write about some of the things I learned during my long career that have application to men and women in today's new information-driven environment. It became clear that what I really wanted to accomplish was to help both the young men and women who are now entering the workforce and the experienced people who have been in the system for a while to realize that they can either be a victim or a victor in the system—the choice is really up to them.

What this book contains is the wisdom that comes only from the hands-on experience of being on the job, of working with fellow employees and with customers, of celebrating the successes and suffering the defeats and disappointments that are part of the territory. Everything I learned during my thirty-six years at P&G came one hour, one day, and one week at a time. There were few guideposts, few maps, and practically no correctional warnings along the way. It was a period of trial and error, of profiting from your mistakes and growing in the process. You might call it "learning by osmosis"; the better you were at absorbing everything you saw, touched, tasted, felt, and experienced, the greater your chances of moving up the corporate ladder. Those who absorbed the most the fastest while learning from their mistakes succeeded. Those who did not fare well in an "osmosis" learning environment and repeated the same mistakes fell by the wayside.

Unfortunately, this learning process takes a full career. The process never ends, and when you are finally at the peak of your game, you find that it's almost time to receive your gold watch. Since there is no institutional memory or system for capturing this valuable knowledge base, all of it is lost when senior and experienced people in the organization leave the company through retirement. They walk out the door with their thirty- to forty-year knowledge base, leaving a huge learning void for those who follow. This is my attempt to fill that void by capturing in writing some of my experiences and the wisdom gained during a career that spanned most of four decades. What I want to do is go back into the archives, if you will, and take the stories like mine from the 1960s and 1970s and 1980s, and see what some of us have learned and how we can apply it to the future. I'm a firm believer, you see, in the old adage that those who forget history are doomed to repeat it.

Here's What I'm Driving At.

It's my hope that this guide will serve six basic purposes:

First, to help all who work in any type of system (commercial, educational, institutional, governmental, profit or non-profit) to realize that they are important, powerful, and vital to the organization's success.

Second, so that everyone may learn that commonsense habits and practices, things that most of us know intuitively, can add immeasurable value to the organization's effort.

Third, to have every reader of this book say to themselves once they've finished, "I can control my destiny. It is up to me and me alone whether I become a victim of the system or a victor over it."

Fourth, to encourage the reader to commit to a proactive role in improving his or her company, and at the same time to convince management that the corporation of the future must be driven by empowered individuals, working together in teams and enabled by information technology.

Fifth, to share with everyone who works for a living, from entry level to CEO, some lessons and guidelines in living, learning, and leading. It is my hope that both my victories and my defeats will in some way educate, motivate, and enlighten.

Sixth, to remind people that the name of the game in both business and in life is the same: It isn't to get ahead of others, it's to get ahead of yourself—that is, to improve yourself. As I will discuss at length later on, this idea, ingrained in me from my Boy Scout days, means to play the course instead of the competition. Do *your* best; don't worry about how others are doing, and let the chips fall where they may.

Obviously, each company can have just one CEO out of tens or hundreds or thousands of workers. You don't have to be the CEO. That's fine. But you *can* do your best and use all your talents. Keep these words in mind: "I am unique! My ideas count! I can make a difference! If Pritchett could do it, so can I!"

Over the years, scores of people have come up to me after my speeches and said to me, "Lou, you have made me think. You have challenged me. You have changed my life. You did exactly what I believe needs to be done in my company."

That's the message of this book. Think! Do! Take my experiences and use them to help yourself get ahead. And, while you're doing it, have fun, too.

After reading the text of several of my speeches, Sam Walton wrote me that he was placing my speeches in a separate file, "and when I am asked to make a talk on management, salesmanship, or building relations with companies or people, I will know where to go for my information."

That's what I'm all about, and that's what this book is all about: management, salesmanship, and building better relations among companies and among individuals. I hope that my book will teach you many valuable lessons in each of these fields and that while you're reading it, you'll have some fun, too. Learning and improving and succeeding and enjoying yourself at the same time—in my opinion, those are the activities that life should be all about.

2
Easy Lessons from
the School of Hard Knocks

You're No Einstein? What a Coincidence—Neither Am I.

There's an old saying, "What was so great about the Great Depression?" Well, nothing at all, if you want to know the truth. I was a depression baby, born in Memphis in 1931, and I'm here to tell you that the depression was no fun.

Not that I realized at the time that my family and I were "poor," even though we would have been looking *up* at the so-called poverty line if it had existed in those days. I only learned many years later that we were "deprived" because our house had only six hundred square feet of living space, our clothes were mended over and over and rarely replaced, our "personal vehicle" was a municipal streetcar, and our summer vacations were day-trips to the zoo via that streetcar.

My father was in the belting business, back in the days when most machines were powered by a main drive, and leather belts off the main drive ran everything from pencil sharpeners to huge turbines. My dad worked for a small company that installed and serviced these leather belts for a number of other firms, including Buckeye, a subsidiary of Procter & Gamble that owned and operated several cottonseed oil mills in Tennessee, Arkansas, and Mississippi. So my connection to Procter is literally lifelong.

Back there on the south side of Memphis, my father's salary provided us with all of the necessities, but few of the luxuries. There never was any money to spare. I never went hungry. I never went cold. I never went without a coat. But it was tight for me and my family, just like it was for most people during the 1930s. Our part of south Memphis wasn't what you'd call the slums; more like the other side of the tracks. It certainly wasn't the high-rent district. We even had a cow of our own. Where we lived wasn't exactly a farming area, but there were open fields all around and we'd take the cow out in the field and chain it where it could graze. We also had a dog named Pooch, who, every year, regular as clockwork, delivered five or six new puppies for us to play with.

The outbreak of World War II returned the country to a wartime prosperity and the Pritchetts, like most Americans, were better off financially as a result. But the war also brought two tragedies to my family, ones that would affect the future course of my life. My big brother Joe, who was fourteen years older than me, was a member of the army's famous 531st Engineer Shore Regiment. He survived landings in North Africa, Sicily, Italy, and at Normandy, where he landed on Utah Beach with the first wave at six-thirty on D day. But his luck ran out less than three weeks later, while he was involved in a mine-clearing operation. One of the mines exploded and killed him. (Years later I visited Utah Beach and discovered that his unit had named a road after him there, in gratitude for his sacrifice.) After Joe was killed, my father lost interest in life, and he died the following year, when I was thirteen. He wasn't in good health, and his trade, the belting business, was going the way of gaslights, because single-drive engines were becoming obsolete. But, whatever they wrote on my father's death certificate, I know what really killed him: a broken heart caused by my brother's death in France.

My First Role Model.

My father's death left my mother; my sister, Jeane, who is a couple of years older than I am; and me on our own. All three of us had to go to work so that we could support ourselves. My mother and my sister went to work at Goldsmith's Department Store in Memphis, selling women's clothing. As for me, I started working right then, at the age of thirteen, in retail—I became a part-time clerk in a little grocery store in south Memphis. From then on, the work ethic and retailing have played important parts in my life.

It may sound corny to anyone under thirty-five, but one of the big turning points in my life was joining the Boy Scouts in 1944, when I was twelve years old. Not only for what I learned, but because some forty years later, scouting would lead me to Sam Walton, as I will explain later. If I turned out worth a damn, the credit goes to my mother and to scouting and to one person from scouting in particular, my scoutmaster, Robert L. "Buddy" Irwin Jr.

When I joined the Boy Scouts, I doubt if I could spell role model, and I'm sure I couldn't explain what the term meant. But I was one of hundreds of young boys who had the great good fortune to live, work, play, and mature under the best role model in the world—Buddy Irwin. Buddy, a contractor and builder some twenty years older than me, was a legend in the Cow Hollow section of south Memphis where he spent most of his life. He was a barrel-chested man about five feet nine inches tall and 170 pounds, built like a football running back. I remember that even in his mid-sixties, he could still beat most people in arm wrestling. Buddy was the kind of man who helped neighbors repair their houses when they needed repairing, and, because he was relatively well off and one of the few people in Cow Hollow who owned a vehicle (in his case, a pickup truck), would drive the sick to the doctor's office (this was particularly important because most of us had to rely on the streetcar).

I belonged to Buddy's Troop 97 for ten years, until I went to work for P&G and got married. My friends and I spent many days and nights camping with Buddy in Tennessee, Mississippi, and Arkansas. In the early days we rode in the back of his pickup truck through rain, snow, and heat, but I can't recall anyone ever complaining. To ride with Buddy in that truck, especially up in the cab, as I was allowed to do after I became a senior patrol leader, was the equivalent of riding on *Air Force One*.

Buddy taught me how to swim, how to fish, how to build a fire, how to pitch a tent, how to cook over an open fire, how to paddle a canoe. In fact, I picked the title of this book in part as a tribute to him. He even taught me how to drive a car. He also taught me respect for other people and for authority. From him

I learned that the greatest accomplishment in life is not to get ahead of others but to get ahead of one's self—playing the course instead of the competition, which I will elaborate on later. Buddy even introduced me to archaeology, which became a lifelong avocation of mine—he took me on field trips looking for arrowheads around Memphis. He also taught me respect for this country, for the flag, and for all those before us who had paid a price to provide all the opportunities that lay before us. I will never forget the way he described my brother's death on the beach at Normandy: "Joe gave up all his tomorrows so that others could have theirs."

When I was a tiny, scrawny thirteen-year-old, Buddy told me that I had to learn to swim if I ever wanted to be waterfront director at one of the Boy Scout camps. I was terrified of the water, and learning how to swim seemed impossible, even though one of my dreams was to be waterfront director. Buddy insisted that I could learn, and he arranged to teach me in the private pool of one of his customers. This one-on-one instruction gave me room to struggle, fail at first, break down in tears, and complain about how difficult it was, all without being observed by my peers. Four years later, at the National Aquatic School at Fort Jackson, South Carolina, I placed second among 110 young men in canoeing at a ten-day course on swimming, lifesaving, rowing, and canoeing taught by former members of the navy and marine Underwater Demolition Teams, better known as frogmen. The following year I succeeded my lifelong friend George Billingsley—the man who later introduced me to Sam Walton—as waterfront director at Boy Scout Kamp Kia Kima in Hardy, Arkansas—the very place where Sam Walton and I would go canoeing down the river nearly forty years later.

One other Buddy story stands out in my memory. In 1950, while I was waterfront director, I spent so much time in the river teaching other young boys to swim and canoe that I developed a serious ear infection. Neither the camp medics nor the local doctor could cure me, so I called Buddy in Memphis. He drove the 150 miles from Memphis overnight, loaded me into his pickup, and delivered me directly to Baptist Hospital in Memphis. I spent a day there, and then Buddy picked me up again and drove me back to camp. Then, as now, there were no expressways, and Buddy made two round-trips totaling six hundred miles. I offered to pay him out of my meager savings from selling shoes in a men's store, but he refused. At the time I thought he was giving me special treatment, but I later learned that Buddy did this kind of favor for any of his boys who needed help.

Buddy was a scoutmaster for some fifty years until his death in 1992. He truly was my surrogate father; I called him "Dad" for the rest of his life, and he was one of the two best men at my wedding, while I was one of the six pallbearers from Troop Ole 97 at his funeral three years ago.

With my mother and my sister out working, I was home a lot of the time. I was a rambunctious teenager, always looking to get into mischief. But scouting saved me from all that. A boy without a father really needs a lot of guidance, direction, and control. Losing my father when I was so young and having Buddy and scouting as an organizational, family kind of structure around me was where I learned to work with people, to tolerate different points of view, and to assume various leadership roles—Eagle Scout, patrol leader. I was looked up to as the leader, in scouting as well as in high school and college. I learned all about leadership in scouting's institutional environment.

Then, when I joined Procter & Gamble, I found the same sort of environment. I was very, very comfortable in it and very well prepared for it. I'm the kind of guy who needs walls and parameters. I need to know, "Hey, you walk twenty feet this way and you're going to hit a wall."

Please Don't Step on My Blue Suede Shoes, I'm Just Trying to Get My Foot in the Door.

I graduated from Memphis State in 1953 with a degree in social sciences—geography and history—which was useless for anything except teaching. I knew that Procter & Gamble owned Buckeye, the company my father had been associated with for years. Plus, my mother was a die-hard fan of *Ma Perkins,* a radio soap opera that was sponsored by Oxydol detergent, a Procter brand. So we were a real Procter-Buckeye family.

At my mother's urging—and it seemed logical enough to me—I went out to the Buckeye plant, where a personnel man named Dave Dunlevy interviewed me and gave me some tests. Instead of offering me a job, Mr. Dunlevy finally said to me, "Son, if I've ever seen anyone in all my years who was cut out to be a salesman, it's you. I'm going to send you downtown to the Procter & Gamble district office and let you talk with S. G. Collins," the district manager. In that era, district offices were fiefdoms. Those were the days just before Madison Avenue and the advertising departments began calling most of the shots at companies like Procter. The sales department was much more important back then while television was still in its infancy, and S. G. Collins, better known as "Red," ran the place as his personal fiefdom; he truly had an iron hand. He was a hard-drinking, hard-charging, hard-cursing stereotype of a district manager of that era. Well, I walked in, wearing my standard outfit that I had worn all the time I was selling shoes at a Bond's store in downtown Memphis to put myself through college—a maroon corduroy sport coat, a tie of indeterminate color, gray pants, and blue suede shoes. (Carl Perkins and Elvis didn't just happen to sing that song by accident; that's what we all wore down there.) Not to mention that I had a crew cut and had used peroxide to turn my color into a few shades of blond; putting peroxide on your hair in those days was kind of like wearing an earring is today. As you can imagine, I was quite a sight. Collins's door was closed, but his secretary took one look at me and told me that Mr. Collins was out of town. She did have me take two personnel tests that had been designed by P&G's own psychologists. One test measured your management, analysis, and reasoning skills, and a second evaluated your aptitude for sales. Each test consisted of about fifty questions on such subjects as personality, logic, mathematics and general knowledge. I scored a perfect 10 on both, which wasn't all that extraordinary, I discovered later.

I hadn't even had a job interview with anyone, and this secretary thanked me and told me they would call me if they had any openings. I took the elevator down to the first floor and started walking to the bus stop to catch the bus home, when all of a sudden the secretary comes running after me, perspiring like mad and yelling, "Mr. Pritchett, Mr. Pritchett, come back! I'm glad I caught you. We didn't know it, but Mr. Collins *is* in. And he wants to see you. Will you please come back upstairs?" I went back up to see Collins and he hired me as a sales representative on the spot. I later found out he wasn't about to hire me because he didn't have any openings. Back in those days, P&G Sales didn't recruit at small colleges and never in advance of a specific opening. They recruited only as a reactive thing when they actually had a vacancy. As it happened, while I was leaving Red Collins's office and heading home, he was fielding a call from Grady Collins (no relation), the P&G manager for the state of Mississippi. Grady Collins had just had his salesman in Tupelo resign, and when Red hung up the phone, his secretary told him that a young man had just been in to apply for a job and that she had turned me away. Red Collins asked her how I had done on the test, and she told him I had scored a double 10. "Go find him!" Collins bellowed, and she did. And that's how I got hired by Procter & Gamble.

I guess I should thank my lucky stars that P&G, like most companies, did not prerecruit in those days and that I just happened to walk in the day someone else quit. No telling where I would have wound up otherwise.

"Hail to the Chief"—and Hell from the Boss.

I spent one day in the Memphis office reading the sales manuals and all kinds of other Procter literature, and then the next day Red Collins gave me a ticket and put me on the bus to Tupelo, Mississippi. There, Grady Collins was waiting for me. A homegrown product who used to say he had grown up so far out in the country in Mississippi that he couldn't even hear the train whistle, Grady had gone on to navy flight school during World War II. I stepped off the bus, wearing white bucks, sporting a flat-top haircut, and looking like the cheerleader I had been in college. Grady looked at me, and it must have been like a drill instructor who says to himself when the recruits step off the bus at boot camp, "Boy, do I have some work to do!"

From my standpoint, the highlight of my first day in Tupelo was when Grady handed me the keys to a company car, the blue-gray 1952 Chevy that my predecessor as sales rep in that area had driven. Even though I didn't own it, that was the first car that had ever belonged to me. In fact, Barbara and I took our honeymoon in it after we got married a year and a half later. The car had a fourteen-inch decal of the old P&G symbol with the man in the moon on the door and a four-inch "No Riders" sticker on the right side of the windshield; who needed anything tacky like tin cans attached to the rear bumper of the car after our wedding, when the car came equipped with decorations like that?

Grady's getting me out of those white bucks and making me grow some hair, plus teaching me the tricks of the sales trade, became sort of a legend inside the company, and it grew as the years went by. Fortunately, I had an aptitude for my job—then, as now, I absolutely loved meeting people, which is the first requirement for selling. Under the tutelage of Grady Collins, I sold a lot of soap and other Procter & Gamble products, which marked me as a comer.

After I had been working out of Tupelo for a little over a year, two top executives of Procter—Jack Hanley and Mark Upson—flew down on the company DC-3 to look me over. Red Collins drove down from Memphis for the occasion. I knew that their visit meant I was being considered for promotion, so I went all out to impress them.

Now, having two bigwigs come all the way from Cincinnati was a pretty big deal in Tupelo in the mid-fifties. Having been a cheerleader in college, I was oriented toward rah-rah and everything, and it was natural for me to line up the Tupelo High School band to be at the airport when Hanley and Upson arrived. As Hanley and Upson walked down the steps from the plane, the band broke into a rousing rendition of "Hail to the Chief." I had also arranged for the local newspaper to send a photographer and run a picture in the paper. Well, this particular photographer was very demanding. In those days, practically all men wore hats, and this picture-taker from the small-town newspaper was ordering these bigshots around: "You, the short one [Upson], put your hat on. You, the tall one [Hanley], take your hat off. And you, the other one [Collins], move over there." It was like the Three Stooges there for a while, with guys taking their hats off and putting them on and moving around under the wing of the plane so you could see the company logo in the pictures, and the band was playing "Hail to the Chief" the whole time. And I was patting myself on the back all the while for how well this was working out.

Wanting to put my best foot forward, I had planned a route that would take us to my best customers and show Hanley and Upson what a bright young man I was. After all, you don't show off your garage, you show off your living room. As I started to drive out of the airport, Hanley ordered me to turn left.

"I need to turn right to go to the stores I want to show you," I protested.

"I said, 'Turn left,'" Hanley insisted.

So I turned left. We went into the first store we came to; it was okay, but it wasn't one of the stores I had primed for the visit. And things went downhill from there.

Hanley started asking me about market share. I had no training in numbers, and I started rattling off these numbers that added up to about 143 percent of market share. Hanley had to be thinking to himself, "What the hell have we got here?" As the day wore on, with seconds passing like hours, Hanley took me apart bit by bit. I mean, he cut me to ribbons. I have seldom cried in my life, but I came close to it that day. It wasn't so much that I just knew I was going to lose my job, it was the embarrassment of absolutely being humiliated in the presence of a very bright man. I think he had a degree in chemical engineering and one from the Harvard Business School as well. He was definitely a big hitter.

At last, the time came for me to drive Hanley and Upson back to the airport for their flight home. To add insult to injury, it had poured much of the day, and now it was practically raining sideways.

By the time we reached the airport it *was* raining sideways. I was trying to get as close to the plane as I could, and when I was about a hundred yards away, I ran my two right wheels off the pavement and into the soft, mushy ground and got stuck. Mr. Upson hadn't said too much all day, but now he spoke up: "Well, this seems to be your first management problem, young man. What do you suggest we do?"

"That's easy, sir," I answered. "Everybody get out and push." All of us did get out and push. By the time Hanley and Upson got on the plane, they were wet and their nice dress shoes were muddy. Red Collins and I said good-bye to them and got back in the car, and Collins said to me, "Let's just sit here awhile and watch them take off." The pilot started the engines and the plane came rolling down the runway in that storm, and Collins looked over at me and nudged me and said, "Wave like your life depended on it, you son of a bitch! Because the moment that plane is in the air, I'm going to kill you!"

And he just about did. We went out to dinner, and the rest of that night Red Collins lectured me on how stupid I was, kept telling me that I didn't know the first goddamned thing about business. I mean, he took me apart, piece by piece. It was the greatest lesson of my life, because until then I thought I was invincible. I was a real bigshot. I had never known anything in life, in scouting, in school, in business, but success. I didn't even know how to spell "defeat." But that day I hit the wall. This was really my first lesson in humility. It was the best lesson I ever got taught. And I have never forgotten it.

But that night, after Red got finished reading me the riot act, he promoted me. I guess he and the others must have already made the decision and must have seen something in me above and beyond my performance that day, something that suggested I must have *something* to offer. Collins later told me that he felt, "This can be one of the great challenges of my life, to see if this son of a bitch can be molded into anything." And I think he and Hanley and Upson must have seen that at least I was a guy who had a lot of creativity, what with the band and the pictures and everything. I think Hanley saw a fellow free spirit, like he was. (Hanley later left Procter and became president of Monsanto. He's been retired for years, but at Monsanto he's still a god to this day. He lives in south Florida now, and he's told me that he has repeated the Tupelo story over and over, especially the part about the band and "Hail to the Chief.")

Skip ahead five years. Had I learned anything about entertaining the top brass? Judge for yourself.

From Memphis I moved on to Columbus, Ohio, as unit manager. Columbus was considered a very important test market for P&G products because it was just the right size, was a well-contained television market, and had the right demographic mix. That combination gave young sales managers like me a great opportunity for exposure to upper management.

In 1959 I received word that our chief executive, Howard Morgens, accompanied by vice-president Jack Hanley and Central Division sales manager Brad Butler, was coming over to spend half a day inspecting me and my territory. You didn't have to be a genius to figure out what their visit meant: I was being "looked at" for a big promotion.

For days before their visit, I studied every number and factoid I could think of that might impress them. I was truly primed. (Incidentally, I always found that these prep sessions made me much sharper at my job. Later in my career I sometimes announced a visit to the field to work with a sharp young manager whom I felt might be getting a bit stale or jaded. My announcements invariably tended to send a shot of adrenaline through the person I wanted to motivate.)

Mr. Morgens and his party were due to arrive at the Columbus airport at noon. As was customary, I got to the airport at eleven o'clock. And waited. And waited. Noon came and went. One o'clock passed. Finally, at twenty after one, the DC-3 carrying Morgens, Hanley, and Butler landed and taxied up to the private plane terminal. I drove out onto the tarmac and greeted Morgens and the other two executives this way: "You fellows are almost an hour and a half late! What happened?"

I was still in my twenties, had been with the company only six years, and thought that truth was the best policy. From the looks on my visitors' faces, I sensed immediately that this was not the kind of truth they wanted to hear.

Hanley and Butler spent the next six months on my case, making sure that such a faux pas would never be repeated. As the years passed, I finally succeeded in mastering the unwritten corporate rules, which had somehow eluded me at Memphis State.

My Boss Swore, "I'm Going to Make Something Out of You, Even if It Kills Me"—and, Sure Enough, It Did!

Fifteen months after I left Memphis for Tupelo, I was transferred back to Memphis as "office head salesman" there under

Red Collins. I had been in Memphis about a month when Red wrote me a letter I have kept all these years. It was typed on onionskin paper, and Red's signature was in green ink—he signed it right after writing, "I am going to train you if it kills me, and I am not going to use kid gloves." A lesser manager than Red Collins would have said, "Why should I care about this kid?" Here was a manager who was interested in an individual as an individual. Here was a manager who saw in a person a skill, a talent, perhaps an ability to do more. Here was a guy who said, "I'm going to take the time, I'm going to make the effort, to try to coach, to try to teach, and I'm not going to use kid gloves." We need a lot more managers like Red in business today.

Little did Red know how soon his prediction would come true. Here I was, this wild young kid with all these ideas about how Procter ought to change everything it had been doing for years. I was always challenging him, questioning him, asking why, that kind of thing.

Plus, I was a real hard-charging young Turk. One of my customers liked to say that if he placed an order for a carload of sons of bitches and the railroad car arrived on his siding and he cracked the seal and opened the door and only Lou Pritchett fell out, he wouldn't feel short-shipped. I mean, I just wouldn't take no for an answer. If I couldn't get in the front door, I would go in the back door, and if I couldn't get in the back door, I would go down the chimney. Not long ago, when I gave one of my speeches and recounted some of my experiences, the CEO who had invited me to speak to his top executives came up to me afterward and told me that during my presentation, he leaned over to his vice-president sitting next to him and said, "Boy, I would have hated to compete with that son of a bitch!"

I guess I was a little bit too aggressive. And I learned it the real, real hard way. One Friday afternoon I worked with Red Collins until about three o'clock, and at about four o'clock on Saturday morning he dropped dead of a heart attack. He was only fifty-five or so. To this day, old-timers at Procter & Gamble maintain that I killed him, that dealing with me was what did it. I can hardly argue that they're wrong.

I Fell in Love with the Company I Worked for, but It Was Only the Number Two Love in My Life.

In 1952, when I was a junior at Memphis State, a coed I was friendly with told me about one of her sorority sisters in Alpha Xi Delta, a freshman named Barbara Burnette. My friend, Patsy Newton, said she thought Barbara and I were made for each other and that she would arrange a meeting. The plan was for Barbara to be with Patsy in the Tiger's Den (the student lounge) at a certain time. I would "drop in," see them together, and be introduced to Barbara.

I will never forget the feeling I had when I walked into that crowded, noisy room and saw Barbara from about a hundred feet away. If you don't believe in "love at first sight," think again, because Barbara and I are proof positive. The instant I laid eyes on her, I thought she was the most beautiful creature I had ever seen, and right at that moment I made up my mind that she was going to be my wife, or else. Barbara was not only gorgeous but a very intelligent girl from the cotton farming hamlet of Lula, Mississippi, which is on the river about sixty miles south of Memphis. At that time, about four hundred people lived in Lula, which had two grocery stores, one dry-goods store, one drugstore, one school, and, like most towns in the Mississippi Delta, a cotton gin.

On our first "date," we went to a Memphis State football game. Some date—I had to be down on the field, performing as a cheerleader. But we went out together after the game and then began going to fraternity and sorority parties, movies, and hayrides together.

I graduated a year after I met Barbara and went to work for Procter & Gamble in Tupelo, Mississippi, which is about a hundred miles from Memphis. Every weekend, I drove to Memphis, stayed at my mother's house, and saw Barbara Friday night, Saturday night, and Sunday. Each Monday morning, I would get up at four-thirty, make the two-hour-plus drive to Tupelo, and be ready to start calling on my customers by eight o'clock. My boss, Grady Collins, approved of this arrangement, as long as I did not leave my territory before 5:00 P.M. Friday and was back in the stores by eight o'clock Monday morning.

Just to make sure that he was getting a full week out of me, Grady would periodically drive up to Tupelo from his home in Jackson, arriving at about quarter of eight Monday morning. By then, I usually was on my second call of the day, and Grady would give me his big, broad smile and comment, "You're going to do well in this company."

I proposed to Barbara in the old-fashioned way, asking her first and then driving to Lula to ask her father for permission. On the evening of December 19, 1954, she and I were married by her cousin, the Reverend Billy Harris, in the Lula Methodist Church.

So, P&G, much as I love you, sorry, but you'll always have to settle for only number two in my affections.

3
Partnering Procter & Gamble with Wal-Mart

"Hello, Sam Walton? This Is Lou Pritchett of Procter & Gamble. How'd You Like to Go Canoeing with Me?"

My main claim to fame during my thirty-six years with Procter & Gamble was conceiving and helping to create a partnering relationship between P&G and Wal-Mart. Sam Walton and I used to tell people that when I first called him in 1987 and suggested we get together, my call came out of the blue and he was so surprised that a P&G executive would call anyone in the Wal-Mart hierarchy that he accepted my call. Actually, I didn't place my initial call to Sam until after he and I had been introduced by a mutual friend. More on that in a minute.

Procter & Gamble to Its Biggest Customer, Wal-Mart: "Don't Call Us, We'll Call You."

Virtually everyone familiar with the situation agrees that I helped improve the relationship between Procter and Wal-Mart. But that wasn't hard to do; until I picked up the phone and called Sam Walton in 1987, there was hardly any relationship at all between these two giant companies, other than us shipping products to Wal-Mart and them sending us money. Eight or ten different P&G divisions were calling regularly on Wal-Mart, but it was a completely uncoordinated effort. As Sam used to put it, it was as if we communicated by slipping notes under each other's doors.

It's hard to believe, but as recently as 1987, no top corporate officer of Procter & Gamble had ever contacted any top corporate officer of Wal-Mart. As Sam Walton, Wal-Mart's founder and principal owner, put it in rather an understatement in his

1992 autobiography, *Made in America*, "Sometimes it was diffi-
cult getting the bigger companies—the Procter & Gambles,
Eastman Kodaks, whoever—to call on us at all." And Wal-Mart
was—and is—only P&G's largest customer in the entire world!
As Sam Walton pointed out, Procter sells more product to Wal-
Mart than we do to the entire nation of Japan.

My company didn't just ignore Wal-Mart, we actually insulted
them. One time, before I got involved, Wal-Mart named Procter
as its vendor of the year. This was a very big deal to Wal-Mart,
but was of such little consequence to P&G executives that they
ignored the honor and didn't even bother picking up the award.

Procter's attitude toward Wal-Mart wasn't so surprising.
Ever since the 1940s, P&G's strategy had been driven by two
strategies:

- P&G product superiority, and
- P&G advertising copy superiority.

Little else mattered. Three generations of Procter managers had
grown up in this environment; the concept of top management
having anything to do with customers was totally foreign. P&G,
after all, had a huge sales organization to "handle" customers.

Nor were Sam Walton's and Wal-Mart's complaints about
Procter & Gamble's attitude new or unique. As far back as
1969, *Forbes* magazine had observed: "Without a doubt, P&G
is the most disliked company in the supermarket industry.
Most supermarket executives will do almost anything that's
legal—and some things that may not be—to keep P&G from
growing. The reason is simple. Supermarkets make very little
money on P&G soaps and detergents and feel like helpless
pawns in the P&G marketing machine."

Once I was named vice-president of sales in 1985, I became
convinced that allegiance alone to the narrow concept of product and ad copy superiority was simply not enough. So I made
a personal commitment to change P&G's historical relationship
or nonrelationship with our customers.

As to Wal-Mart specifically, I found that there was no sharing of information between the two companies. There was no
joint planning; there was no systems coordination or compati-
bility. All there was were two separate corporate entities going

their own ways, burdened by, but oblivious to, the excess costs that were being created by this obsolete system.

In short, instead of having an "us and them" type of alliance, it was more "us against them."

Sam Walton and I Paddle the Boat Together—Literally.

After assessing the relationship between P&G and Wal-Mart and determining that we had to completely revolutionize it, I set about finding a way of getting an introduction to Sam. As it happened, one of my closest childhood friends dating back to our days as Boy Scouts, George Billingsley, has lived for many years in Bentonville, Arkansas, where Wal-Mart's headquarters are located. Bentonville is a little town of about ten thousand in northwestern Arkansas, and I figured just about everyone had to know everyone. So I called George and asked him if he knew Sam Walton. To my astonishment, George's answer was: "Know him? Hell, he's a dear friend. We play tennis nearly every day."

I told George that I wanted to meet Sam Walton so that I could try to improve the relationship between P&G and Wal-Mart, and, if possible, recast that relationship from being adversaries to being partners. George's reaction was: "I can get you in to see Sam, Lou. But you don't want to go in the front door and try pitching him on this idea of yours from the git-go. The way to deal with Sam is off-site. What we ought to do is get some of the boys together, some of us old Eagle Scouts, and invite him on a canoe trip."

George's plan sounded fine to me. He told Sam what I wanted to talk about and Sam said, "Yes, I'll go." So George made the arrangements for the canoe trip on the South Fork of the Spring River in Hardy, Arkansas—Sam Walton's home territory. Everything was set for the trip in July of that year, 1987. I appropriated a plane from the Procter & Gamble fleet, a luxurious Gulfstream that our CEO, John Smale, used to fly around the world on business, and Barbara and I flew down to Arkansas. All of us were going to meet over dinner the night before we went out on the river in canoes, and everyone showed up on time—everyone except Sam Walton. As time went by and still no Sam, I was getting worried and more worried and even more worried. I thought they'd kill me back at headquarters for taking the company Gulfstream down there and then have Sam not show up. But he finally did arrive about three hours late—he had had some kind of problem with his own plane.

Just about the first thing Sam said to me after George Billingsley introduced us was to ask, "Lou, were you in [Boy] Scouting?"

I told him I had been.

And he said, "Were you an Eagle?"

I told him I was, and he gave me the Eagle Scout grip and just lit up; Sam had been the youngest Eagle Scout in the history of Missouri, where he grew up. He had grown up in the same era I had, the '30s, '40s and '50s, during the depression and World War II, when scouting was very, very important for a lot of young men.

And from that first moment on, after he established that I, too, was an Eagle Scout, he and I got along famously; "Never have a pair been better suited," in George Billingsley's words.

The next morning, Barbara and I were driving Sam to where the canoes were. We stopped at a service station, and Sam wanted to buy a banana flip to take with him, but he was wearing his swimming trunks and didn't have any money on him. So he said to me, "Lou, you got any money?" And I handed him a dollar. Here was one of the richest men in the world borrowing pocket change from me! He bought his banana flip, and it felt like he and I had known each other all our lives; Sam was just able to establish great rapport with people.

Now this canoe trip was for pleasure, but it was for business too, of course; that was my whole reason for asking George to arrange it. Sam was famous for carrying a yellow pad everywhere he went so he could jot down notes, and, sure enough, he had it with him. He was in a canoe by himself, and Barbara and I were in another canoe, and all day long Sam would paddle up next to us and we would hold our two canoes together and he and I would talk business.

Sam said he was so shocked by my approach that he agreed to go on the canoe trip. Also, he was extremely curious to see what a Procter executive was like in person. "I have been so disappointed in the way your company has behaved toward us," he declared. "Your people act like a bunch of guys who just don't have time for us."

One problem that absolutely drove Sam crazy was when any of his stores ran out of merchandise. If he didn't have the stock on the shelves, he couldn't sell it. The customer would probably go to one of his competitors, and Sam would lose that sale forever—and maybe the customer, too. And Sam told me that running out of Procter & Gamble products was not at all unusual in his stores because our systems weren't integrated.

Sam also complained about different consumer product companies like P&G and our focus and how narrow it was. The sales reps would come and call on his buyers and say, "Take this promotion. Take this toothpaste or this diaper or this candy bar and buy into my allowances or my promotion and promote it next month."

Sam's point to me was, the thing that most of the vendors don't realize is that "I also sell a product, which is the total makeup of my store." He sketched a schematic of his store on his yellow pad and he said, "For example, your brands are very important to my product, my stores. But in total, your brands are just a small portion of what I sell. And yet, every month, your salespeople come and call on me and want me to change my product mix to conform to yours.

"Let me give you an example," he continued. And this is what really drove his point home for me. "I know you've got a formula for making Tide. And that formula is probably so many ounces of chemical A, and so many ounces of chemical B, and so many ounces of chemical C, whatever. Suppose a chemical salesman called on you every thirty days and said, 'Hey, I've got $200 a ton off on sulphur this month. Why don't you change your Tide formula? Why don't you put more sulphur in it this month?'" I thought that was an outstanding example of how a retailer feels about a vendor calling on them and saying, "Hey, twelve times a year, change your product mix or your formula, so you can sell more of my product." As we paddled along, Sam began firing questions at me about our company and what my plan was. "Sam," I said, "I'm absolutely convinced that this dual system that we've got, this almost adversarial system, where we've created our independent system and you've created yours, we're not planning together, we're barely talking to each other. Both of us focus on the end user, the consumer, but we do it independently, without consulting each other. What we need to do is revolutionize the way we do business and move away from the we-ship-you-the-product-and-then-you-do-whatever-you-do-with-it mentality. We need to become partners."

My point was that since their system and ours failed to complement each other, it cost us a lot more money to do business together than it should have. And these excess costs could result in one of only two things:

• Either they got passed on to the consumer, making our products more expensive than they should be, and thus potentially reducing sales.

• Or they came out of profits and hit us or Wal-Mart or both companies where it really hurt, on the bottom line.

I explained that I thought our two companies needed to create a shared vision of doing business with each other—not *their* vision or *our* vision but a mutual vision. What I could see our two companies doing was joining together in order to achieve goals that would benefit both of us.

As I outlined my perception of the relationship between Wal-Mart and Procter & Gamble, Sam kept confirming everything I said and embellishing on it. You could see that he agreed with the whole concept and that he and I were on the same wavelength. As Sam said during that trip, "Just think, Lou, what we could do if we could think of each other as extensions of one another's operation! If only Procter could have a mind-set that my stores are their stores and that what we are doing is going to affect your product on that shelf."

It was obvious from the start that Sam and I were soul mates. There was just a chemistry between us. After the first twenty minutes, I felt as though I had known Sam for twenty years. George Billingsley later told me that the other fifteen people on the trip had immediately noticed that Sam and I hit it off so well and became so engrossed in our conversation that it was as if, for Sam and for me, no one else on the trip existed.

In retrospect, I know that what George says is true. I distinctly remember that during the trip we had to portage the canoes for several miles, and the company that had rented us the canoes picked us up at the portage point in an old, worn-out yellow school bus, with a trailer behind it to transport the canoes. The seats on that school bus were torn, there was no air-conditioning, and the noise from the motor was deafening. Sam and I moved to the back of the bus so we could continue our discussion about our companies and our business. We sat across the aisle, facing each other, and it was so very hot that all the windows on the bus were wide open. We were traveling on an unpaved back road in northeastern Arkansas, and thick clouds of red dust poured in on us. Sam and I were so involved in our conversation that neither the heat, the dust, the noise, nor the bumpy road distracted us. In fact, when we reached the spot where the canoes were placed back in the water, everyone but the two of us got off the bus, loaded the canoes, and prepared to paddle away. It was then that Barbara started pounding on the side of the bus and yelling, "Lou! Sam! We're going to leave without you if you two don't come out here and get going! You can continue that world-shaking discussion on the river. Let's go!" Only then did Sam and I realize that the others had just about abandoned us and were ready to paddle away without us.

In spite of our instant and close friendship and in spite of our agreement on most aspects of creating a partnership between our two companies, the ultimate decisions were not up to the two of us. At least not on my side. Sam was Wal-Mart, but Lou Pritchett was just a cog in the Procter & Gamble operation.

Toward the end of that first day on the river he said to me, "Well, Lou, do you think you're going to be able to pull this off with all those Yankee bosses of yours?" Sam's calling them Yankees struck me as a riot because I had never thought of Cincinnati as "Yankee." It was strictly the Midwest to me. But to Sam, anything north of Arkansas was "Yankee." I told him I thought I could pull it off because a couple of my bosses were in my corner. And he said he would do anything he could to help because he thought that what we were talking about was absolutely essential.

Looking back on that first ride down the river of ours, where he and I conceived the basic formula for the alliance between our two companies, Sam later characterized it as "the most productive float trip I ever took with George [Billingsley]." In Sam's words, he and I were able to take "a basically adversarial vendor/retailer relationship" and turn it 180 degrees into "a win-win partnership" that he considered "the wave of the future." All I can add to that is, "Amen!"

The Win-Win Partnership Is a Lot Like a Successful Marriage.

The outcome of that first canoe trip with Sam was the consummation of what George Billingsley refers to as "the magic marriage" between Wal-Mart and P&G. To the best of my knowledge, this was the first time that two companies that big—each one with revenues of several billion dollars a year—had formed such a partnership. Within three months, the top ten officers of Procter & Gamble traveled down to Bentonville and spent two whole days exchanging ideas with Wal-Mart's top ten executives. Within three months of that session in Bentonville, our two companies had created a joint working group to team up as partners and revolutionize the relationship between the manufacturer and the retailer. We brought in representatives of most of our major departments, including sales, marketing, systems, manufacturing, distribution, and finance, to devise new ways of doing business with their counterparts at Wal-Mart in each specific segment of business. This "partnering" approach proved vastly cost-effective and productive in every way for both Procter & Gamble and Wal-Mart. Initially, we assigned twelve of our people and moved them to live permanently in Bentonville. One of the best comments on our partnership with Wal-Mart came from a couple of executives at Kroger supermarkets, which is based in Cincinnati. It's also a telling view of P&G's arm's-length relationship with all its major customers, pre–Wal-Mart. Jack Partridge, then the public relations manager at Kroger, was a friend of mine, and a couple of years after we got the Wal-Mart deal going, Lyle Everingham, Kroger's CEO, came to him and said, "Jack, I understand that Procter & Gamble has moved twelve people to Bentonville, Arkansas, to work as a team with Wal-Mart. I can't believe them [P&G] having people in the same city as their [Wal-Mart's] headquarters."

And Jack's answer was, "Mr. Everingham, they [Procter] got ten thousand people here in Cincinnati, *your* headquarters."

Eventually, Procter & Gamble would have more than seventy-five executives and employees living in Bentonville. And basically, we invented the whole partnership as we went along, and it worked out beautifully.

Take Sam's complaint that his stores often ran out of P&G products. We solved that by tying our computers together. Today, if you go into a Wal-Mart store and buy a tube of Crest toothpaste or a package of Charmin toilet tissue or a bar of Ivory soap, the inventory control people at both Wal-Mart and Procter & Gamble know it instantly, and a replacement is on the way. The result is that P&G sells lots more product to Wal-Mart, and they in turn sell it to the consumers, and everybody's happy.

Partnering and Partners—in Practice, Not in Theory.

So, what does the partnership between Wal-Mart and Procter & Gamble that Sam Walton and I conceived and nurtured, what does it all mean—not only for our two companies but for *all* companies? Partnering is more than just playing golf and having lunch with people and hoping that your volume will increase and theirs will, too. What it really is is getting in and instead of having two dual, unconnected, incompatible systems, it's becoming extensions of each other's operation. Not to make you feel better, not to make the other company feel better, but to drive cost out of the system and deliver a better value to the end-using consumer.

When I speak of partnering, I don't mean only in the Procter & Gamble/Wal-Mart sense. I mean that no matter what business you are in, you should try to become partners with every person and every company that you do a substantial amount of business with. But as to the specific example of manufacturers like Procter & Gamble, I'm talking about forming partnership relationships with both vendors and suppliers (and especially with the company's own employees) in order to make the whole process more efficient and less costly. Lower costs result in a combination of lower prices and higher profits.

Wal-Mart has made the P&G/Wal-Mart system available to all its vendors, and that's good. That's where the real advantage in partnering comes. You can't be selfish in this business game today. Your approach has to be, "How can I help? What can I do? What systems will work? What approaches? What strategies can I help you with, sir, that can be applied to all of your vendors and help you in toto?" The reward from that comes because the company you become partners with never forgets that you were the one who helped them streamline their operation. And so you always get the extra spoonful of sugar from them.

But you can't patent your method for your company only. And you don't want to. Also, you do that for someone else, and they're going to do the same for you. Because they're going to have ideas or get ideas from someone else that will help you and they're going to be feeding those ideas back to you. With Sam Walton, for instance, he asked us all about company planes. When is it smart to own one? When is it best to lease one? Those are subjects that are a million miles removed from selling soap. The exchange of ideas, the exchange of strategies, the exchange of thoughts, of programs, of systems—that's what partnering is all about.

The last word on the partnership between Wal-Mart and Procter & Gamble and between Sam Walton and Lou Pritchett has to be Sam's. In 1991, about a year before he died, he wrote me a letter and reminisced about what we had accomplished together:

"I think back on our first canoe trip and how we evolved our partnership process with Procter & Gamble. It was one of the best things that ever happened to our company and I think time bears out that many other companies are beginning to view the supplier as an important partner."

A Guaranteed Rx for Failure: Forget to Treat Both Your Customers and Your Suppliers as Partners.

For many years at Procter & Gamble, our attitude toward our suppliers was, "Deliver it to us at the lowest price and the highest quality. If you can't do it, we'll turn it over to somebody else who can." Well, we learned a very simple truth: If you insist on hammering your suppliers down and demanding the last quarter cent out of them, that last ounce of flesh, they're not going to have money left to invest in retooling, capital improvements, and research and development. They're going to be so narrowly focused, they're going to be so strapped, that in the end they're going to go down. And you're either going to go down with them, or else you're going to have to find a replacement for them, whether you want to or not. Fortunately for P&G, the Purchasing vice-president, Marv Womack, was a follower of Dr. Edwards Deming and his Total Quality teachings and began in the mid-eighties moving the company toward aligning strategically with a limited number of suppliers. In fact, Marv's excellent work with suppliers strongly influenced the efforts started later in sales.

Put the squeeze on your suppliers, and you're liable to wake up one day and wonder why your packages are falling apart, why the ends are coming unglued, why your toothpaste tastes like—well, like something you wouldn't voluntarily put in your mouth. Then you go talk to that supplier and you find out that he's been cutting every cent to the bone, that there's been no R&D, that he's just been trying to survive day to day. It's the old penny-wise, pound-foolish approach. That's why it's best to deal with one or two or a small number of suppliers and make them your partners. You have to be as interested in their survival as they are in your survival; you have to become extensions of each other's company. If your suppliers are just making it on a shoestring, on the basis of being the low bidder, without being able to make any profit and devoting any planning to servicing your needs in the future, you are eventually going to reap the whirlwind. That's life. So you have to deal with your suppliers, as well as your customers, on a partnership basis, and become extensions of each other's operations.

The days are over when suppliers are willing to tolerate the attitude of "Strangle me. Strangle me. And when I die, someone else will take my place." Before you can sell, you have to have a product to sell. Kill your suppliers—and you kill yourself.

In my opinion, the absence of supplier-customer trust and the lack of supplier-customer integrated systems will be the leading causes of business failure and bankruptcy in the new game that will be played in the second half of the 1990s and on into the twenty-first century. Those companies that continue the traditional "we sell and you buy" relationship with their customers will find their costs soaring. It will become increasingly difficult for such outfits to gain an audience with future decision makers.

Replacing confrontation with cooperation and trust will be necessary in order to play this new game. That means that companies will have to refocus their efforts from simply producing products and transferring them to the customer's warehouse into aligning with the customer in partnership and thinking and acting as extensions of each other's businesses. This new system, driven by the explosion of information technology, will be won by those companies that are willing to trust, share, and partner with their customers. The companies that are willing to settle for getting only what they are already getting (or less) should just keep on doing what they have always been doing.

In short, a guaranteed prescription for failure is to treat those you deal with, whether they be your customers or your suppliers, as simply people you buy and sell from—rather than as your partners.

Pritchett's Precepts of Partnering.

My theories on customer-supplier partnering evolved over many years. As I reflect on this subject, it seems as though I was probing the partnering concept as early as the late 1950s, when, as a young Procter & Gamble unit manager, I used to ask the managers of Safeway, Kroger, Malone & Hyde, and other key customers in the Memphis district to help me develop some thoughts and ideas about how we could work together more closely.

My feelings, and that is all they were at the time, were that we needed to find a way for P&G to offer more to our best customers than simply a "we sell, you buy" relationship. I distinctly remember being at Winn-Dixie's headquarters in Jacksonville, Florida, one day during that era and telling one of their vice-presidents that P&G was the best in the business at obtaining and analyzing data on consumer habits and practices, but that we needed to find a way to share this information with companies like his in order to make both of our businesses more profitable.

This idea of wanting to go beyond the traditional "buy-sell" model stuck in my craw for years before I figured out how to handle it or convert it into reality. In 1981, when I reached the Philippines as president of P&G's subsidiary there, I clearly saw not only the need to move beyond the buy-sell model but also an opportunity to test my theories that had been marinating for so long, thereby bringing the supplier and the customer together to share information and deliver superior service to the end-using consumer. In October 1982, the Philippine Association of Supermarkets (PASI) invited me to share my business beliefs. My speech marked the first time ever that I crystallized my thoughts on the partnership between the retailer and the vendor, and it marked my first use of the word that embodies a now popular business concept, *partnering*.

Here's what I told the members of PASI about what I'd require from suppliers if I were in the retail grocery business:

1. Suppliers must change the way they think about my operation. Rather than simply trying to sell me bigger orders, they must bring me solid ideas that, when implemented, would automatically result in large orders. And we must seriously consider "partnering" with each other as customer and supplier.

2. Suppliers must think in terms of specific category growth—I as retailer have no preference for selling Brand A over Brand B but for increasing sales of the total category.

3. Promotions absolutely must be 100 percent consumer oriented with the clear objective of bringing more customers into my stores—to increase my total customer count and total revenue per checkout transaction. Any promotion that encourages the retailer simply to cut the price is self-defeating and inefficient, and the whole system would do better without it.

4. Manufacturers must *not* use the aisles of my stores as a battleground for their own personal disputes and gains. Instead, they must work with me in individual partnerships to draw more customers into my stores.

5. Suppliers should try to discipline themselves in the dealer allowance area and think in terms of long-range plan-

ning, because "short-term" volume gains for them or for me rarely benefit either of us and usually escalate the cost of doing business for both of us.

6. Suppliers must help me manage the inventories throughout my store, in the back room and on my shelves. Shelf-management programs should be built around the "space according to movement" principle: My selling area is finite in size, and the true genius resides in allocating shelf space for maximum return, not simply in "selling it" (the shelf) to the highest bidder.

7. Manufacturers must help me move quickly into use of computers by sharing their expertise and technology. This service is sorely underdeveloped and untapped but potentially can be a profitable resource for both partners.

8. My partners and I must share sound training techniques for our staffs—from the stock clerk to the checker to the store manager. I would capitalize on the enormous training capabilities of my suppliers in terms of both quantity and quality.

9. Dialogue with my suppliers—meaning in-depth discussions of the problems facing our industry and the economy and what we must jointly do to help answer and/or correct them—must be open and ongoing. No exceptions.

10. My partners and I must spend more time discussing the principles, programs, and strategies that work to build customer count and store distinctiveness and less time haggling over free labor and an additional dealer allowance. Manufacturers must help me become more strategic and long range in my planning approach to the business.

11. All my suppliers would know that I'm a good listener and willing to experiment and to find the better way. They would understand how my taking the longer view is in their best interest, that their success is totally dependent upon mine.

4
How *Not* to Succeed, No Matter How Hard You Try

Good business management and good government are analogous. In each you need a system where feedback from the constituents or employees filters directly up to the managers and then back down to the constituents and employees. This continuous loop, when operating properly, keeps everyone in the system informed as to the issues and opportunities and allows for learning on both sides. Problems in government and in business are born when political leaders or corporate executives start thinking they have all the answers, that they know what is best for the constituents or the employees. The movers and shakers come to the conclusion that more government or management control is better than less, and proceed to create their own little world with its own rules and regulations.

In any government or business, when the leadership loses touch with the people and sends them the wrong signals, disaster is imminent. Too many employees in companies today are suffering from the erroneous belief that their company owes them a guaranteed job for life. This misconception is the result of management sending the wrong signals over the years. The same is true for government. By promising cradle-to-grave care for every citizen, government trains the constituents to believe that it owes them something and that "entitlements" are the state's obligation. Until both government and corporations begin involving people in the entire process, we will continue to be a country of poorly managed, poorly led, frustrated individuals who let resentment and anger sap our creativity and pride.

Managing and governing are not quite as complicated as brain surgery. They simply are not that difficult if business executives and politicians understand the basic needs of human beings and the basic rules of managing.

All managers and all politicians need to learn only four elementary skills:

- How to listen.
- How to learn.
- How to help.
- How to lead.

Every outstanding politician and business manager possesses these talents. Unfortunately, the demand for outstanding politicians and business managers has always exceeded the supply.

Pritchett's Law: Bottlenecks Are Always at the Top of the Bottle.

Bottlenecks in what I call command-and-control organizations are almost always at the top of the bottle. Command and control by its very definition says you've got one or a limited number of people making the important decisions. That means that you are automatically disallowing the brains, the skills, the thought processes of all the other managers and people in the organization. In a classic pyramid organization, where top management is doing it to the middle and the middle is doing it to the bottom, one thing's for sure—nearly everyone is getting screwed. Autocrats who create a classic pyramid structure tend to cultivate a system in which they screw the people below them; those under them screw the ones beneath them, and on down the ladder, until everyone gets screwed.

That's why the traditional pyramid structure has to be flattened. It may have been the perfect organizational structure for its time, during an era when corporate communications had to be handled vertically. There was no better way to communicate. The guys at the top had to have a cadre of servants, if you will, mid-managers in between, whatever you want to call them, directing those at the bottom. My concern with the pyramid organization is not that it is evil and always has been but that it has outlived its usefulness. What we've got to do is find ways to create a new, flatter, more democratic form of organization. It will be one, given the new methods of electronic communication, where you don't have all that unneeded structure. After all, in many instances, the people at the bottom of the organization will receive information at the same time as those at the top.

Also, today's rank-and-file workers are much better educated and more qualified than they used to be. They aren't simply hod carriers any longer; they're capable of making decisions on their own, and we've got to find a way to capitalize on that. The pyramid is the worst way in the world to capitalize on it because that type of structure promotes only vertical communication. What we have to do is motivate corporations to encourage horizontal or lateral communications, where people are talking to each other, functions are talking to each other, they're interlocked, and they're sharing data.

I once heard the board chairman of a large company, a corporation with a typical pyramid arrangement, tell the sales force, "You people have a job to do, and it's selling. I want you to put blinders on, like a mule, and do this job. The advertising people will do their job; trust me. The manufacturing people will do their job; trust me. Each function will do its job. You just do your job and it will all come together at the top and management will play the pieces and the parts like a pipe organ and everything will work."

In business jargon, that was the old stovepipe structure, all those vertical tubes of command. Contrast that with what Ford Motor Company did when it was in the process of inventing the Ford Taurus during the 1980s. Instead of having various departments—engineering, design, manufacturing, and so forth—work independently of each other, the company, from day one, integrated these units into a multifunctional Taurus team. The result was that a number of potential problems with the Taurus were discovered and fixed early on. That's the way all businesses should do it.

In the modern world, that stovepipe structure, looking neither left nor right, is the *worst* model. You have all this talent, and if you try to keep the left hand from knowing what the right hand is doing, you can imagine the cost to the system. So today's concept is multifunctional teams, knocking those stovepipes over on their side in favor of coordinated communication. That's what the new structure has got to look like.

I've been around a long time, and I have yet to come across one person who's as smart as ten. My whole management philosophy, always, has been to surround myself with competent people and let *all* of them do their jobs. That kind of group, over time, is always going to whip any command-and-control group.

Trying to Shove Loretta Lynn into a Stovepipe Just Won't Work.

In 1986 Tom Quinn, one of my protégés, was trying to persuade Wal-Mart to enter whole-hog into the food business. Until then, basically the only food items Wal-Mart was selling were snacks, candy, and soda pop. Tom was in our food division at the time—where peanut butter, cake mix, oil, and shortening formed the core of our food business. He requested an audience with all the key Wal-Mart people to sell them on the concept that if they really wanted to be the largest retailer in the world, they had to sell food along with everything else they stocked.

Tom knew the only way he could get all of the Wal-Mart brass together to listen to him was to have a hook. As it happened, Loretta Lynn was doing television ads for one of P&G's brands, Crisco. Figuring that Loretta Lynn would certainly win the attention of Wal-Mart's executives, Tom went to the Crisco brand managers and asked if they could spare her for a day. The initial answer was, "No, we only get her for eight days a year and we need her for important things." Which didn't include dinners with Wal-Mart, which didn't sell Crisco. The Crisco people, not surprisingly, were interested only in their own brand, not in helping the entire P&G corporation.

Tom was finally able to show the Crisco people how much product they could sell if he could get them into Wal-Mart, and they reluctantly agreed to loan Loretta Lynn for the occasion. Next, he had to get her to agree to go. She appeared at a P&G sales meeting in Nashville, and Tom went up to her afterwards and asked her, "How would you like to meet the richest man in the world?"

"Great!" was her answer. "Sign me up for that!"

The plan was that she would have dinner with Sam Walton and most of the Wal-Mart hierarchy at the Bentonville home of

Jack Shewmaker, who was then Wal-Mart's chief financial officer. In return for Tom bringing Loretta Lynn in, the Wal-Mart
people agreed to listen to his pitch for an hour and a half the
next morning.

After Tom had arranged the whole thing, one final hitch
developed: He learned at the last minute that Loretta Lynn
never flies commercial, and he had been planning to escort her
on an airline flight from Nashville to Bentonville. So Tom called
Tom Laco, who was then vice-chairman of our board of directors, and invited him along. Tom, being a very smart man, said,
"You really just want me for the plane, right?" And Tom Quinn
answered, "You got it! Loretta won't fly commercial." So Tom
and Tom picked her up in Nashville in the company Gulfstream
and flew her to Bentonville.

At Jack Shewmaker's, they all had dinner, and Ms. Lynn sang
a few songs and hugged and kissed everybody. All the Wal-Mart
executives loved her, and on top of that she spent part of the
next day signing autographs at Wal-Mart's general offices and
main distribution center. She must have signed two thousand
autographs, which spread all kinds of goodwill for Wal-Mart
and Procter & Gamble, as well as for Crisco, a brand that did
not exist until then at either Wal-Mart or Sam's Wholesale Club.

The payoff was that Tom gained the undivided attention for
an hour and a half of everybody at Wal-Mart except (to the cha-
grin of our featured attraction) Sam Walton, who was up in
Canada hunting with his grandson and missed the whole thing.
Tom was able to convince the Wal-Mart people that they had to
be in the food business; after that they completely came around
and started selling food—including Crisco, of course.

Not only were the Crisco people unreceptive to Tom's proposal initially, but even after they agreed to let Tom use Loretta
Lynn for a day, they thought the whole thing was so unimportant that they sent one of the Crisco brand assistants along
instead of the Crisco brand manager. Aside from sparing
Loretta Lynn for one day, all they were really interested in all
along was their narrow little slice of the business with Crisco,
given the internal reward system. Their attitude was, "It has to
benefit Crisco first; if it's good for the rest of the corporation,
too, that's okay."

Thanks to Tom Quinn's persistence, the Crisco brand managers succeeded on this occasion—in spite of themselves. What they should have said from the first time Tom proposed it was, "Hell, yes, we'll do whatever we can that will benefit the entire company." If they didn't learn a lesson from that episode, I hope that they have since or that they will.

Those Who Most Need Change Often Resist It the Most.

As Tom Quinn's experience with Crisco and Loretta Lynn demonstrates, in traditional, functionally structured organizations, "turf" becomes a major issue that can adversely affect everyone in the organization. Most corporate functions evolve into independent fiefdoms that cause the members of each unit to view those in other units, and sometimes even the company itself, as "the enemy."

I experienced this firsthand in the mid-1980s after I returned to Cincinnati from the Philippines and was named vice-president of sales. I tried to make changes, to turn the sales organization into a function that did more than simply take orders from customers, to forge a whole new relationship with the customers (which is what eventually led me to Sam Walton). A number of P&G vice-presidents invited me to lunch, at which they planned to serve me as the main course. They told me that I was treading on their turf and that they wanted me to stop trying to recast the sales organization in accord with the rules I had been preaching for years and am outlining in this book. These managers were deeply concerned that my efforts to empower the sales department and change it from solely a product-driven organization into a customer-driven one were posing a threat to their power. Part of their concern was the product of the company's internal reward/recognition system, which was based on short-term (spelled monthly) sales volume. If I succeeded in making the sales department listen to and better serve the customer, short-term sales might be sacrificed in favor of long-term ones—to the overall benefit of the company.

One vice-president challenged the statement in my memo, "My Vision for P&G Sales," where I asserted that I would provide the needed leadership for the sales department. Staring at me face-to-face, he declared, "We don't need your leadership. We have our own leader. He's called 'the sales manager.'"

The executive who took issue with me never has learned what leadership is all about. To this day, he continues to think that leadership is something that can be granted by the stroke of a pen. Which, I suppose, explains why he never has been recognized as a leader.

As recently as 1988, I had a senior vice-president of Procter & Gamble tell me that my real worth to the company was to teach the sales organization to beat the bushes harder and faster than ever before. He wanted me to focus 100 percent on short-term sales volume. I refused to accept this, because I knew that in the rapidly changing customer environment brought about by information technology, to blindly pursue short-term volume was the equivalent of rearranging the deck chairs on the *Titanic*.

What you have to do if you run into bosses who are intractable, you have to find out what they want to accomplish, what's important on their screen. From my experience, the best way to proceed is to find out what's on someone else's agenda and show them that your new way helps them to get there better than the methods they've always used. At that point, you can say, "If I help you achieve that, will you give me enough space to prove something different to you?" I have many a scar on my back from being less than diplomatic, and I've discovered that you can't bully people, you can't make them feel stupid, you can't act like you have all the answers and they don't. You have to create an environment that makes it easy for people to get on board, no matter when they catch on, and you have to be patient until they do catch on.

In other words, leaders make it easy for people to follow them.

It's the Unwritten Rules That May Drive You Nuts.

While flying to New York recently, I found myself sitting next to a fellow about forty years old who had recently moved from one high-tech company to another. I'll call my seatmate "Jack." When I told Jack that I earn my living by advising corporations, he described two mistakes he had made in the brief time since he joined his new company. The first was to respond to his boss's boss's request that Jack write down one of his ideas for improving the company and send it to him in memo form. Trying to follow procedure, Jack wrote out his idea, sent it to the "big guy," and copied his immediate boss. When Jack's immediate boss received a copy of Jack's memo, he went through the roof. He called Jack in, and while acknowledging that Jack's idea had real merit, said that that wasn't the issue. The important thing, the supervisor declared, was that Jack had violated the chain of command. "That's not the way we do things around here," Jack's boss declared.

Jack said he made his second mistake when he called the big boss, to whom he had responded in writing, and apologized for "breaking the rules." Upon hearing that, the big boss's comment was, "Nonsense—what rules?" As Jack, a twenty-year veteran of corporate infighting, told me, he did not understand the unwritten rules at his new company, and it had gotten him in hot water. How, he asked me, do you learn the unwritten rules during your first ninety days on the job? By trial and error, or what?

The result is that Jack is worried about his career. To make matters worse, his immediate boss, ostensibly in jest, asked Jack if he was out to get his job. Moreover, Jack is afraid that no one is interested in the objectivity he brings to a totally new environment. There is simply no opportunity for him to be critical or to outline what might be a better or different way of doing things.

This attitude paralyzes many corporations. If you want to get ahead, don't break the unwritten rules; do cover your ass; do what everyone else does; don't rock the boat or make waves; and don't try to tell us what you've learned from your own experiences. Just do what you are told. Is it any wonder that so many corporations are bedeviled by middle managers who would rather cover their ass than help transform and grow the business?

If You Are to Succeed, You Must Ride Toward the Sound of Battle.

Why don't managers encourage new approaches? In general, they fear economic reprisals; if my new approach doesn't work,

I may not get promoted, I may not get the salary increase, I may lose my job. And there's an element of pride; in order to be willing to accept that change, you have to admit, "Some of the things I said yesterday aren't true."

I have noticed four specific obstacles to change: ignorance, incompetence, ego, and fear.

1: *Ignorance.* Some people don't have a clue that things need to be changed. Too often, senior management listens only to other senior management, because the top leaders are exposed only to others of similar rank. In many organizations, there is no system that allows—or, better yet, forces—management to mix and mingle with the workers throughout the company. As a result, the top executives have no way of knowing what is really going on further down in the organization. Conversely, the underlings have no idea what issues or opportunities confront the senior group. This lack of communication is very costly and counterproductive.

2: *Incompetence.* Some managers know their system needs to be changed, but they don't know how. Executives like those tend to purposely surround themselves with the opposite of the best and the brightest—the worst and the dimmest. They envelop themselves with second-stringers, people of marginal quality, so that their own marginal quality won't stand out.

Another reason for an incompetent boss to surround himself with incompetent people is that those people are loyal to the death. It's like the Mafia. These inept aides are well aware that they aren't very good and that they owe everything they have to the person who hired them.

What's required is a totally new thought process, a totally different relationship between supervisors and subordinates. I don't care whether we're talking about on the shop floor or in the executive suite. My experience, both with Procter and with the 150 or so companies I've dealt with since I retired has been that you still have the over-fifty school who tend to believe that information is something to be controlled, that information is something to be parceled out sparingly. They are from the old school, which operated on the "need to know" approach to sharing information. The new breed, I think, is going to have to say, "Hey, in the new age, there will be these empowered individuals who have access to information and are allowed to participate in the decision-making process."

Now, I don't mean that corporations become democratic institutions where the rule is one employee, one vote. A lot of people misread what I have to say. Their reaction is, "Well, you talk about empowerment and sharing information and all, and that means you want a guy on the shop floor or the lowest-ranking salesman in the field to be making *corporate* decisions?" Not at all! What I'm saying is that these people should be entitled to participate in the decisions at their level and have a voice, have some input all the way up the corporate structure, but it's still top management that ultimately makes the vital decisions.

What I'm saying is, it's amazing how you can open people up when you allow them to think and reason with you. Once, when I was in P&G's industrial-products division, I was working with a salesman out in New Mexico. He had a brilliant idea about how we ought to change the marketing strategy of one of our industrial brands that we manufactured for the car-wash business. And eventually we put his plan into effect, but it took a long time. I asked him how long he had been thinking about this, and he said, "Well, I've been with the company about nine years. So maybe seven years, I've been mulling this over." So I asked him, "Why in the world didn't you ever come forward with it?" And you know what his answer was: "Nobody ever asked me."

By the same token, I was once working with the owner of a supermarket chain who couldn't figure out why he wasn't doing well. "My pricing is right," he told me. "My product mix is right. My advertising is right. My stores are clean. The lighting is right, the layout is right. What the hell can be wrong?"

The cause of this chain's inability to keep its customers was that the employees had an attitude problem. They were surly and nasty and unfriendly and uncommunicative to consumers. So the consumers decided it was not a pleasant place to shop. There were hundreds of stores in town, and a lot of the customers just decided to go somewhere else. The customers were saying, "There are other stores with the same products, the same prices, the same locations. And I can go there and be treated like a human being."

A lot of CEOs, a lot of managers, don't understand why their business isn't doing better. They seem to be doing all the right things, but it isn't working the way they want it to.

That's the time when you start asking your own people, as well as your customers and your suppliers, what they see as the problems. You start using all your resources to help you figure out what is wrong. A fresh perspective, fresh input, can be invaluable. It becomes self-perpetuating: If the business is bad, you push the managers harder to make it better. The harder you push them, the harder they push the employees. The end result is that everybody is under pressure, everybody is unhappy. It begins to be reflected in the employees' attitude toward the customers. A customer walks down the aisles, someone is stocking shelves, and the customer says, "Pardon me, sir, can you tell me where the ketchup is?" "Don't know. I think it's aisle seven. Ask somebody else." That's the kind of thing that really turns off the customer. You don't have to hit the customer over the head with a baseball bat to have them say, "Hey, I don't like shopping here." All you have to do is one rude thing like that— "Sorry, can't help you"—and it torpedoes thousands and thousands of dollars' worth of advertising and all the efforts you've made to attract business.

What I'm saying is—and Sam Walton was a master at this— you have to understand what your business is. If you're in retailing, for example, your store is not fifteen thousand products along with some brick and mortar and a cash register up front. What your store really is is the employees in the store, the ones who have contact with the public. But a lot of retail executives can't seem to understand that.

If you tell your employees, "Here is the new way to wear your uniforms and to approach the customers," you will fail miserably. You have to go back to square one and say, "Here is the issue. Here is the problem. And here is why we're doing this." This is why you don't treat the symptoms, you treat the cause.

But your employees will never change unless you explain to them your rationale, your reasoning, why you're asking them to do what you do. If you just tell them, "This is what you're going to do if you want to work here," it's meaningless, it's dead. You have to invest time and energy to explain to them *why* you want them to do it a certain way.

3: *Ego*. That's one of the biggest problems in American business today. If you don't hold the keys to your desk loosely, if your main motivation is fear of being fired, you probably aren't helping your company. Because you're not able to be an advocate for anything. What you're being is a politician. You'll sacrifice the better way for doing it the way that will advance your career. I wish I had a dollar for every meeting I've attended where someone makes a comment and the boss goes the other way and everyone's underneath the table eyeing their loafers: "Yes, S. J. You're right, S. J."

4: *Fear* and the lack of confidence to enter a new arena, where you may not be the expert, you may not be in control. The way it is in traditional organizations today, the higher you advance, the more you're in control. And if you want everyone to stand in the road and wave a flag, they do that. Because you're the boss and they seek to please you.

Bosses like that not only don't want capable people around them, they'd be delighted if the capable ones fell into a manhole today. In fact, this type of boss would hold the manhole open for anyone he perceived as a threat. Of course, that boss's boss ought to fire him. The type of managers I'm talking about think there's no way they can call on their subordinates for advice. Because their power is that they've got that job and they're afraid to let anyone know they don't know anything. In their state of anxiety, they fear that asking subordinates for their opinion would be viewed by the organization as an admission of weakness. There's always been a lot of that in corporate America, and there still is.

One of the biggest problems in American companies today is that too many of them have systems that reward managers for control. Many managers believe that information is power—"If I have it, I'm strong; if you don't have it, you're weak."

Some managers I've known have appropriated control and refused to share it with their people. Their approach is,

"Look, if I share it with you and let you know as much as I know, then you will be my equal. And if you're an equal, you're a threat." Managers like that are going to be on extremely thin ice and very, very nervous in this new information age, where almost everybody is going to have access to most information just as rapidly as the boss, if not sooner. That's why the new management paradigm is going to be one in which everybody says, "Look, we're going to live or die by the information technology sword. And we've got to come together and organize ourselves and learn how to work together, based on all this information we have, and then based on how we collectively decide to act, react, or not act on that information."

Ego and fear are also what cause senior managers to resist visionary types. Since these managers are by definition older, they may fear that they could become redundant or be viewed as over the hill if they allow people with vision and revolutionary ideas to get too close to power; it could be personally dangerous for them. Plus, many of them are afraid to seek out advice for fear that people will take that as an admission that they don't know how to do their job.

Not only are executives from the old school likely to run scared themselves, they purposely sow fear within their organizations. "Disagree with me, and you're history" is their line. This "technique," naturally, terrifies their people and stifles the prophets and dreamers within their companies, as survival becomes more important than creativity. This bunker mentality takes over; as a former executive of one company whose top managers operated that way complained to me, "Those bastards have ruined this wonderful company."

Today, there's a new game, and managers have to change those old rules. Changing the rules means that both sides are going to have to trust each other. And when you trust each other, you open yourself up, you make yourself vulnerable. If you're unwilling to be vulnerable, if you're unwilling to think about things differently, you're bound to come up with the same solution you always have. Only, you probably won't be part of whatever the solution is.

To be sure, courage among leaders in business and elsewhere

is at a premium today. During the Civil War, General Stonewall Jackson told some of his young officers, "Gentlemen, if you are to succeed, you must ride toward the sound of battle." I don't think enough current *Fortune 500* executives are intentionally trying to ride toward the sound of battle.

Why Use One or Two Heads If You Can Use One Hundred?

A corollary to fear is the unwillingness of many managers to understand, accept, or appreciate the learning and insight they can gain from their subordinates. Strangely, it seems the higher the manager rises, the less sensitive he or she often becomes to what those farther down in the organization can contribute to the manager's personal learning and growth.

I have spent a lot of time trying to understand why so many senior managers behave this way. I've concluded that, given the power of their rank and position, many executives assume, often falsely, that once they have attained their position, there is nothing more to be learned—in their exalted station, they have become both omnipotent and omniscient. It may be as simple as them thinking that no one else can know what they know or think as well as they think, because if someone else could, that someone else would have their job. Perhaps the exalted position itself actually causes the individual to think that he suddenly is intellectually superior to the balance of the workforce and now has the burden of doing all the thinking for the corporation. Or perhaps the individual feels so insecure in the position that it requires all his being to hang on to the job, leaving him no time for learning or listening. Regardless of what causes this behavior, these "self-contained" managers, as I call them, do tremendous damage to the organization not only in the present but also in the future. Their conduct becomes the model that many of the younger managers emulate. Senior managers like the ones I've described are, in my judgment, the greatest threat to an organization's future, because they have in effect stopped learning and stopped growing.

One prime example of how this works manifested itself several years ago when I was involved in training members of the P&G multifunctional team for their roles in the new partnership between P&G and Wal-Mart. Our team had spent about six weeks analyzing and creating the model for the company's first major multifunctional team endeavor. The members of the team had done some extraordinary work, and they were excited about presenting it to one of P&G's top executives. I arranged for him to meet with my people. When all of us had assembled in the conference room, I told the executive that the team wanted to share with him its learning and plans for creating the partnership with our largest customer. No sooner had the words left my lips than he frowned and said in no uncertain terms that he didn't have time for a presentation; rather, he insisted, he would proceed by asking all the questions.

The meeting, of course, was a disaster. First, because the executive did not know enough about the customer relationship, about partnerships, or about the team's learning to even ask the right questions. Second, his behavior was the very opposite of the team's—we had spent hundreds of man-hours learning to listen to each other, to share in problem solving, and to respect the other fellow's opinion. The team leader and I had to spend the next month trying to rebuild our unit's spirit and enthusiasm. I guess I should have known better than to invite this particular executive to meet with our "partnering" team, which, in and of itself, was a new concept, at least at P&G. I knew very well that he felt that everybody should be "wired" just like he was and that those who weren't just were not acceptable. If you didn't share his "DNA," you were a strange, malformed, abnormal son of a bitch.

The only positive impact that resulted from the session with this executive was the collective lesson on how *not* to behave that the team members learned by personally witnessing his behavior. In a way, this one meeting was beneficial—worth months of training time.

The bottom line is that companies that completely utilize the talents of all their people will always outperform those that do not. Otherwise, no matter how much talent you may have stacked up throughout the organization, you run the potential risk of having fifty thousand watts of power producing only fifty watts.

Before You Blame Your People, Consider That Most of Them May Be Experts within a Lousy System.

Along the same lines as the managers who surround themselves with second-stringers are the ones who simply encircle themselves with *too many* subordinates, whether those underlings are good staffers or not. What they are creating is one of the most dreaded of all phenomena that can plague an organization: a *bureaucracy*! One of the companies I consult for is First Union, the Charlotte, North Carolina–based megabank. First Union's chairman and CEO, Edward E. Crutchfield Jr., puts it best: "First Union has never knowingly recruited or hired a bureaucrat. Rather, First Union management has created an environment where bureaucrats are allowed to be born, to grow, and to flourish." This is a very profound statement by Crutchfield. The fact that Ed Crutchfield is aware of the problem means it is less likely to grow into a serious one at the company he runs. Remember, bureaucrats are not born, they're made!

And who makes bureaucrats? Management, of course. If your company is faced with creeping bureaucracy, or, for that matter, most other problems, it's almost always management's fault. Management has the responsibility of reinventing itself in order to help employees reinvent themselves. If workers have been taught and required to do certain jobs certain ways and have been rewarded by management for doing so, who should bear responsibility when technology or other changes in the system render the traditional methods obsolete? The workers must be guided and directed from above toward the new techniques that make the entire operation more efficient.

How *Not* to Win Friends and Influence Your People: Insult Them.

Several years ago, a well-regarded midlevel sales manager at Procter & Gamble made up his mind to accept a job at another consumer-products company. When he went in to explain his decision to the top brass, one of them commented to him, "You know, those people you're leaving to go to work for, they're the pinky-ring crowd." The man was just trying to say something derogatory about the competitor that had hired away a valuable asset. But what the P&G official who made that remark failed to notice was that this particular individual was himself wearing a little pinky-ring. He later let some of us know that he probably would have been receptive to an offer to stay with P&G. Instead, as he walked out of the room where he had announced his decision and prepared to leave the corporation, he was muttering to himself, "These guys don't have a clue. Now I know for sure that my decision to leave is correct."

Not only had that offhand remark strengthened his resolve to leave Procter, it also made it extremely unlikely that he would ever consider returning.

Leadership Usually Gags in the Executive Dining Room.

An old friend of mine, Jack Ruppert, who joined Procter & Gamble several years after I did and spent thirty years there, tells a story from his days in the Marine Corps. In 1956, Jack and about two hundred other second lieutenants were undergoing intensive training in riflery at the Quantico Marine Base in Virginia. For two weeks, they arose every morning at three o'clock to start their arduous days at the school the marines refer to as "the University of Death and Destruction." The first thing they did each morning was eat breakfast, and one day before dawn they were joined by Colonel (and future General) Lewis B. Walt, then the commanding officer of the school and later the commandant of the entire Marine Corps.

Not only was Walt unquestionably in charge, he was a bear of a man. As he approached the chow line, Jack Ruppert and the other trainees saluted and made room for Walt and his entourage to cut into the line and get their breakfasts. Walt proclaimed, loudly enough for about thirty of the men, including Jack, to hear him: "Gentlemen, don't you ever get out of my way when you are in line for chow! You are the men doing the work. My staff and I can go without eating if that's what it takes to feed all of you. Now, hear what I am about to tell you, and hear it well. If I ever hear of any of you eating before your troops eat, I will personally do you great harm!"

Another dear friend of mine ever since my Boy Scout days, Jim McWhorter, offers similar wisdom from his days as a colonel and Army Ranger through several tours of duty in Vietnam. I once asked Jim what the secret of military command is, and he said the cardinal rule of command is, "The troops always eat first."

Compare and contrast the philosophy of Lewis Walt and Jim McWhorter with the lessons we learn from the executive dining room.

I have never read or heard how the executive dining room came into existence, but I'm sure that whoever created it thought the concept was a great idea. The thinking no doubt was that those who ran the company were in need of a private place, a special sanctuary, to discuss the earth-shattering issues that confronted them. Obviously, captains of industry could not do this in a public place—that is, out among their lowly employees.

Over the years, the executive dining room has become a signal that top management is different—meaning better—than the workers, and is therefore entitled to a private place to eat. It also sends a message that all that teamwork we talk about does not apply to the executive suite. If I were a CEO, I would go to great lengths to maneuver my competitors into installing executive dining rooms; nothing is more likely to create divisiveness within a company.

If memory serves me correctly, I ate lunch in the executive dining room a total of twice during my four years as a vice-president of Procter & Gamble. Two times in four years!

I decided not to eat in the dining room for the best of reasons, but the result was, to some extent, the worst. Many of my fellow executives came to regard me as "that arrogant son of a bitch! He doesn't want to join the Old Boys club. He thinks he's better than we are. To hell with him!" Yes, some of my colleagues took my refusal to dine with them as a slap in the face, and I can't say they were wrong, although shunning them certainly was not my motive.

As time went by, it became a given among top management that I seldom showed up in the dining room. The times that I did eat there, I noticed a pecking order that was virtually set in concrete. If the senior guy at the table decided he wanted to talk football, guess what subject was discussed? If he wanted to discuss politics, you discussed politics. In my opinion, that was crazy. The last thing I wanted to do was to become one of the top officers of the company and suddenly hear nothing but what the other officers were saying. I know it may sound like a cheap political stunt, but I honestly felt I could help the company by being closer to the troops. I couldn't persuade any of the other officers to do it my way, but *I* did it my own way. Even today, some of my fellow former officers tell me they still can't believe how brave I was, how I stood by my convictions.

Why did I do it? As I say, I feel that the closer you are to your troops, the more you can learn what's *really* going on. During my years as a vice-president, I felt I could learn a lot more by eating lunch with six, eight, twelve different employees every day in the employee cafeteria than I could by sitting down five times a week with the same group of officers. Furthermore, eating in the company cafeteria instead of in the executive dining room meant that I had to walk a long way from my office to the cafeteria and back. Usually, during those daily walks, I was able to meet as many as twenty-five different people—people I would not have had an opportunity to talk to if I had been sitting up in the executive dining room, talking to the same people every day about the same things and listening to everyone agreeing with each other.

Of course, executive dining rooms are also a symbol of the divisions within management itself as well as between management and labor, because only a select few managers are allowed to eat in them. At many companies, the key officials tend to split management into the serfs and the nobility. The serfs—the mid- and low-level managers—aren't allowed to do anything except process information; the nobility then takes that data and makes all the important decisions.

After I became a regular in the employee cafeteria, the rank and file started saying, "At last, we have someone at the top level who can speak for us." They knew that I was not a phony. My eating with them sent a message that we were all part of a team. At Procter & Gamble, the same as at most other companies, we made a lot of speeches about how the company and the employees were inseparable, about how we loved the employees, but in the final analysis the employees were saying, "Well, if you really love me, why won't you come eat with me?"

What executives accomplish by isolating ourselves at lunchtime is to show the workers that management says one thing and does the opposite. Which, of course, creates a "We're important and you're not" attitude. I don't think there's a single executive perk that projects a we-against-them attitude more than segregated eating facilities. And segregation is exactly what I mean: separate, but not equal. Having management dine in private, luxurious surroundings, being presented with the finest food by their faithful, loyal retainers, the *servants,* is the most blatant manifestation of the air that "We are better, we are higher, we are richer, we are smarter. And everyone else is beneath us—*beneath* us!"

About six months after I retired, P&G closed its executive dining room. The rationale offered was that it was too costly to maintain a separate dining room for thirty or forty officers now that we were in this belt-tightening mode. More recently, in the summer of 1994, one of America's largest corporations, Mobil Oil, closed its executive dining room, reasoning that the trend in American industry is clearly away from "limited membership." Not long before Mobil shut the facility down, a bogus memo was circulated among employees, declaring that although the company was trying to reduce costs in other areas, "the executive dining room remains secure."

Procter & Gamble's executive lunchroom recently reopened, but I hope the current top management avails itself of the opportunity to mingle with—and dine with—the rank-and-file employees as often as possible.

If Everyone's Looking Out for Themselves, No One Is Looking Out for the Whole Enterprise.

For many years at Procter & Gamble the division sales managers, who practically lived on airplanes as they traveled from district to district, flew first class and stayed in top-of-the-line hotels. Those perks helped compensate them for all their time away from their families. They and other employees were allowed to accumulate frequent-flier miles while traveling on company business.

One day during the mid-1980s, an edict was abruptly handed down from the executive suite: "Under no circumstances will first-class travel be authorized, and from this day forward, all frequent-flier mileage accumulated on business travel will belong to the Company."

A number of old-line sales managers understood the need to curtail expenses; moreover, as stockholders, they were happy to do whatever was needed to improve P&G's profit position. Still, they were understandably miffed by this new way of doing business.

The problem wasn't the policy change itself. No, the problem was the total lack of humanity evidenced by management's way of announcing and executing the new procedures. If top management had said, "Look, times are tough. We need to take some extreme measures, including travel expense control. At the same time, we, your management, are going to restrict our own use of corporate aircraft," or, "We are passing up our own stock options this year," everyone would have agreed and pitched in to help, and the changes in travel policy would have been accepted and would have disappeared without a ripple.

Instead, these changes in travel policy and the way in which they were announced served to create two distinct and widely separated classes within P&G. The first—corporate management—would continue to enjoy the perks of company aircraft and the traditional financial benefits. The second caste—the huge majority of underclass employees—would continue to ride in the back of the plane, both figuratively and literally. This Marie Antoinette system of management created dissension when none was necessary. Top management had forgotten a fundamental principle of leadership: "Don't ask your people to do anything you're not willing to do yourself."

Furthermore, the high-handedness with which the new policy was implemented caused open rebellion in the ranks. Most of the senior sales division managers simply ignored the edict or found ways to get around it. The intent of the new rule was correct, and everyone knew it, but it was executed so ineptly that it produced untold cost in terms of unproductive bitching, devious behavior, and reduced respect for and loyalty to the company and its top executives.

Decisions, Decisions, Decisions—*Somebody* Has to Make Them.

Among my least favorite management types are the ones I call string collectors. They collect information as if each individual piece of data they gather amounts to a twelve-inch piece of string that they then tie together. They just keep collecting more and more string—that is, data—and tying it into a ball of string until it gets so damned big they can't push it through the door.

They accumulate every possible piece of information, and yet they still want one more piece, always one more, one more. It's like they're constipated. They keep saying, "Well, I don't have quite enough data to make the decision yet." All they're doing, of course, is creating a mechanism that allows them to avoid making decisions. You can never give that sort of person enough information to make a decision. In the words of industrialist-philanthropist Nathan Cummings, "Nothing will ever be attempted if all possible objections must first be overcome." The kind of managers to whom Cummings is referring spend so much time trying to avoid making mistakes that they don't perform as well as they're capable of and don't allow staffers to perform as well as they're capable of.

People who sit on the fence and can't make a decision are way, way down on my list. One trait of the true leader is decisiveness; if you can't make a decision, you probably aren't cut out to be a leader. And when I talk about decisiveness, I mean just that. Yes, consult your people, solicit their input, and weigh it carefully. In the end, though, only the true leader can make the important decisions. Decision making by consensus is not leadership; it's followership. In the words of Abraham Lincoln, after he voted yes on an issue and every member of his cabinet voted no: "The ayes have it!"

By the same token, I'm not suggesting that anyone confuse decision making per se and mere motion on the one hand with progress on the other. Too many managers today seem to think that they must always be moving or doing something to justify their jobs. This is normally a tremendous waste of time, energy, and productivity. I maintain that the typical manager wastes 30 to 40 percent of his time busying himself with make-work projects. All managers need to focus on doing just a few things extremely well. When they're not working on one of those things, that's when they need to prop their feet up and do some serious thinking. Unfortunately, that isn't going to happen until the internal reward and recognition systems are changed to allow this kind of behavior. Propping up one's feet and just thinking—*just thinking!*—often produces nothing more than the boss's wrath. Today's CEO must let it be known that, in the words of the famous GE commercial, progress—not simply motion—is the company's most important product.

I know that whenever I sat in my office with my feet propped up and tried to just *think,* I felt a tremendous sense of guilt. I don't think anybody would have reprimanded me for doing that, but the environment was such that you just didn't do it. Nobody ever finished all their work. If you had five projects to do and you finished those, you'd better have three more waiting. Because no idle time was allowed.

A lot of this is brought about by the overall management environment. There was no feeling of "I've got to stay busy, even if it's make-work busy" in Silicon Valley, especially back in the early days. But those people work incredibly long hours because they love their work. Some of them sleep in sleeping bags in their offices and work off and on around the clock. Instead of it being a nine-to-five job, you set your own hours. Some of those creative geniuses were night owls. They might not even come to work until normal people were going home. Nobody cared. And look what they created. But that wouldn't be tolerated in most of the button-downed corporations.

Damn the Torpedoes! Full Speed Ahead!

An old-time Procter & Gamble unit manager named Art Glenn had a favorite story about managerial inflexibility and its potential for disaster. Many years ago, a senior sales manager traveled by train from Cincinnati to Jacksonville to review Art's market with him. When the executive arrived in

Jacksonville and Art picked him up, there were hurricane warnings flying.

Glenn advised his boss that they should stay inside that day, but the sales manager, not being from hurricane country, didn't have much respect for a little wind and rain. He insisted that they stick to their plan. The first thing that happened as the two of them walked out of the hotel where the sales manager was staying was that both of their hats went flying over a three-story building. Art said he knew right then that that was an omen that bad things were in store. But the sales manager was insistent, and they got into Art's car and headed toward the first store on the route Art had mapped out. By then it was raining so hard that the windshield wipers couldn't handle the rain, so they were just creeping along.

Up ahead was an underpass where the road dipped beneath the railroad tracks. As they approached the underpass, Art saw a ton of water on the road and he thought something looked unusual, so he slowed down. The sales manager ordered him, "Well, go on through! Go on through!" But, as Art got closer, he could see a man standing in water up to his knees, waving his arms furiously and motioning them to stop. The sales manager kept urging, "Go on! Go on! Pass him!" Art inched toward the man and rolled his window down. When Art and his boss got close enough to hear the man over the howling wind, he was shouting, "Go back! Go back! I'm standing on top of my car!" So he must have been standing in about eight feet of water.

The sales manager finally decided that maybe it wasn't such a bad idea after all to return to the hotel and wait out the storm. Of course, he had ignored Art's advice that they never should have set out in the first place on a day like that.

The Third-Base Umpire Doesn't Call Balls and Strikes.

One of the cardinal rules of baseball is that the umpire at third base doesn't call balls and strikes (except, occasionally, on the question of whether or not a lefthanded batter swung at a pitch).

There's a very simple explanation for this practice. It's not because the third-base umpire is stupid, it's not because he isn't qualified, it's not because he doesn't know the game of baseball. The reason is that he is out of position. I have noticed that the way many American corporations are structured today, senior officers and managers are often out of position. CEOs at the top of the pyramid are making decisions that affect not only employees in the middle of the pyramid but those at the bottom—even though the CEO frequently knows hardly anything about what's going on down there. He or she is out of position to know what's really going on.

If you're not in the correct position, you simply shouldn't be making the calls or the decisions. But too many CEOs say, "I'm too busy to be in all of those positions to make those calls. That's why I've got all this staff reporting to me." What they fail to realize is that by the time much of the information is filtered up to the CEO—and given our desire to please the boss, we all filter—the information that he receives will have been tailored or doctored or slanted toward telling him what he wants to hear. That's because so many of the managers reporting to the CEO do not want to be the bearers of bad news.

I used to make a point of telling employees who visited me in my office that what you see depends on where you stand. Behind my desk was a row of four huge windows overlooking downtown Cincinnati; on the wall opposite me was a large and beautiful Japanese screen I had bought on one of my trips. I would ask my guests to describe my office, to tell me what they saw. Invariably, they would answer, "It has a large desk and four large windows." And I would insist, "No it doesn't. It has a large desk and a large Japanese screen." Then I would make the point that to me, the office did not have four large windows. It only had a desk and a large screen. Because what I saw depended on where I stood or where I sat. And what they saw depended on where they stood or where they sat.

That used to make quite an impression, particularly on my younger people. To really understand someone else's perspective, the first thing you have to do, as the American Indian saying goes, is walk a mile in their moccasins. If a CEO stands in one particular place and looks at his organization, he may see it as a triangle. But people standing in other positions or facing in other directions may see it as a trapezoid.

And if management sees it as a triangle and the workers see it as a trapezoid, they're never going to be able to come together and you're going to have labor problems, on top of everything else.

We need more managers who are willing to admit that they don't know it all, that they must see things through the eyes of other people, and that what they see is determined by where they stand. They have to make sure that they stand in enough positions within their company to really understand what is going on throughout the organization.

Never Assume Anything!

In 1955, after I had been a unit manager in Memphis (my first management job) for a few months, I took my first crack at recruiting new employees. I went over to my alma mater, Memphis State College, which was an unusual place for large companies to recruit. Back in those days, college recruiting was in its primitive stages, particularly in small state-supported colleges in the South. College recruiting itself was just about brand-new; until then, most new hires had been picked on an as-needed basis, which is how I went to work for the company. And the primary vehicle for finding candidates had been newspaper help-wanted ads. As recruiting in person evolved, the initial emphasis was confined to Ivy League and engineering schools. Nevertheless, the company viewed the opportunity to establish rapport with college faculty and recruit students on campus as the wave of the future, a much better way of bringing qualified candidates into the company than through the traditional approach of help-wanted ads in newspapers. I was excited to lead the effort at Memphis State for a number of reasons, not the least of which was that I had been a "BMOC" at MSC only a few years earlier; the idea of returning to campus as a manager with a major corporation was indeed heady stuff for a twenty-three-year-old.

I studied the material available and went about the recruiting process exactly as my instruction manual specified. First, I talked with several professors I knew, as well as the dean of students (in those days no one person or office at MSC was responsible for job placement). My contacts spread the word via the campus newspaper, fraternities, bulletin board notices, and class-room announcements. When the actual day of interviewing arrived, I was swamped with over twenty-five candidates who turned out to talk about working for P&G. The first day, either I rejected about 80 percent or else the applicants themselves concluded that they had no interest in selling soap to grocery stores in Mississippi, Tennessee, and Arkansas. I tested the remaining five and eventually arranged for other unit managers and my supervisor, the district manager, to interview the finalists.

One young man in particular impressed me from the moment we shook hands. He was tall, good-looking, and conservatively dressed, with an air of command about him. He fit the P&G model perfectly, and I was convinced that on my first venture into college recruiting, I had hit the jackpot. After lengthy interviews, which included scores of questions about his past and his future goals and ambition, and after a battery of tests, I was positive that we had a real winner. I offered him a job, provided he passed a background check; he did, with flying colors, and we hired him.

The following Monday I drove the company car, which would be assigned to him, to the parking lot of a local super-market where we were to meet and begin week one of a thir-teen-week indoctrination program. My new salesman arrived at the appointed time, and the two of us exchanged pleasantries and spent about an hour discussing the training program and exactly what we would do that first day. At the end of the hour, I handed my prized recruit, my blue-chipper, the keys to the company car. His response buckled my knees: My perfect candidate, the future CEO, could not drive a car! He didn't even have a driver's license! During all the questions, all the tests, all the interviews, I had never asked him the most basic of questions—could he drive an automobile?

From that day forward, my first question to the hundreds of job applicants I interviewed was, "Can you drive a car?" Without exception, the job applicants answered that of course they could, and many of them couldn't keep themselves from looking at me like maybe I wasn't quite playing with a full deck. But I had my reasons for asking that question—damned good ones. Live and learn, as the adage goes.

Behind Every Successful Man There May Stand a Woman Who Thinks His Boss Is Trying to Work Him to Death.

Hey, I'm definitely not saying that *I'm* perfect. The idea is to learn from your mistakes instead of repeating them. After all, there are times when you think you are doing the right thing for both your company and your people, but it all blows up in your face and leaves you wondering how your best intentions could backfire so badly. Neglecting to ask my "perfect sales rep" if he knew how to drive was one of those times. Another involved the wives of some of the men who worked for me.

One of the many lessons I learned the hard way was to never, ever, assume that an employee's spouse feels the same way about the company and the job as you do and as the employee may. I discovered this truism in 1979 while I was serving as sales manager of the paper-products division. Our part of the company had been thriving for several years; the perpetual challenge was to continue to deliver greater sales volume, year after year after year. In the company in general and in the paper-products division specifically, it was completely unacceptable for sales not to grow each year, regardless of breakthroughs by the competition, changes in the consumer's taste, or any other rationalization. There simply was no such thing as an acceptable excuse! If the growth bubble were to burst, you sure as hell didn't want it to happen on your watch, so you did whatever it took to deliver more volume.

One Sunday afternoon, while revving up for the coming workweek, I had a brainstorm: I would involve the wives of the managers in my sales division in the quest to produce an all-time record quarter. My reasoning was that if I could induce the wives to feel like a part of the business, they would develop a sense of proprietorship. This, in turn, would motivate them to encourage their husbands to work a little harder. I could hardly resist congratulating myself for my masterful concept of "micro teamworking" at its best. A husband-and-wife team focusing together on the most important things in life, like generating the movement of historic tonnages of toilet paper and paper towels, could hardly fail.

Bright and early Monday morning, I composed a letter to the

wives of each of my six division managers. I explained our sales goals and the importance of our meeting them, praised their husband's efforts to date, and asked each wife to encourage her husband to dig just a little deeper and add another gram or two of energy to our campaign. I ended by offering a free dinner for four at Cincinnati's finest restaurant to the husband-and-wife "team" who increased their volume the most. My secretary typed the letters on my finest stationery and mailed them to each of the six wives.

Then I sat back and awaited what I knew would be an outstanding response, providing yet another example of creativity to sales managers throughout the company on the part of yours truly. Four days later, I received my first reply. It was not exactly what I had expected. In fact, this lady was so mad that, had she been a man, I suspect she would have asked me to "step outside" to settle our differences. Her message, written in beautiful longhand, informed me that her husband already worked as hard as any individual could work and that he spent many more hours on business than he did with her and their family. Furthermore, according to her, he was contributing far more to the company than his salary warranted; the last thing he needed was even more pressure from home to make him work harder. Contrary to what I had been hoping for, she suggested that I find a way to influence the managers, especially her husband, to slow down and smell the roses. In closing, she told me exactly what I could do with both the volume contest and the dinner for four.

In retrospect, I realized that my fatal mistake was to assume that all wives thought and reacted exactly like mine, that other wives also shared their husbands' business interests and would rush enthusiastically to the battlements. That was the last time I attempted to involve spouses in company projects. It also marked the first time I saw clearly that there were some people whose lives did not revolve around selling toilet paper.

Epilogue:

I felt this lady's complaints were entirely justified, and her husband's career was not harmed in any way; no one but me knew about her letter. I'm not even sure her husband was ever aware of the letter she had written me. To this day, Barbara and

I exchange Christmas cards with that couple, and they visited us at Hilton Head several years ago. Neither the lady nor I has ever mentioned her letter. Her response was the only one I received to my "stroke of genius" letter to the wives. I have always assumed that the wife who chewed me out in no uncertain terms must have expressed her sentiments to the wives of the other managers, and none of them felt it necessary to elaborate on her views.

Practice What You Preach—Especially If It's Advice You Paid to Obtain.

I have spent almost forty years in corporate America, but the mistakes, blunders, and all-around ineptitude on the part of some business executives still amaze me on occasion.

Several years ago a major corporation paid me a hefty fee to come in and speak to several hundred employees on how to improve their operations and their sales techniques.

I had worked with this company, starting a couple of months in advance of my presentation, and senior management seemed to be in complete accord with my advice that the wave of the future is to be totally honest, totally trusting, to be caring and sharing with your customers and your suppliers, as well as with your own people.

I was certainly under the impression that the top managers of this company were already on the same page that I was and that my presentation was just going to jell this and confirm it.

Now, as a provider of my speech, I became one of this corporation's suppliers. My contract reads that I'm to be paid 50 percent upon signing, with the balance of my fee due within five days of my speech. I gave my speech around the twentieth of the month, had a very pleasant time, said my good-byes, and waited for them to send me the rest of my money.

The five days passed. Then a week, two weeks, a month. I didn't want to be pushy, but finally I called the CEO's office and asked where my money was. "Oh," the CEO's secretary explained, "we pay our bills at the end of the month"—the month *after* my speech, that is! So, right there, they're talking about a delay of approximately six weeks, even though they had signed a contract with me in black and white that specified that

I was to be paid within five days. Nor had they paid my expenses, which were also due immediately.

I got paid, of course—eventually. But the point is that the very thing they hired me to talk about was fairness, trust, and developing caring, sharing relationships with their suppliers, among others. So, here I was, a supplier, and the very next week they violated the lesson I taught them.

Their end-of-the-month policy amounted to them saying, "Our internal systems are for our convenience, for *our* good. We can't be flexible, we can't change, because this is our policy. And you will have to adapt yourself to us." And no matter what my contract said, their position was, "We're sorry. But we only write checks at the end of the month." And they expected me to accept that—like it or lump it.

Obviously, holding me hostage to their "corporate policies" was no way to create a trusting partnership with their supplier. What if I were a small supplier, someone who does not have a huge cash flow? Someone who provides something for that company on the first of the month, but they're going to use his money for at least thirty days until he gets paid?

But, back to the bottom line: *They paid me to teach them how to improve themselves!*

It's Not What You Don't Know That Will Hurt You, It's What You Do Know That Ain't So.

History is filled with predictions that turned out to be 180 degrees opposite the truth: "Columbus is sailing off to his death, because the world is flat"; "Airships will never fly"; "Babe Ruth never should have given up pitching to be an everyday ballplayer"; "Most women aren't interested in the right to vote"; "The atomic bomb will never work"; "No way a second-rate actor could be elected president of the United States."

A lot of business executives and managers claim they *know* things to be true that are patently false. For instance, they feel that the average worker is a lazy son of a bitch who gets up in the morning and says, "I'll go to work and screw up today." Believing things like that, which are inherently untrue, is a tremendous weakness for managers.

In my main field of expertise, sales, I worked with many a sales manager who felt that if you went to customers and asked them for input, all they were going to do was try to get their hands deeper into your pocket. A lot of sales managers used to say that what you needed to do was really load up the retailer with your product. If you could take up as much of his shelf space and his backroom space as possible with a huge inventory of your merchandise, he would have to sell your stuff because he couldn't afford not to. But what you were also doing was causing internal problems for the retailer by tying up his capital, which diminished his ability to compete; you weren't helping him at all. There always has been a certain selfishness in the selling game. What it amounts to is, "If I can swap my product for your dollars, I am better off, and I really don't give a damn what happens to you after that." I think that in the new age, in a partnering relationship, you can't be that selfish. You can't just say, "Well, that's your problem." Companies that have that attitude are doomed to lose out in the twenty-first century. You have to be as sensitive about the retailer's money, his cash flow, as he is. In the new sales environment, you can no longer follow the old rule of "Load 'em and leave 'em."

And that applies across the board, to all kinds of businesses, whether you're in sales or anything else. If you *know* something—absolutely, positively know it—you had better be right. Otherwise, you're in big, big trouble.

Because it's the visionaries who have always led us into tomorrow by ignoring the common knowledge and going against the grain. Like Columbus establishing that the world wasn't flat, and the Wright brothers demonstrating that the airplane wasn't just a concept out of science fiction. And in this era, Ted Turner with his idea that there was a place for an around-the-clock, all-news television network—something called CNN; and Al Neuharth with his silly notion that people would buy a daily newspaper that contained no local news and short, punchy, mostly upbeat stories. "MacPaper," it's often dismissed as. But millions of people read *USA Today,* day in and day out. And imagine the "nut" who suggested a few years back, "Let's put a machine filled with money in the middle of a shopping center and leave it there, without an attendant." He must have been laughed out of the room or even stoned, but today the ATM (automated teller machine) is everywhere, because it fills a need. It's people like that who are inventing the future.

A Boss Who Is a Lemon Should Be Traded for Another Model.

Some bosses, like some dogs, simply cannot be housebroken. That doesn't mean they're of no value. I like to tell young people today, whether you stay with one company for your entire career or change jobs a number of times, one of the things you ought to be sensitive to is observing both the strengths and the weaknesses of the people you work with and the people you work for.

You can learn from your bosses as much about how *not* to manage as you can about how *to* manage. I once worked for a boss who would have made a Harvard Business School textbook example of how not to manage. He endlessly compiled data in order to avoid making decisions. He lied to his people as well. Working for him wasn't fun, but it was one of the most valuable learning experiences I ever had.

A lot of people are so eager to learn how to manage when they enter business that they dismiss bad management as an aberration within the system. They regard a bad manager as just one bad apple in the barrel. What these employees—young, old, or in-between—should do is make the most of a bad situation. Observe the way bad managers do what they do and then try to avoid doing it, just as I did.

Spectators Versus Leaders.

Some managers are what I define as spectators rather than leaders. Spectatorship means managers who *appear* to be letting their people run the game, perform, and do their best, but the whole time they're standing on the edge of the field, watching the action, and almost letting events happen randomly. When things start going bad, the spectator will claim that he was just an observer and that everything bad is someone else's fault. But when something good happens, he will be the first to attempt to take credit for it. Spectator-managers make it a noncontact sport. When you're sitting up in the bleachers or on the edge of the field and not directly involved, not engaged, then you can avoid getting harmed or tainted by disasters. You get none of the negative fallout. Most people who work for a spectator as opposed to a leader are able to sense it immediately.

I read somewhere years ago that among the differences between spectators, who practice a "hands-off" style of management, and leaders, who come from the "hands-on" school, are:

• The spectator says, "This is our objective. You know what to do and what results you are expected to deliver. Now go do it, and come back and tell me how you did it."

The leader says, "We all agree on our goals. I think I can help you achieve them best by being involved with you in this effort."

• The spectator says, "Keep trying until you get it right."

The leader says, "Where are you having trouble? How can I help you?"

• The spectator says, "*You're* supposed to be the manager. *You* figure it out."

The leader says, "How do you think we could do it? Maybe we can figure it out together."

Pritchett's Ten Rules for Stifling Innovation.

1. Regard any new ideas from below with suspicion.
2. Insist that people who need your approval to act must first go through several other layers of management to get to you.
3. Express your criticism freely, and withhold your praise.
4. Treat identification of problems as a sign of failure.
5. Control everything carefully.
6. Secretly make decisions to reorganize or to change policies.
7. Make sure that requests for information must be fully justified, and guard against letting data be given out to employees freely. Follow religiously the "need to know" rule—you never can tell when the right information might fall into the wrong hands.
8. Assign to lower-level managers, in the name of delegation and participation, the responsibility for figuring out how to cut back, lay off, or move people around, or to otherwise implement threatening decisions you yourself have made. And by all means, make them do it quickly!
9. Operate on the assumption that nothing will work as well without you as it will with you.
10. Above all, never forget that *you* are supreme and superior and that *you* already know everything important there is to know about this business.

Pritchett's Twelve Deadly Sins of Management.

1. Being product driven instead of customer driven.
2. Focusing internally instead of externally.
3. Believing that the formula for success, which got the company where it is today, will carry the firm into the future.
4. Allowing the traditional pyramid structure, the primary cause of low productivity throughout an organization, to dominate.
5. Forgetting that it's not what you *don't know* that can cripple you; it's what you *do know that ain't so.*
6. Avoiding risk altogether rather than managing it effectively.
7. Discouraging your people from telling you the truth.
8. Failing to understand that all management is the management of people, not of things.
9. Failing to recognize that an organization's most precious resource is its people and not knowing how to deploy them.
10. Failing to realize that it is the people in the organization who will either make or break the organization.
11. Silencing the internal dreamers, poets, and all other dissenting voices.
12. Teaching your people that their most important mission is not to screw up.

5
How to Manage Successfully

> "Come to the edge," he said.
> They said: "We are afraid."
> "Come to the edge," he said.
> They came.
> He pushed them . . . and they flew.
> Those who love us may well push
>   us when we're ready to fly.
>
> —Guillaume Apollinaire,
>   poet and contemporary of Picasso

Those words of Apollinaire, which constitute one of my very favorite messages, should be inscribed and framed in the office of everyone who aspires to be a leader. A true leader must always keep that carrot a little further out there and always question you and always challenge you and always push you. There is a time when everyone needs to be pushed, and the leader should know when that time is.

The Education of Lou Pritchett: Learning All My Life, from Day One Right Up to Today.

I mentioned that you can learn a lot from a bad boss—namely, how *not* to manage. Good bosses, naturally, provide a much more valuable opportunity to learn. I think everyone, from the CEO of the company to the newest hire, should keep track of what they learn from the people they work for. Then, as the years go by, do what I have done: Make a list of the best bosses you worked for and what you learned from them. Keep this list on paper, retain it in your head, and use it to improve yourself and to teach the people who eventually go to work for you.

When I was thirteen, soon after my father died, I had to go to work. My first job was in a grocery store named Weona, which was owned by an Italian named Valente Ugolini. He looked just like a grocer ought to look—the big belly, the apron, the whole nine yards. He never said to me when he hired me that he felt sorry for me because I was thirteen years old and my father had just died, but he gave me a job and I worked there for several years during the summertime and in the afternoon after school. By his nuances, by what he allowed me to do in the store, by his trusting me to run the cash register, by all these things, Mr. Ugolini let me know that he believed in me. It was an outstanding example of trusting a young person and helping to groom him without forcing him, a tap-to-the-left, tap-to-the-right kind of thing.

Another Memphis grocer who taught me a lot about selling and about life was a man named Roy Good. He owned an independent market that was right across the street from an A&P. That was formidable competition, but Roy Good had one big advantage: The guy who ran the A&P was just a manager, but Mr. Good was the owner of his store—if he didn't run it right, he would lose his business and his only source of income.

Roy Good won his customers' loyalty by always doing a little bit extra for them. With my mother, knowing that we were struggling to make ends meet, he always gave her an extra ounce of meat or coffee or whatever she was purchasing. He believed that you did anything you could to gain and keep customers.

During the early 1940s, the war years, when I was ten or so, Mr. Good had a big display of candy that cost a penny for five pieces. If you wanted some candy, the clerk had to come up, slide the cabinet open, get a paper bag, go in, get the candy, take it out, and measure it for you. I used to stand out in front of the store, and when a housewife would come out with a load of groceries, I would carry them home for her in my little red wagon. Very few people had cars of their own in those days; mostly, they used the streetcar to get around. Mr. Good kept an eye on me, and one day he came up to me and told me, "Anytime you want some candy, Lou, you go in and help yourself. I don't let the other boys do that, but I'm going to let you do it." Then he motioned toward a Dixie cup that sat on the counter and said,

"You just put your money in this cup, whatever you owe me." I will never forget that as long as I live. You could have made me the head of General Motors and I wouldn't have been as thrilled. The man trusted me. Do you think there's any way I would have violated that trust?

That way of doing business helped Roy Good survive against that big national chain, which could always beat him with lower prices. But he knew there was nothing more important than the way he treated his customers, and there was no way the A&P could match him on service.

Years later, I went to high school with Mr. Good's daughter. One day she said to me, "You know, my daddy is more of a preacher than a merchant. And his customers are almost like his flock." That may sound a little ridiculous or a little melodramatic, but the way he treated me was one of the major lessons I learned early on about the relationship between customers and vendors.

Yes, treat your customers like your flock instead of merely like people whose money you want to transfer from their pockets to yours. It works every time!

During my thirty-six years at Procter & Gamble, I worked for many bosses, including those I reported to indirectly, as well as directly. Some had great strengths and some had great weaknesses, but six of them had all the right stuff—the right combination of intelligence, integrity, compassion for others and humility. Raw and unpolished as I was when I joined the company, I know that I never would have been a success had it not been for what I learned from these six bosses. Those six (in order of when I worked for them):

Grady Collins, 1953–1955
Jack Hanley, 1954–1972
Ernie Baker, 1955–1959
Jim Edwards, 1975–1980
King Fletcher, 1981–1984
Tom Laco, 1985–1989

Grady Collins, my very first boss at P&G, set the standard for all the others. I can still see the stunned look in Grady's eyes in September 1953 when I stepped off that Greyhound bus in Tupelo, Mississippi, to start my career. As I mentioned, I had a crew cut and was wearing my very best college outfit—blue suede shoes, gray trousers, and a maroon corduroy sport jacket. Grady had not been involved in selecting me for the job but had taken me into his unit on the recommendation of his own boss, district manager S. G. "Red" Collins. In those days, it was a real black mark for a district or unit to have a vacancy, because an opening translated into lower orders; no one would be calling on "the trade," as we called our customers. Grady had accepted his boss's selection, and now here I stood at the bus station in Tupelo, saying, "Hello, Mr. Collins, I'm your new salesman."

During the fifteen months I worked for Grady Collins, my learning curve soared! Never had I imagined the wonders that Grady showed me—how to plan for a call, how to estimate the needed P&G volume, how to outsell and outthink the competitor, how to gain the customer's confidence. One of the most effective training tools Grady used was to alternate customer calls with me. He would accompany me out into the field, and each of us would handle every other call. After I had been on the job for several months, he and I would have "Who Can Sell More" contests on these alternating calls.

Grady was a master teacher with unbelievable patience, and I hung on his every word. I was absolutely convinced that the gods had smiled on me and allowed me to work with the crème de la crème of sales managers. Many years later, I realized that Grady Collins had done more to shape my thought processes and selling skills than four years of college had. Grady taught me the real rules of selling, of business, and of human relationships, as well as the value of integrity in dealing with others.

When I was starting off in Tupelo in the mid-1950s, back in the days before the proliferation of supermarkets, my responsibility was to sell P&G products to retail stores that by today's standards would be classified as "mom-and-pop" stores. My accounts also included ten reasonably large wholesalers in the northeast corner of Mississippi. When I called on the wholesalers, I would go into their warehouses, which were suffocatingly hot in summer and freezing cold in winter, and take a count of all their P&G inventory. An employee from the customer always accompanied the sales rep to make sure that the inventory count was accurate, so that the wholesaler would not be misled into ordering more than he needed.

I called on each wholesaler about once a month, and after some six months on the job and half a dozen visits to each customer, I stopped by the New Albany Wholesale Company in New Albany, Mississippi. One of the employees told me that the owner, Hank Powell, wanted to see me. I went back to Mr. Powell's office, and he sat me down and said, "Lou, I've been watching you during your calls on us. You have impressed me with your honesty, so from now on, you just go ahead into the warehouse by yourself and take your own count."

I can't tell you how much this man's trust meant to me, a brand-new sales rep who was eager to advance. Before long, the other nine wholesalers entrusted me to do the same thing. This experience taught me how important it is to have someone trust you, and to do whatever you can to earn their trust.

Jack Hanley never was my direct supervisor. Rather, he was always my boss's boss. Nevertheless, I saw and felt Jack's influence as much as I did that of any immediate supervisor. Jack Hanley was my personal hero from the day I first met him in 1954 until he resigned from P&G to become president of Monsanto in 1972. Perhaps he represented a father figure to me, that strong male character I needed so badly from the time my own father died. Jack Hanley was such a positive influence on me during my formative years with the company that whenever other companies approached me with job offers, I always said to myself, "If P&G is good enough for Mr. Hanley, it has to be good enough for Lou Pritchett." To this day, forty years after I first encountered him, it's still difficult for me to refer to Hanley as "Jack." Calling him "Jack" seems like referring to the Queen as "Liz."

Hanley possessed the most dynamic personality of any individual I have ever encountered. He could walk into a room filled with people and take charge, just by the sheer force of his personality. I have seen him enter meetings in the company of heavyweights such as Neil McElroy and Howard Morgens, and even though Hanley was junior in rank, it was he who radiated command. There was just something about Hanley that caused other people to stop talking when he arrived in order to hear and observe "the great one." To fully appreciate this, you should know that both Neil McElroy and Howard Morgens were extremely impressive, authoritative, and self-assured men. Nevertheless, it was Jack Hanley who always stood out. Although he was always "onstage" and in control, by no means did Jack Hanley dominate a meeting or a conversation.

My colleagues and I used to bet on when Jack would become president of Procter & Gamble; there just wasn't any doubt that he was destined to run the company. All of us believed that that would ensure the company's growth and continued preeminence in the consumer goods business. I once described Mr. Hanley to my mother by explaining that his leadership skills were a combination of MacArthur's and Patton's and that his vision and compassion were comparable to Churchill's. My mother's response was that if I was correct, why wasn't Hanley at least president of the United States? And my answer was that he no doubt could be if he wanted to.

Jack Hanley worked me harder—and taught me more—than any other boss I've ever had. He had a unique ability to bring out the very best in people, to make them want to become all they were capable of becoming, and then some. I have often wondered what P&G would look like today, and how much more I might have contributed, if Jack had remained with the company and become CEO.

The first boss who taught me how to think as a manager rather than as a salesman was Ernie Baker. Although Ernie was a super salesman, he definitely understood the need for a salesperson to be first and foremost a manager and to think beyond the case volume or the short-term order. Ernie knew instinctively that true success depended upon the salesperson's ability to communicate with the customer. As he used to say, "If you really know the customer and the customer knows you, you've got a leg up."

Ernie taught me the value of thinking strategically rather than tactically, and also that strategic thinking could be applied to the smallest sales challenge as well as the largest. He also knew the value of challenging and stretching his people. As a unit manager, Ernie assigned me responsibility for the largest customer in the Memphis district, Malone & Hyde Wholesalers. In most districts, the district manager always handled the largest, most prestigious customers. But Ernie didn't follow that rule. He believed in training through challenging, and it worked. To his credit, Ernie never looked over my shoulder and tried to micromanage the district's most important customer through me, even though we lived and died by how well I handled that customer. By the same token, Ernie never got so close to a person that he lost sight of his mission, which was to train that person. I can recall that whenever I started to get too big for my britches, Ernie always sensed it and brought me back to earth. He had a very agreeable manner that allowed him to lead while training. To this day, I value Ernie's adherence to the basics and to the integrity of his convictions. Ernie Baker taught me the importance of staying the course and seeing through whatever I had started.

Jim Edwards was a card-carrying, full-fledged genius. An engineer by training, he thought and acted the way an engineer does; he was methodical, logical, linear, inquisitive, and challenging. It was under Jim that I blossomed and began to realize that I could compete with the Big Boys, including the ones with the Ivy League backgrounds and the B-school degrees. Jim Edwards never played games or tried to make you look dumb. He was a master at playing the role of inquisitor in an attempt to bring out the best in a person. Jim never put you on the defensive or attempted to capitalize on your shortcomings or lack of knowledge. He was also the best listener I ever worked for. His questions were never designed to show how smart he was; all of them were intended to bring out the very best in you—to make *you* look good. Jim seemed to always ask the not-so-obvious questions that made you really think. I left his office many times wondering why I had not thought of some of the issues Jim seemed to think about continually.

At the same time, Jim had an extremely down-to-earth, human side to him. One of my most vivid memories of him was the time in 1977 when he and I flew on the company plane from Cincinnati to Indianapolis to inspect a test market on Certain toilet tissue. Certain was a special toilet tissue, impregnated with lotion, and was one of Jim's pet products. As he and I exited the plane, the unit manager who greeted us could not help blurting out the news that "Elvis is dead." To which Jim responded, "The King is dead! Long live the King!" That evening, Jim led us on a lively discussion about the legacy of Elvis. Interesting, interested, suave, basic—that was Jim Edwards.

Until I began rising through the ranks at P&G, I never knew that people like King Fletcher existed. By 1981, when I went to work for him in the international division, he was already a legend throughout the company. King was known for his unique combination of intelligence and compassion for the "little man"—the average person buried deep within the organization. Yale-educated and from a wealthy background, King was comfortable with both the powerful and the lowly. He could talk to anyone on virtually any subject; I used to marvel at his breadth of knowledge, ranging from the arts to politics. King loved to recite poems and could entertain for hours with his renditions of "Sam McGee" and other verses.

When I first reported to him, prior to my move to Manila, I was immediately struck by his combination of intelligence and humor. He put me through a painstaking drill to prepare me for my stint overseas, one that I thought had ended for people of my experience twenty years earlier. The retraining program he devised for me proved to have equipped me to handle every challenge of being a general manager in a foreign country. King's visits to Manila were always the highlight of the month or the quarter. He and I would work for ten or twelve straight hours on a plan for a new commercial or a better copy line or a unique strategy. These very intense meetings were invariably followed by a few drinks or a play or the opera. King Fletcher taught me to work hard and to play hard, and above all to enjoy life and to make business as much fun as possible for my people and for myself. I credit him with preparing me for the post of vice-president of sales that was next for me and for the consulting work I have done since retiring. To this day, King Fletcher remains one of my role models.

✲   ✲   ✲

I am convinced that I was promoted to vice-president in charge of sales at the insistence of Tom Laco. I have known Tom for almost forty years, and early on, I recognized that Tom possessed something special that set him apart—a deeply rooted feeling for others and a belief that anyone who had the right leadership in the right environment could succeed.

Tom was my boss for the last four—and most tumultuous—years of my tenure. During those four years, Tom pushed very hard for some of the reforms I was proposing. Many failed, but Tom tried his best to sell them. Many times I saw him walk down the long green-carpeted hall, past my office, on his way from CEO John Smale's office to his own with his chin on his chest, but Tom never, ever bad-mouthed John or the company. Tom was a master at using all of his resources, his bosses, his peers, and his subordinates to accomplish the company's objectives.

If ever there was a company man, it was Tom Laco. He believed in the goodness of the individual and was convinced that the worst among us need but a little direction and encouragement to get back on the right path.

The Best Professor I Ever Encountered in the School of Hard Knocks: Sam Walton.

As the partnership between Procter & Gamble and Wal-Mart evolved, I had the opportunity to observe and become friends with a true business giant, Sam Walton. He and I were friends for the last five years of his life, until his death from cancer in 1992. Sam Walton was a giant of a man. Sam recognized that the people who worked for him—not things, and certainly not money—were his most valuable asset. In my opinion, if we had a few thousand more like Sam Walton—or a few hundred, or even a few dozen—America would dominate world business and have a strong dollar, and every balance of payment with other nations would be decisively in our favor. We would be as powerful and unchallengeable in business as we have been in military power and foreign policy since the Soviet empire collapsed.

I've described how the partnership between Wal-Mart and Procter & Gamble evolved, one that has become legendary in

American business. Now I want to tell you about Sam Walton—what kind of man he was and why we need more like him.

People are always asking me, "What was the secret of Sam Walton's success? Was he a marketing genius? Was he a financial genius? Was he in the right place at the right time?"

And my answer always is, "All of the above." Sam just had a knack for business and for people; as his biographer, John Huey, observed, Sam had a run of "29 straight years of good business judgment." No, Sam wasn't a fluke, and he wasn't a flash in the pan; he was a genuine genius, and he proved it year in and year out.

If I had to single out one thing about Sam that accounted for his success, it would be that he truly understood that people are the most important factor in the business equation. He understood that he couldn't run all the stores himself. He understood that he couldn't drive all the trucks. He couldn't do all those things. He was a marvelous delegator. Maybe it was his personality that allowed him to do this, but when Sam Walton trusted you, there was nothing in God's world that would allow you to violate that trust. You were willing to pay the price, whatever it took, to make sure that you were able to meet his objectives and fulfill his trust in you.

As good as he was in marketing, as good as he was in finance, as good as he was at everything, in the final analysis Sam Walton did it with good judgment, common sense, and intuition. He had a feel for the market. He wasn't a Harvard-trained businessman and he wasn't offered the head job at General Motors or IBM, but he had more business sense in his little finger than some of the leading captains of industry do in their whole bodies and heads.

Don't get me wrong when I say that Sam was a delegator. The main thing is that he knew what to delegate and what not to delegate. But he certainly was a stickler for detail. Until his company got too big, Sam prided himself on visiting each and every Wal-Mart store at least once a year. Right up to the end of his life, the thing he enjoyed most was visiting his stores, even if he couldn't get to all of them every year. And he would go into those stores and talk to as many employees as he could, from the stock clerks all the way up to the manager; he certainly did not confine himself to the top brass. He always used to tell me that most of his best ideas came from his clerks and stockboys. He was a mind-picker—that's the way I would describe him. It was important to him to get out and walk through the stores.

On those visits to the stores, Sam liked to fly his plane and drop in unannounced. George Billingsley often accompanied Sam on these trips, and, as George describes it, "Sam was not always the most careful pilot in the world. He liked to circle over the parking lots of the local Kmart and the local Wal-Mart and have me count the cars in each lot while he circled." And if there were more cars in the Kmart lot than there were in Sam's parking lot, the first thing he would do was ask his store manager to explain what was going on. Talk about a hands-on manager!

On one of my visits with Sam in Bentonville, I had just come from a tour of a number of stores, including Wal-Marts, in Missouri, Arkansas, and Ohio. He spent an hour questioning me on every detail I could remember. In spite of his success, there he was, the head of the company, with a pad and a pen, still probing, still looking for information. And taking copious notes. I remember I told him that one of his stores had been closed because it was Sunday. And he said, "I want to check into that. I thought we were opening all of our stores on Sunday. I wonder why that one was closed."

I also told him that three of his stores had been out of stock of the same product, one of our products. That got him going at length about how the store clerks were supposed to make sure to restock the shelves and keep anything from running out and how much money you could lose by not having the merchandise available for the customer to buy. It almost drove him crazy whenever he heard that one of his clerks didn't react, respond, behave the way *he* would have behaved if he had been in the store in that same situation. He kept trying to instill his way of doing business in every member of the organization.

I think one of the great things about Sam was that he never lost touch with who he was and what his role in life was, whether it was when he was starting out and could barely pay his bills or after he was worth $30 billion. For that reason, he was one of the happiest men I knew, while other CEOs I've observed over the years were often tied up in knots. They didn't get any fun out of the job, even though they were the supreme boss.

Sam was the most even-keeled person I ever met, always just the same. Most people, sometimes they're up, sometimes they're down, they're happy or they're sad. But with Sam there was a straight line. I happened to be with him in Bentonville on "Black Monday"—October 19, 1987, the day the stock market crashed. The Dow-Jones Industrial Average went down more than five hundred points, and Sam's personal shares of Wal-Mart stock lost about half a billion dollars. His reaction was, "It's only paper."

To a large extent, Sam seemed oblivious to money, whether it was his or someone else's. George Billingsley talks about the time Sam went to New York, where *Financial World* magazine was honoring him as CEO of the year. The featured speaker was Michael Milken, the junk-bond king. (This was before Milken went to prison.) Milken gave an outstanding after-dinner speech, and Sam just sat there spellbound. After a while, Sam whispered to a friend sitting next to him, "Who is this Milken fellow? What does he do?" As successful as Sam was, he just didn't pay attention to the news and he didn't even know who Milken was—a man who had been written up in all the papers for making $500 million a year.

Sam truly loved his work. The only things I saw him engage in other than business were tennis and bird hunting. Those were his two true loves outside of business. And no matter what he was doing, he was every bit as focused as he was when he was concentrating on his business.

Can You Picture Rockefeller or Onassis or Trump Cleaning Up After His Dog? Neither Can I.

One incident involving Sam that really sticks in my mind: After my retirement in 1989, I started spending a lot of time with my lifelong friend and current business partner, George Billingsley, in his hometown of Bentonville, Arkansas. Our work sessions were interrupted each afternoon about two o'clock, when George would go over to Sam Walton's home for a couple of sets of tennis on Sam's backyard courts. I always went along, but since my tennis game wasn't quite up to Sam's and George's, I functioned as ball retriever and occasional referee. Whenever Sam and George disagreed on whether a ball was out or in, I'd make the call and both would agree without further comment.

A word about the scene of these tennis games is appropriate here. It's well known that Sam Walton loved to hunt birds about as much as he loved selling Moon Pies, claw hammers, and Thermos bottles. Part of the bird-hunting ritual is to own, train, and work hunting dogs. As is the case with everything in life, not all hunting dogs can be trained to hunt; dogs may be bred for hunting, but some of them just don't like to hunt. Unfortunately, you don't learn this until the dog has advanced past the puppy stage and has absorbed many hours and dollars to be trained in the ways of the hunt. Sam, who liked to train his own dogs, had a real weakness: After he had spent months training the dogs and had gotten to know them as personalities, he could not bear to part with one. As a result, the ones that could not or would not hunt became Sam's pets.

And so it was that one day George and I arrived at Sam's to play tennis, found no one there, ventured onto the court to warm up—and discovered four or five bird dogs lounging on one side of the net, enjoying the early-afternoon sun. Even if the dogs hadn't been there, George and I would have known that they had recently been present, as they had left unmistakable evidence on the court.

George and I had just spotted this "problem" when Sam walked up. Instead of yelling or fussing at the dogs, Sam commented in his normal tone of voice that he was responsible for the mess, since he had left the gate open when he hosed down the court early that morning. He walked to the dressing room, returned with a bucket and scoop, and proceeded to clean the dog latrine. Both George and I offered to help, but Sam insisted that since he had allowed the dogs to get in, it was his duty to clean up after them.

It's amazing how seemingly little events and small episodes make huge impressions on people. I thought that when Sam discovered the mess on his courts, he would have gone through the overhead and yelled, blamed the dogs, and chased them from the courts. No, indeed; this wonderful man immediately knew that the dogs were just being dogs and that what had happened was his fault, not theirs. Sam Walton taught me many invaluable lessons about his life, simply from being around him.

A high-powered Wall Street stock analyst once had an even more mind-boggling experience at Sam's tennis court than I did. Sam was besieged with requests from out-of-town financial experts and news reporters for interviews, and he ducked them as much as he could. But he finally agreed to see this guy. George Billingsley was at Sam's tennis court one day, waiting for their game to begin, when Sam arrived in his pickup truck with this man, all duded up in his pinstripe suit. Sam was also wearing a business suit, but he went right into his quick-change routine. First Sam took off his coat. Then his shirt. Then his trousers. As each garment hit the ground, the Wall Street guy's eyes got bigger and bigger and bigger, according to George. Now Sam is down to his underwear, and the Big Shot is sweating profusely. When Sam finally slipped into his tennis shorts, the visitor gave a huge sigh of relief. Even so, Sam didn't really have time for the guy. This financier wound up spending maybe a total of two minutes with Sam while Sam was switching from one court to the other, and not learning anything that he couldn't have found out by reading the newspaper. Sam had agreed to see the guy, but he sure as hell wasn't going to let it interfere with his tennis match with George.

One thing that really struck me about Sam and his people were how down-to-earth they were. Being from Memphis and having spent much of my career in Cincinnati, I don't exactly qualify as someone from the upper echelons of the New York, Washington, or Los Angeles power game, but these people from Bentonville, Arkansas, really showed me about keeping in touch with your roots and remembering where you came from.

The first time Sam brought his team of about six key people who dealt with Procter & Gamble up to Cincinnati to visit our headquarters, one of our officers asked me, "Where are you going to put them up, Lou? Over at the Cincinnatian?" Well, the

Cincinnatian, which was right near our offices, was a hotel that charged about $200 a night. My answer was, "Oh, God, no. Sam has already let me know that he wants to stay at Motel 6." So he and his team stayed there at the "We'll leave a light on for you" place, over on the Kentucky side of the river. He wasn't about to stay at some $200-a-night hotel.

And he wasn't about to let us pay for the rooms for the Wal-Mart crew, either. They were paying for their rooms; they never allowed anybody to do 'em any favors. They didn't want to be in anyone's debt.

Living simply was just Sam's way. I'll never forget the time he invited me to go bird hunting with him at the place he leased near Falfurrias, Texas. Sam's "hunting camp" consisted of four or five old house trailers. And I mean old ones. They had been formed into a sort of semicircle around a campfire. I was assigned to bunk with Sam's son, Rob. I was thinking to myself that the inside of the trailer was going to be ultraluxurious. When I got inside, it reminded me of my army days. I mean, there was a cot and that was about it. And the plumbing—well, when you peed into the commode, it went right down outside into the grass underneath. At this particular time it wasn't hooked up to even flow away from the trailer. I mean, there were no luxuries, no frills. You think of a lot of hunting camps you go to, and it's like staying at the Ritz Hotel. But this was just barely a notch above camping outside, lying in a sleeping bag with nothing over your head but the stars.

During Sam's first visit to our headquarters, he and several other Wal-Mart executives were walking up to the Procter & Gamble buildings. Sam looked at the buildings, our new twin towers that take up a couple of city blocks. You could see that he was just thinking, "My God, what a tremendous structure!" We got inside and he wasn't saying anything. We got on the elevator and went up to the eleventh floor where the executive offices are. When you step off the elevator there, you're stepping onto carpet a couple of inches thick. There are paneled walls and a collection of fine art from the Ohio Valley—the place is absolutely gorgeous. It's very conservative, but it's also positively splendid. As we left the elevator, Sam turned to me and said, "Well, Lou, now I know who's making all the money in the soap business."

Then we walked down to John Smale's corner office, and Sam kept looking around. Of course, Smale's suite was palatial. Now for the first fifteen or twenty years Sam was in business, even though he soon was doing extremely well, his desk was a door stretched over two sawhorses. Being from south Missouri and north Arkansas, Sam realized early on that in order to make money he had to control his costs. He didn't need a big, fancy office or a big, fancy desk. His office, even when he was being touted as the richest man in America and one of the wealthiest in the entire world, was about one-third the size of my den in Hilton Head.

I also remember our second canoe trip, in 1988, when Sam brought his wife, Helen. When they arrived, she apologized to all of us. "I've got dog hair all over me," she explained, "because Sam made me ride to the plane in his dog truck, and you know the dogs ride up front with him. So excuse my appearance." Here are two of the richest people in the world walking into this canoe trip and in a very gracious way she was apologizing because she had ridden in the pickup truck in the dog seat. Later on she bought him a new pickup truck. I was riding in it with him one day and I asked him what he thought of it. "Oh, it's fine, it's fine," he answered. "The only thing I don't like about it is this durned digital radio. You can't do anything but push buttons to find these stations. I wish this radio had one of those dials where you had a band back and forth. It would make life a lot simpler." Sam was a modernist and he loved new things, but he also preferred the simpler things in life, like a dial radio instead of a digital one. In spite of all the money he made, he never lost his small-town sense of things. And, boy, it wasn't fake, either.

Another time, Sam came to Cincinnati to open two new stores. There was a big grand opening, and then Procter put on a dinner for him. It was raining sideways, but when we got to the restaurant he took me aside and said, "I'll stay awhile and have a salad, but I'm not going to stay for dinner. I have to leave town tonight."

I asked him why he had to leave. "Sam," I said, "you're not going to fly out of here in this weather."

"Well, Lou," he said, "I've got to. You see, I've got two dogs in a pen out in my plane and I'm taking them to St. Louis to have them bred. And if I don't get out of here tonight, I'll be too late."

Here he was opening his new stores, at a dinner with his biggest supplier, it's pouring down rain, he's sixty-nine or seventy years old, and yet he still has the stamina and the interest in those dogs that he was going to go back out to the airport, fire that plane up, and take off in that weather to take those dogs to an appointment they had in St. Louis.

Another thing about the opening of those new stores in Cincinnati: Representatives of major Wal-Mart suppliers as well as rival retail chains were on hand, and Sam was wearing a P&G baseball cap I had given him. He asked me to come over and meet two top executives of Kmart—here he is with that P&G cap—and he said to them, "This is Lou Pritchett. He's a Procter & Gamble vice-president and he's the guy we're doing all this wonderful business with." These guys smiled and shook hands with me; they knew that if we were doing something special for Wal-Mart, we'd do the same for them if they wanted us to.

Gradually, as if by osmosis, what I learned from these best bosses I've listed here and from Sam Walton sunk in on me. What I want to do now is share with you some lessons, both those I learned from others and ones that I formulated myself.

People Tend to Support Best That Which They Help Create.

The leader's real job is to get people to do things because they want to, not because they have to. Leaders must create an environment where the workers support one another, where they want to become all they're capable of becoming, where they're not just sitting back waiting for direction. Instead, the workers take the initiative and become part of the problem-solving process, the process of capitalizing on opportunities. As I keep saying, *people tend to support best that which they help create.* Sam Walton called those the ten most powerful words in American business.

When people are doing things because they really want to do them, not because they are part of the job requirement, the job description, they do them better. When you find a thread and it leads through the maze, under the roots, around the trees, and the thread is that people are doing things because they want to, not because they're told to, when you follow that thread to its end, you will find that it is tied to the ankle of a superior leader.

The motto of the newspaper in Memphis when I was growing up was "Give light and people will find their own way." That's the way I have always operated as a leader—give my people the light and let them find their own way, but don't force them to—and it has *never* failed me! No matter what job I was in, I lived by that maxim, and it always worked.

I decided back near the beginning of my career that in order for me to be successful, I was going to have to learn to lead as well as to manage. That was my experience in scouting, that this whole leadership thing, of getting people to do what you want them to do and have them like it, was very important. I did a lot of reading and I came across a saying somewhere: "The leader's job is to teach so people will know, to share so people will grow, and to enlighten so people will have hope." I have always felt that teaching people was better than directing people.

Allowing your people to give you input is paying them the supreme compliment, because you're asking for their judgment, their opinion, and you're valuing it. At the same time, you're valuing them as individuals. It's a way of making someone feel that he or she is the most important person in the world to you and your business, even if it's only for a minute or two in the aisle of a store, the way Sam Walton did. It's a dignity thing. It's a respect thing. It's magic. And it doesn't cost you anything.

When employees are never asked for their input, never asked for their thoughts, never asked for their ideas, they aren't as productive. The managers who are always broadcasting their ideas from above, telling the workers, "This is what we're going to do and this is how we're going to do it and your job is to execute"—those kinds of managers may get things done, but the managers who allow other people to participate in the process get a hell of a lot more done. That's what I've observed.

If You're Ever in a Position to Do Something, *Do Something!*

One of my idols is Neil McElroy, the CEO of Procter & Gamble during my early years with the company. I was lucky enough to spend time with him on a couple of occasions, and during a two-day field trip he and I once took together, he said something to me that has become perhaps my cardinal rule in business and in life:

"Young man, if you're ever in a position to do something, *DO SOMETHING!*"

Or, as another immortal leader, Winston Churchill, declared during the dark days at the beginning of World War II, "To every man there comes in his lifetime that special moment when he is physically tapped on the shoulder and offered the chance to do a very special thing, unique to him and fitted to his talent. What a tragedy if that moment finds him unprepared or unqualified for the work which would be his finest hour."

Throughout my years in management, I have tried to "do something." I hope that Mr. McElroy would be proud of me; I hope you will learn from me about how to do things, and that if you are ever in a position to do something, you, too, will do it.

You're either moving ahead or losing ground; so if you ain't doing something, you will soon be obsolete. Don't let it happen!

Of course, human nature is fundamentally self-seeking. Bearing that truth in mind, what the true leader has to do is provide a vision that is bigger than self but still allows the things that are important to self to be achieved. One of the masters at that was Sam Walton. He made and allowed people to be part of a team. It's something bigger than just you alone.

Leadership means being able to change on a dime. It's not who's right, it's what's right. You have to be issue focused, not position focused. At the end of the day, you're selling a vision. The vision is intangible, abstract, impalpable, elusive. It doesn't exist on paper or anywhere else. If the vision existed, I could sell it to you as a product; I wouldn't have to sell it to you as a vision. I could demonstrate it to you, bring the dirt in, dump it on your floor, and show you how my new vacuum cleaner cleans it up. But if it's a concept, a vision, I have to have enough of your trust to act until that vision can come to life.

Effective Organizations Are Made Up of Ordinary People Doing Extraordinary Things.

It takes extraordinary managers to get ordinary people to do extraordinary things. Please don't be put off by the word "ordinary." I use this word in its most positive sense, to describe people of character who are willing to pay the price in hard work and personal sacrifice to attain their goals. These people respect others and are willing to go the extra mile for the good of the whole. These "ordinary people" are the same ones who plowed our fields, dug our mines, built our cities, expanded our national boundaries from the Atlantic Ocean to the Pacific, fought our wars, and who today pay our taxes. They are "ordinary" only in the sense that they are the ones who collectively rise to the occasion and serve without fanfare. These "ordinary people" are found in every corporation and at every level in American business. It is they who do the extraordinary things that make companies successful—when management does what it is paid to do: provide leadership and a proper working environment.

Bricklayers and Architects.

Very early in my career, soon after I was promoted to my first management position, a low-level manager in Memphis in 1955, I sensed that *any*body could do the product forecasting, the production schedule, the company automobile expense budget. Those jobs didn't require any added skill. I sensed that mastering those tasks was *not* the secret to success. Even if you master those skills and do a superb job, all you've accomplished is X. The secret is to create an environment where everybody in your organization, whether you've got five people working for you or five hundred, it's X times 500 or X times 25 or X squared. The real secret to success is to try to multiply your strengths through others. And to try to multiply and capitalize on the strengths of others. If you create an environment where everybody is allowed to participate, you're going to have a leg way up on the people who are just managing statistical stuff, which I maintain is a clerical job.

What it boils down to is that the real secret of management success is the difference between treating your people as brick-layers and treating them as architects. And, by the way, both jobs are respectable; one isn't any better than the other. The difference is that the bricklayer is a manager who runs a business, while the architect is a leader who builds a business. Who are the people who can get the greatest input, the greatest contribution, the greatest heart out of their organizations?

A classic case of a company that has been led rather than managed ever since the start is Federal Express in my old hometown, Memphis. Fred Smith was so motivated and so committed because of his ownership of the company and the trust that was placed in him that he was able to motivate his employees to perform the same way he did.

What the leader—as opposed to the manager—must do is see to it that every single employee is focused on the ultimate customer. It doesn't matter whether you're manufacturing automobiles or toothpaste, building buildings, designing computers, or operating a retail chain. The company's mind-set, which originates at the top, must be that whether you have direct contact with the customer or not, you should be thinking about the customer at all times and be intellectually and emotionally engaged with the customer, even though you may never see that customer. The average employee in the future is not going to be able to say, "My job is simply to sweep this floor." Or, "My job is just to tighten the bolts on this machine." No, the employee of the future is going to have to say, "My job is essential in delivering either the product or the service to the customer. Whether I do that physically or intellectually, just thinking about it, I can make a contribution." The objective is to focus everyone in the organization, including all those who aren't out in the salesroom selling cars to people, on the need to think about the customer during every single waking hour.

To Err Is Human, to Allow Your Employees to Make Mistakes Is Leadership.

Equally important is to encourage your employees to grow on the job by allowing them to make mistakes without getting killed for it. In raising children, if you come down on your child every time they're about to do something new, even if you know that what they're going to do is wrong, you're going to have one frustrated kid on your hand. The same holds true in business: You have got to allow people the luxury of living their lives and doing their jobs and making their mistakes, so that they can learn by trial and error.

Instead of having your hand around their throats, telling your workers when to speak or not speak, think or not think, move or not move, what you have to do is guide them with your arms open wide. Give them a little tap this way, a little tap that way, to help them stay on the right track, but allow them to make mistakes. The greatest training program in the world is trial and error. If you disallow it, or if when people make mistakes, you threaten them with firing or verbally abuse them, you'll force people to stop taking any kind of chances, any kind of risks. It's the turtle syndrome—the turtle can't move without sticking its neck out. Any time you find a manager who says, "I'm going to kill you if you make a mistake," you will find all the people sitting back in a corner, waiting for orders. Talk about a crime! Talk about a recipe for disaster!

Of course, managers must believe in themselves. But they have to resist the temptation to get so involved in picayune details and other people's business that everyone else stops using their creative talents and develops the attitude, "What difference does it make? Hell, he's going to come in and tell us how to do it anyway." There's a real danger in that.

Whether it's an individual or a corporation, weaknesses are generally an extension of strengths. I've seen that in my case and many others. If a manager's real strength is the ability to look over people's shoulders and see insights and points they haven't seen and you do that and it really helps the case, that's a great strength. But if you carry it to such an extreme that you force the people in the organization to say, "Well, why do I want to use my talent or my brainpower or my input, because it's going to be second-guessed, changed, corrected, anyway?"—that's when it becomes a weakness. In other words, delegate some of the responsibility—and then stay out of the picture. Don't fall victim to the "Nothing will work as well without me as it will with me" syndrome.

That's the kind of leader I always tried to be, and I think it worked. I've received hundreds of compliments on my style from many of my subordinates, and nothing could mean more to me. What I'm talking about works!

If You Trust People, They're More Likely to Trust You. And the Opposite Is True—Many Times Over.

As a young (twenty-eight-year-old) unit manager in Memphis in 1960, I learned firsthand a very important lesson on trust.

Among the basic responsibilities of a P&G field manager was to conduct two "follow checks" or "audits" each year to ensure that your sales reps were making the calls they reported in their daily records and that they always had on their person the "company cash" they were required to carry. The company gave each salesperson $100 in cash, which was known as "imprest money." It was to cover such expenses as gasoline, lunch (we were allowed a dollar a day for lunch), reimbursing store owners for P&G discount coupons that consumers turned in, and paying the retailers for damaged merchandise. If a sales rep was short on his company cash, I either had to write him up and report him to higher-ups or accompany him to his home or bank while he replenished any shortage.

On this particular occasion, I discovered that the senior sales rep in my unit, a man twenty years older than I, was $42 short. I suggested that we go to his bank and get the money, and he agreed. That brought his cash on hand up to the mandated $100. End of incident.

But not the end of the lesson I learned from it. Here was a man of forty-eight who had been with the company for twenty-three years, being shepherded to his bank by his twenty-eight-year-old boss. By doing this, I was only following orders—just like the defendants in the Nuremberg trials testified they were doing after World War II.

The problem was, my orders didn't fit the situation. How demeaning this was for my salesman, a valued employee who had never done anything to warrant suspicion. Although he never said a word about the incident, I never forgave myself for "carrying out orders." The company rule itself was wrong because it left no room for a manager to exercise his own judgment and because it put managers in the position of having to treat our senior employees as being untrustworthy. I knew that this sales rep had the money; he simply didn't have it on him at that moment. My act embarrassed him and made him feel less of a man. Enforcing this rule without being allowed to take all the circumstances into consideration was simply bad management. This was one of the first lessons I learned about trusting your people, striving to understand them, and meeting them at least halfway.

Trusting Your People Results in Empowering Them.

Empowerment requires a very simple, basic act of trusting the individual or the members of the organization. And until you trust them with the power, they aren't empowered. I think too many managers of the old school are holding back. After all, trusting someone makes you vulnerable. And no one wants to be vulnerable.

Nor does anyone seek to voluntarily give up power. And yet giving up power is the definition of empowering others. To me, the best example in this era is Mikhail Gorbachev. As bad as things are today in the former Soviet Union, they would be much worse had Gorbachev not voluntarily given up much of his power by encouraging *perestroika, glasnost,* and similar policies. As the supreme leader of the USSR, he was one of the most powerful men in the history of the world. And yet, Communism was falling apart when Gorbachev took the reins. Had he tried to cling to power, the result almost certainly would have been a bloodbath that would have stood out even by the standards of Russian history.

Open Your Ears, Open Your Mind, Wake Up Your Business.

Corporate executives who are unable to listen to their subordinates, as well as those outside the company, are almost doomed to fail. To repeat, whether they want to admit it or not, there's a huge element of trust required in good corporations. Corporations have to send out forward observers, as they do in the military, to tell them what the situation is. If your forward observers say to bomb at certain coordinates, then, by God, you'd better bomb there. In an army, it's the infantryman or the cavalryman on the front lines who has the eyes and ears to know what's going on, to see what the enemy is doing. If you're not able to accept the information that's reported to you, you might as well not bother sending out the scouts. But a lot of organizations seem unwilling to ask for outside data and to believe it after it's reported back to them. A lot of executives are happy only when the data that comes back fits with their paradigms, confirms what they already believe. Otherwise, they simply will deny what they haven't been conditioned to believe.

To paraphrase a famous remark of Winston Churchill's, we shape our buildings and then they shape us: Corporate structures, internal reward/recognition systems—over time they shape the company. People hear what management says, they hear what the CEO says, but they do only what they're rewarded for doing and avoid what they're punished for doing. The sooner CEOs understand that, the better off they'll be. In some respects, the weakest person in a company is the CEO, because often he or she is so isolated and insulated they don't understand what the rank and file are thinking. A classic case was President Nixon, who—at his own direction—was insulated by his advisers from what was going on. They told him only what he wanted to hear. And eventually that helped cause Nixon's downfall. CEOs—corporate emperors, if you will—don't like to be told they have no clothes, and no one within the company wants to break that news to them, either, for fear that the messenger will be blamed for the message.

I remember that at Procter & Gamble, when we started working with Wal-Mart, we went down to Arkansas, we saw a lot of important things, and we reported back to headquarters what we had seen. Well, some of P&G's top executives, ones who had never been in Bentonville, insisted, "That's not what you saw!"

"Well," we said, "that's what we think we saw. Why don't you come down and take a look at it, because if you stand in the same place that we did, we think you'll see the same thing."

They said, "We're unwilling to do that, but, by God, what you're seeing isn't right."

Another time, I brought Rosabeth Kanter, author and visionary expert on business at Harvard, to visit Procter & Gamble headquarters. She was working with us as a consultant, helping develop new approaches to business. One of P&G's top executives, a traditionalist whose point of view was, "The way we've always done things is the best way," asked me who this woman was, and whether she worked for Procter. I told him it was Rosabeth Kanter, editor of the *Harvard Business Review* and author of *The Change Masters,* and I mentioned some of her other credentials. I asked him if he had read *The Change Masters,* and his answer was, "Nope! If a Procter person didn't write it, I don't read it." There's a classic example of someone with a closed mind.

Procter & Gamble was by no means the only company in which some of the top managers have that attitude. I've encountered many a manager in many a company whose attitude is, "Why the hell should I work with him? He's three notches down, or four or five notches down, below me on the organization chart. What the hell could he tell me, a seasoned, bright, experienced, Harvard Business School grad?" On the other hand, if you can ever buy into the proposition that everyone is a unique source of knowledge and information, it is amazing what you can learn.

I used to go into stores and interview store clerks. They were men and women who worked eight to ten hours a day, putting our merchandise onto the shelf. We got the A. C. Nielsen numbers, surveys of how merchandise sold in the stores, but they were always sixty days late. Nielsen always told me what *had* happened. But Nielsen never could tell me what *is* happening. And we lived and died by the Nielsen sword. You didn't have to be in the fast-learning group to understand that the clerks could tell you what had happened *that very day*. The clerks could tell you what was selling; they told you what was not selling; they told you what you weren't shipping enough of; they told you what the competitors were doing in promotion; they told you what the customers really wanted in terms of packaging, like if a package tended to leak or was the wrong size.

I'm a firm believer in marketing surveys, like Nielsen (as long as you're very careful about how they're done), as well as in focus-group interviews, which are essentially the same thing as a marketing survey. Unfortunately, some marketing surveys are not worth the paper they're written on. The problem is that too many managers today, given the internal reward/recognition system, are driven to make a certain thing happen. So they tailor the questions on the marketing surveys to get the answers they want.

But in general, most marketing surveys have a real value. If you don't know where you're going, any road will get you there. I don't think a company can survive without polling-type knowledge. In my opinion, the failure of General Motors to find out what consumers thought of their cars and what consumers wanted their cars to be like is what really crippled them. That's why I always say that GM hurt themselves—it wasn't the Japanese. General Motors simply was not doing enough market research to determine what their customers liked and didn't like! And, apparently, corporate arrogance kept them from believing whatever information they did obtain.

Obviously, the results of a public-opinion survey depend upon the questions. A good company tells the marketing research people, "Don't tell us what you think we want to hear. In fact, you'll get fired if we think you're telling us what you think we want to hear. What we want you to do is tell us what the truth really is, what people are really thinking." The market research people need to operate in a vacuum—they simply provide the evidence and let the company executives do with it as they will.

I have observed that quite often, people—employees, customers, outsiders like store clerks—present a lot of good ideas, both in discussion or in writing. These ideas get kicked around for a while, but then, because they don't fit into a corporate strategy or a function strategy, they're pretty well put aside and dismissed as interesting but useless. For example, the concept of the personal computer at an affordable price had been around for years. Steve Jobs of Apple, with his dream that "a few smart people could change the world," and visionaries like him did not invent it. But they acted on that idea and IBM didn't. The Japanese car manufacturers acted on the idea that the basic premise in Detroit was wrong: Customers *do* want quality. That *is* important to them. Trading up for a new car every year was a false premise.

But so many great ideas get cast aside. The genius of management is the ability to recognize a great idea when it comes along and to apply it. It doesn't necessarily have to be an idea that no one has ever thought of. It just has to be an idea whose time has come. This is why you have to make room for dreamers and poets instead of mocking them as lazy-crazy sons of bitches and isolating them from the herd. Those people need to be nurtured and nourished and hothoused like an orchid. They may not produce miracles ten times out of ten, but one out of ten ain't so bad in today's environment. Every human being needs to understand that he or she can bring their total person to the workplace. That means you bring your emotions, your concerns, your fears, your desires, your hopes, your visions, just as much as you bring your back, your fingers, whatever. It's not that difficult for management to create that atmosphere.

Street smarts, intuition—whatever you want to call it—has always been and always will be indispensable in business. One concern I have is that during the '60s and '70s, under some managers, we became very clinical in our approach to sales and selling and most every other aspect of business. There were formulas for doing everything. You either did something in specified fashion or you didn't do it at all. You proceeded on a linear basis—one, two, three, four. There simply was no room for intuition. It was just, "Give me the facts. And nothing but the facts." Then you studied the facts to death, interpreted them, and that supposedly told you what to do.

It's the people out in the field, like the sales reps, where intuition has always been valued. When you walk in and call on fifteen dealers a day and some of them have personalities at one end of the spectrum and some at the opposite end, you can't go in there with a preset approach. You'd better have a feel for what you're doing, or else you're not going to make the sale. You go in and talk to one of them about baseball, slap him on the back, while to the other one you go in and talk cold, hard facts.

It's instinct that makes the best sales reps superior. Some managers had the attitude, "If you've got it, you're lucky. Good! Use it! Thank you very much. So what?" There was no appreciation for what a gift you had and no effort made to bring that skill out in people or to encourage it or to allow it to happen. And the managers and top executives who feel that way don't even know what it is to set foot in a store. I've even known a lot of sales executives who would feign everything from an attack of appendicitis to a migraine headache to avoid calling on an actual customer.

I'll never forget the conversations I used to have with a guy who was in effect out in the field—that is, removed from management—at the Ford Motor Company. He had been just another guy on a Ford assembly line at a plant in Lorain, Ohio. The house where Barbara and I lived in Cincinnati had about three acres of grass, and sometime later this fellow, I'll call him "Ernie," mowed our lawn. Ernie was a very bright guy who wanted to open his own welding company, and eventually I loaned him $500 to buy his own welding machine. He used to talk about how boring his job at Ford was. Ernie said he stood there and about every eight seconds he took a drill and put a bolt on a piece of the car. I asked him what he thought about while he was doing that mind-numbing job of his. "I try to figure out how to steal that $800 drill I use, without getting caught" was his answer. Nobody from management ever tapped in and asked, "Ernie, are you smart, dumb? Have you got anything else to offer?" It was just, "Here's this machine. Go bolt the damned car together."

The sad truth is that most major corporations don't really want their employees to express their opinions about the business. Many companies give lip service to change, which is the worst of all possible worlds. Why bother having employees participate in meetings about change if you have no intention from the beginning of changing at all and no interest in their answers to your questions? You not only waste a lot of time and effort, you unnecessarily create a lot of bitterness and frustration on the part of those who take part in a sham process and then find themselves ignored or worse.

A friend of mine who is an executive in retail marketing told me about a man named John Ryder, who conceived a number of visionary ideas at the A&P grocery chain. But A&P didn't afford him the opportunity to put his ideas into practice, so he quit and joined Basics/Metro, a Baltimore-based supermarket chain, where he has been given more freedom and is helping create the supermarket of the future. Among his ideas are banks and fast-food restaurants inside the stores, and better placement of high-priced items, to increase sales volume. I believe that before long, John Ryder will be recognized as a prophet in the supermarket industry, and all the major chains, like Safeway and Winn-Dixie and Kroger, will adopt his techniques. This guy has broken the code. But A&P didn't reap the payoff from Ryder's innovative capacity; someone else did.

In practically every situation, there is somebody out there who knows the best way to do things. If you can only find that person and give him the freedom and the resources, there's no stopping him. Look at companies and entire industries that didn't exist a few years ago, like Apple Computer, Blockbuster, and Federal Express. Those companies have encouraged free thinkers, and everything has come together for them. That's the kind of outrageous result you can get.

I would love to work for Herb Kelleher, the CEO at Southwest Airlines, or Bill Gates at Microsoft, or to be a CEO in their image. It would have to be a totally off-the-wall company where they would let Lou Pritchett be Lou Pritchett.

A lot of CEOs insist that's the kind of company they want. But when push comes to shove, it ain't true. I can't tell you how many times I've gone out to give a speech and at a cocktail party or a dinner the evening before, the CEO or the president of the company or whoever will say, "Man, what you're going to talk about tomorrow will reinforce the way we've been doing things—this is exactly the way we operate." Then, the next afternoon, after I've made my presentation and I'm in private meetings with some of the middle managers, they're saying, "Bullshit! Doesn't work that way around here." Many top execs talk the talk, but they don't walk the walk, and the last things they truly want are change and new ideas.

The fact is, if you cannot volunteer ideas to your boss and argue with your boss, he isn't worth working for. A boss who wants yes-men surrounding him is not a good boss. Bosses like that don't listen, they're not responsive, they're self-centered, they're looking out for themselves and not for their employees. They don't encourage their people to stand up and say, "This is wrong."

One secret for corporate success is that great ideas must be solicited and leaders must teach people to dream. It's all part of understanding human nature, which is the first thing that managers should be able to do. There ought to be courses at the business schools that teach students why people do what they do. Courses that turn future business executives into human engineers. "Human engineer" is something I've been called several times, and it's the most flattering title I could be given. You come to realize that the only resource that's really important isn't your hardware, it's your human resource. In the old days, executives spent more time on and were more concerned with managing machinery and hardware than with managing people. All that has changed, and we have to change with it.

I want to encourage every CEO to be a human engineer. After all, you, too, were once a human engineer, were you not? Yes, back when you started out in business, and each time you joined a new company, you had a fresh perspective and a raft of new ideas, did you not?

This is what I call my litmus test for CEOs. Think back to your youth: What did you not like about the systems that were in place at that time? What did you not like about the rules and the regulations you confronted early in your career? What did you not like about the way your bosses treated you? What did you not like about the way the company was progressing? What did you not like about the necessity to conform and the fact that *con*formance was just as important, if not more important, than *per*formance? And then ask yourself whether you are guilty of doing the same things to your own organization now that you are running the show.

Step back and try to look at yourself and your company as if you were an outsider. You may discover that your company is mismanaged or that it's crumbling from within, or that your competition—no matter how weak it has been all these years—is overtaking you. You may have started taking it for granted that your competitors will keep screwing up forever. Well, maybe not. One of these days, one of them may wake up and start doing things right. Unless you do, too, you'll be left in their wake.

So go back to being an outsider-insider. Today—before it's too late.

People Tend to Behave the Way You Treat Them.

It is a universal truth that people tend to become that which they think others think they are. Think of them as dogs and they will behave like dogs; think of them as losers and they will behave like losers; think of them as winners and they will behave like winners.

That's important to remember not only because of its implications for your employees' productivity but because your people are going to treat your customers exactly like you treat your own employees. If you treat your people like they are not to be trusted, your people will treat your customers like they're not to be trusted. If you treat your staffers like dogs, they're going to treat the customers like dogs.

When I walk into a restaurant or a grocery store or a gas station or a factory, I can almost tell you what kind of management there is simply by looking at the way the employees behave, by the way they treat the customer.

Enthusiasm is like the measles or a cold; it's contagious. But so is dissension. And dissension isn't the same as criticism. Dissension doesn't mean you should stifle constructive critics. You can be enthusiastic about a problem and its solutions, just as you can be enthusiastic about the way things already are. One response to one of my speeches was, "He has given my organization a good case of enthusiasm," which I consider the highest form of tribute there is.

People who are enthusiastic are going to outperform those who aren't. And I don't mean false enthusiasm, either. This is not just cheerleader rah! rah! I'm talking about employees who really are committed and believe in something and want to share it with others and get them to participate in the process.

I think enthusiasm is a learned trait. It's trainable. It comes from working with people. One of the first things you have to do in order to breed enthusiasm is teach your people about human nature and about why humans do what they do.

I firmly believe that you cannot become a 100 percent customer-focused company until you've become a 100 percent employee-focused company. But the converse is also true: If you become a 100 percent employee-focused company, you almost certainly *will* become a 100 percent customer-focused company.

Clothes Do Not Necessarily Make the Man or the Woman.

American Management Systems (AMS) of Fairfax, Virginia, a defense-related consulting and technology-services company, has gone out of its way to be "a good place to attract and retain talented people to work on clients' problems," according to Chairman Charles O. Rossotti. AMS hires quality workers and then stays out of their way and lets them do their jobs. Teamwork and individual initiative are encouraged, and workers are allowed to work flexible hours and to dress casually unless there's a reason to wear their Sunday best. "We assume our employees are smart enough to know that if they're meeting the head of a bank that day, they'll dress appropriately," says Rossotti.

AMS must be doing something right: Profits have increased 25 percent each year for the ten-year period through 1994. The firm has the kind of enlightened management I'd like every company to have. AMS management clearly recognizes that *people* will make or break an organization and that the real secret to increased productivity is *not* a manager standing behind the workers, wielding a whip.

AMS's dress code is typical of companies that are on the cutting edge of American business today. At what I characterize as the "hippie-type companies," like Ben & Jerry's, Apple Computer and many of the other firms in Silicon Valley, Nike, and Celestial Seasonings, what do they wear to work?

Sandals, jeans, T-shirts—whatever they feel like. Because these companies don't want to stifle their employees' creativity. If you could interview the CEOs of the top one hundred corporations in America and you showed them pictures of sandals, jeans, and T-shirts, people eating pizza and drinking Cokes at their desks, most of them would respond, "Nonconformists. Hippies, maybe. Maybe even ne'er do wells and goofing off."

But look at Apple Computer and Microsoft and how well they're doing.

So many of us, me included, still tend to eyeball people and make a value judgment based on the way they look. I was on a plane recently, and the guys behind me were on their way to Hilton Head for a golf weekend. They were loud and obnoxious, and one of them had on a tank top and shorts and a straw hat that looked like something somebody might have first bought back in the Eisenhower era. I was shaking my head and mumbling to myself, "What a bunch of jerks!" These guys were playing cards and talking real *loudly*. About halfway down, though, they started talking about their business, which was the marketing of computers and software back up in Boston. I couldn't help overhearing them. The guys were brilliant! Absolutely brilliant! They weren't talking about today's software and what it can't do, will do, should do; they were talking about where they're going to have to go from here. They were saying that five years from now, three years from now, people will look back and consider today's technology to be buggy whips.

The moral of that story, which I'm learning all the time and having drummed into my head by my wife and my two sons, is, "Don't make value judgments based on the way people look." You still have CEOs of my vintage who look at someone and decide that the way they dress, the way they talk, the way they behave, indicates whether the person is good, bad, smart, dumb, efficient, inefficient. And it just isn't so. I'm sure that if the IBM executives could have peeked into some of the Silicon Valley labs several years ago, they would have said, "We sure as hell don't have to worry about this. There's no threat from these guys."

And speaking of IBM, can you believe what happened in February 1995? Glory of glories—the company announced that the 880 staffers at company headquarters in Armonk, New York—at the direction of Chairman Louis Gerstner, who favors golf shirts—are shifting from business suits to casual wear!

Always Play the Course, Not the Competition.

My scoutmaster, Buddy Irwin, was the first person who told me, "Most of us go through life looking at our peers, our bosses, our subordinates, as competitors. Especially our peers. Most of us go through life thinking that in order to get ahead, we must beat out people in like positions. In other words, for you to win, somebody has to lose. For you to get ahead, somebody's got to be behind."

But, Buddy explained to us, "The way I lead my life and the way I'd like you boys to lead your lives is to think about it as a game of golf. In most sports, like football or baseball, you play to kill the other guy. But in golf it's different. In golf, what you really do is pit your skills, your strengths, your talents, versus the golf course. It makes no difference how good or how bad the competition is. You're playing against a fixed set of circumstances there. And that's the way I think you ought to play life." That has stuck with me through the years, playing the course, not the competitor. What I learned from Buddy Irwin has been a great underpinning, both in my business life and in my personal life.

I have always believed in competing fairly and winning fairly, but, above all, winning. By winning, I mean simply doing my best. Whether I came in first or last, if I did my best, I won. I've never felt that in order for me to win, somebody else had to lose. Shipping volume to outsell other divisions, as I did for thirty-six months in a row when I was in charge of Procter's Southern division early in my career, was not something I did to personally beat *other managers* but simply something I did in the course of trying to do my best.

Procter & Gamble lived by the same philosophy that Buddy Irwin did. At Procter we had many hard-and-fast rules, and perhaps the first was never, never, never mention a competitor by name, especially in a derogatory way. The idea was that by tearing down the competition, you were lowering yourself to their level. Instead, we were taught, directed, and commanded to always take the high road. If we were trying to sell one of our products to a dealer and he or she asked us about a competing product, our stock answer was, "That's a good company and they make a good product. But we believe ours is better." This lesson was hammered into our heads regularly, by everyone from Procter's CEO on down.

I'll never forget when we introduced Comet cleanser a few years after I joined the company. Comet was a breakthrough product because it contained bleach and really erased the stains from porcelain sinks, bathtubs, and toilet bowls. Until we developed Comet, Colgate's Ajax was the industry standard to the extent that it had practically become a generic name, just like "Xerox" is used as a verb for "copying."

We introduced Comet to the grocers with a dealer demonstration kit that had been prepared by the sales merchandising department. The demo kit contained an eight-by-eight-inch piece of porcelain, a small sponge, a small bottle of water, a small bottle of brownish-black stain (we were told that this blotch represented the typical stains in a household sink), a can of Comet, and a can of another cleanser, which we identified simply as "Brand X." We would ask the grocer to take us to a comfortable, private spot in the store and proceed to demonstrate our new cleanser by staining two sections of the porcelain plate and then applying Brand X to one of the stains and Comet to the other. We would then let the dealer use the damp sponge to try and remove the stain—first with Brand X and then with Comet. Obviously, no amount of rubbing would make the stain under Brand X disappear, but a couple of passes and the smear under Comet would vanish, as if by magic. The final step was to sell the dealer a ton of Comet, get him to agree to a prominent location to display our new product when he received it, and set the date for his tie-in newspaper ads, which would coincide with the beginning of our own radio campaign. (This was before television supplanted radio as the main advertising medium for products like ours.) Never once—not during our in-store presentation and not in our advertising—did we refer to Ajax by name. Of course, it was obvious to everyone what "Brand X" was.

As I rose through the company hierarchy, up to and until the time I became vice-president of sales, I worked with sales reps all over the world. Every time I was in the field, I checked my reps' sales materials to make sure that they never mentioned a competitor.

This rule remains in effect at Procter to this day. It strikes me as a classic example of how a company formulates the proper basic principles and beliefs and then lives by and enforces those rules. And this canon, which I first learned from Buddy Irwin and then had ingrained in me during my tenure at Procter, remains an integral part of my own personal code.

The Shortest Route to a Subordinate's Heart Is to Let His Baby Pee on You.

The winter of 1960 found Barbara, me, and our first son, Brad, living in Columbus, Ohio, where I was a unit sales manager. That January, Barbara was shopping in a grocery store when a rack of soft drinks exploded, embedding a sliver of glass in her left eye. For six weeks, Barbara couldn't lift her head or otherwise put pressure on her head or neck. That left me, with help from Barbara's mother, to care for both Barbara and newborn Brad, as well as try to do my job. I was rising through the ranks of management and didn't want to do anything to jeopardize my advancement, but my family was my primary concern during this crisis.

That's when I really came to appreciate what a wonderful company I had joined. Not only did management tell me to take as much time off as I needed to be with Barbara and the baby, but the senior vice-president, a wonderful Bostonian named Rowell Chase, visited our house and bounced Brad on his knee as only a grandfather would. Rowell Chase was a legend at P&G, an ad man who had helped launch Tide detergent shortly after World War II. Even so, he took the time to help out a young employee and to follow up for years after this traumatic period in our lives by asking about Barbara and "the baby" whenever he saw me. Nearly thirty years later, when the company held my retirement reception, it was Rowell Chase, himself retired for many years by then, who asked one more time about Barbara and Brad.

Rowell Chase's concern about Barbara and my family, and the concern on the part of the entire Procter & Gamble company, wasn't simply paternalistic. It showed a genuine interest in my wife who was injured and in my brand-new baby and in me. I wasn't making much of a contribution to the business, staying home and taking care of my baby, and it was bothering me. Rowell Chase knew that, and he put me in that comfort zone because of his sincere interest in the well-being of me and my family.

That's classic leadership—making an employee feel so good about himself and about the company and about my work— that to me was more important than more pay. Chase's thoughtfulness also taught me that if this was the way my superiors treated me, I was going to be sure to show care and concern for the people who worked under *me*. That's the kind of thing that pays huge dividends that there's no way of measuring; the dividends are so huge. This simple act of concern from a senior officer helped ensure my everlasting loyalty to the company.

Rowell Chase's kindness toward me was by no means unique at P&G. One of the most beloved members of the sales division was a field manager named Pete Brady. At the age of forty, Pete suffered the first in a series of heart and vascular problems that would take his life ten years later. When Pete had that first bout with heart disease, Brad Butler, one of the top executives in the sales department, decreed that Pete was to receive his full salary for as long as he was ill. That edict remained in effect until Pete's death; regardless of whether he was able to work or not, he was paid in full. Brad Butler's willingness to go the limit to take care of one of his people set a tone within the sales organization that kept many talented people at P&G in spite of efforts by other companies to lure them away. Brad Butler practiced and genuinely believed in the most fundamental principle of leadership: "Take care of the troops, and they will take care of you."

The Best Way to Treat Your Employees Is Not to Treat Them as Employees at All.

Previously, I discussed the executive dining room approach and the "us-against-them" attitude P&G provoked with its edicts on first-class travel and frequent-flier miles. Compare those with the policies of Warner-Lambert, the New Jersey–based pharmaceutical company that my friend Tom Quinn joined in late 1994. At Warner-Lambert they don't just mumble all the usual corporate buzzwords about how we're going to empower people and treat everyone as equals. They genuinely care about how people treat each other as they go about their business. For example, everyone is referred to as a colleague. Similarly, at Giant Food, the Washington, D.C.–Baltimore–area supermarket chain that's famous for being a wonderful company to work for, the workers are referred to as associates rather than employees. There's no rank, so to speak, when folks in companies like these are discussing things. Obviously, it would be naive to say that there aren't Warner-Lambert or Giant Food people who are full of themselves or pompous or meek or whatever, but these companies have recognized that how people communicate with each other, whether it's open and honest, or guarded and dishonest, has a lot to do with the ability to bring about change and to exchange ideas.

Be a Benevolent Boss, but Never Forget Who the Boss Is.

Among the more colorful characters in P&G history was one of my predecessors as vice-president of sales, T. J. Wood. During his reign, after World War II and into the 1950s, Wood was feared and loved at the same time. Feared because he asked extremely probing questions as he grilled his salespeople, and enforced the strictest discipline. To many employees returning from the war, T. J. Wood embodied their worst nightmare of a drill sergeant. But he was also loved because he never asked anyone to do anything he would not do himself. Moreover, beneath his gruff demeanor was a compassionate man. He epitomized the demanding, loving father of nineteenth-century fiction, believing that discipline and hard work build character in his sons and daughters.

During the early to mid-1950s, the country reaped the benefits of wartime technology. One of the major examples of high tech in those days was air-conditioning, which was steadily becoming the in thing for both buildings and automobiles. Millions of Americans who had lived all their lives without air-conditioning began insisting they could not live without it.

As vice-president of sales, T. J. Wood's responsibilities included selecting office space and company cars and deciding whether or not they would be air-conditioned. The staff pressed harder and harder for air-conditioning in both offices and automobiles, but Wood stubbornly resisted. At last he compromised in an unusual way: He drew an arbitrary line across a map of the United States from east to west and decreed that air-con was authorized in all offices and cars located below the line, but not in those north of the Wood Line.

Employees south of his line thought they had died and gone to heaven, but everyone north of the line protested. A man named John Harris was then running the Chicago district office, and he didn't want to take no for an answer. Harris set out to convince Wood that during July and August, it was every bit as hot in Chicago as it was in New Orleans. Wood obligingly scheduled a trip to Chicago in August, and Harris prepared for Wood's visit like a general marshaling his troops. Upon Wood's arrival at the offices in downtown Chicago, Harris put his plan in motion. Papers and reports were strewn all over Harris's desk, and, with every window wide open, Harris started reviewing the district's activities for Wood's benefit. As Harris had anticipated, the wind swept through the open windows—Chicago is not known as the Windy City for nothing—and the papers began blowing all over the place. The noise from the trains, trolleys, and street traffic below made it necessary for both men to shout most of the time in order to hear each other, and the heat was nearly unbearable.

With both men wilting, Harris finally turned to Wood and declared, "Mr. Wood, I think now you can understand why Chicago needs to be authorized for air-conditioning."

Without glancing up from the reports in front of him, Wood answered, "John, if you would get your ass out in the field with your customers, where you belong, instead of sitting in this office, you could enjoy their air-conditioned stores and offices most of the time!"

Another decade passed before the Chicago office was air-conditioned.

Tune in to Your Employees' Need for Real Wheels.

J. S. "Dutch" Janney followed T. J. Wood both in the job of vice-president of sales and in Wood's footsteps. Just as there had been pressure on Wood to pay for air-conditioning, the sales force constantly urged Janney to upgrade the company cars, which for years had been notoriously stripped-down, bottom-of-the-line vehicles, dull gray in color. Was it too much, the sales staff asked, to have a major option like *radios* in the cars where we spent so much of our time? Out of the question, Janney insisted.

All the salespeople in the Pittsburgh office ultimately decided that the next time Janney dropped in on them, they would gang up on him and vigorously plead their case for better cars. The discussion lasted about half an hour, and the session ended with Janney refusing to yield an inch. He countered every argument with some strong points of his own:

- Imagine how expensive it would be to upgrade the thousands of company cars the sales division operated across the United States.
- What difference did it make what the cars looked like or whether they had options like radio, as long as they were reliable and capable of transporting the sales rep from point A to point B?

As the meeting was breaking up, Janney announced that he wanted to inspect some of the retail stores in the Pittsburgh area. He and one of the district managers left the office and headed out to the DM's car in the parking lot. As they reached a row of cars, the DM put his briefcase on the ground behind a car and began searching through his pockets for his keys. While the man was occupied, Janney placed his hand on the car they were standing near and began walking around it, pointing out how great it looked, what with its chrome trim, its snazzy color, its nice wheel covers. All in all, he concluded, this was a damned nice-looking hunk of automobile, and no salesperson had a right to be ashamed of it. Just then, the district manager located his keys, opened the trunk of the drab gray entry-level Ford next to the car Janney had been admiring, and declared, "Mr. Janney, that's not our car."

Within a few months after that episode, the upgrade process began with each new car the sales division purchased. There was no quantum leap, but at least it was a step in the right direction.

Be Observant, and You Won't Wind Up All Wet.

During the mid-1950s, when I was a sales manager in Memphis, Jack Hanley, who was in charge of soap sales in the South for Procter & Gamble, visited me occasionally. On one of his trips, in 1955, he and I stopped by to inspect a new supermarket that was state-of-the-art for that day and age. Hanley and I spent over an hour inside; when we started to leave, it was raining bucketloads. It was our practice to always park our company cars far away from the store in order to let the customers have the close-in slots. On this particular day, I must have parked a half mile from the front door of this huge new store. Unfortunately, Mr. Hanley's plane was scheduled to leave shortly, so we couldn't wait until the downpour ended.

In honor of Mr. Hanley's visit I was wearing one of the new drip-dry seersucker suits—my latest pride and joy. As we stood in the front door, gazing out at the rain, Hanley looked at me and asked innocently, "Is that one of those new drip-dry suits I've been reading so much about?"

I was truly delighted that the boss was impressed with my new clothes, and I answered, "Yes, sir!"

Without hesitating, he shot back, "Good!!! You go get the car!"

Of course, I would have had to get the car anyway, but by taking notice of what I was wearing, Jack Hanley at least gave me reason to console myself while I dashed across the parking lot, growing wetter by the minute.

Knowledge Is Power. And the Lack of It Is Just the Opposite.

Fairly early in my career, one of the longtime and legendary fixtures in the sales department taught me quite a lesson about knowing your territory. This occurred in 1966, when I became manager of the Southern sales division and Bill Evans was in charge of the Jacksonville, Florida, district. I joined Bill while he made his rounds in north Florida, near the Georgia state line.

Bill was then about fifty-five, some twenty years older than me, and he had been with the company for over twenty-five years. He was from the old school: smart, frugal, honest—and dedicated, really dedicated, to the premise that hard work and long hours were good for the soul, mind, body, and wallet. To Bill Evans, hard work meant getting up at first light or earlier, putting in a full day, and then going to bed early and getting a good night's sleep.

Bill started each morning with breakfast promptly at six o'clock, and then hit the road to call on his customers until six in the evening, when he stopped for dinner. After a particularly long day working with Bill, I was ready to drop. So I asked Bill if we could start a little later the next morning, perhaps at six-thirty. Bill pondered my proposal for a minute or so and then answered with a wry smile on his face that that was fine with him. In fact, he agreed, to my surprise, that we would get up whenever we woke up. This sounded like a great idea to me and I went to bed about nine-thirty, anticipating a long and restful night.

What I did not know was that the small hotel where we were staying, the only one in the little town where we were, was situated about thirty feet from the main line of the Florida–East Coast Railroad, which ran all the way down the coast to Miami. Bright and early the next morning, a twenty-car train went by under a full head of steam, blowing its whistle and bell at the crossing in the center of town—and no more than forty feet from my hotel room.

The combination of noise and vibration seemed to last ten minutes. When the racket finally died in the distance, I heard a knock at my door and Bill Evans calling, "Roll out now! You're burning daylight!" It was 5:00 A.M.

Knowing the turf a lot better than I did, Bill had no trouble agreeing that we could "sleep in" until six-thirty or even later. He was well aware that everyone within the sound of that train would be wide awake at five the next morning.

By the same token, Bill Evans's lack of familiarity with a place once cost him any shot at making a fortune.

A year or so before Bill snookered me on the "sleep-in," I held a meeting with all my district managers, including Bill, on Hilton Head Island, South Carolina. This newly developed island paradise seemed like the ideal spot for a new management team to come together and plan how we would take the high ground.

We convened at the original hotel on the island, the William Hilton Inn. This property had been built by the founder of this new community venture, Charles Fraser. As I recall it was a small, intimate hotel with a feel of being the most private place on earth. The hotel was positioned on the beach in a grove of oak, pine, and palm. During dinner the first night, as the five of us sat in the small dining room, we were approached by one of the locals, who asserted that he had a very special deal for us—we could buy a half-acre oceanfront lot for several thousand dollars. At that time, that much money sounded like $5 million to most of us. With the exception of Bill Evans, who was about twenty years older, we all were in our thirties. The concept of investing $5,000 in something as impractical as a lot on the ocean in South Carolina seemed totally ludicrous. Second homes and real estate investment for the "golden years" were totally out of the question for us.

Bill Evans sensed how tempting this local wheeler-dealer's offer was to the rest of us. Knowing pretty well what our financial situations were, he attempted to relax us by commenting, "Who the hell would want to buy a lot in this damned swamp? I wouldn't take a piece of this alligator-infested bog if you gave it to me for free!"

Today, I live in this "alligator-infested bog" on a lot that's worth many times what Charles Fraser's asking price was in 1965. I only wish I had had the money and the foresight to buy that oceanfront lot; today, if you're sitting in the barber chair and you hear that an oceanfront lot is for sale for $1.5 million, it's sold before the barber finishes cutting the other side of your head. The question remains, how do you tell the difference between a good investment and a poor one in real estate, in stocks, in life? Things are rarely what they seem to be at the outset. Perhaps nothing is as great or as controlling as a vision and faith to see it to completion.

But the best way to make the correct decision is to know thyself, thy fellow man, and everything else you can find out—one thing in particular. As the song goes in *The Music Man*, "You got to know the territory."

To Be a Good Leader, You Must Be a Good Communicator.

Among the many lessons I learned from P&G vice-chairman Tom Laco was how to write a memo. Tom taught those of us who were privileged to have direct contact with him that in good memo writing, you shouldn't even have to read as much as two or three paragraphs to learn the writer's basic message. Plant the seed early! State from the beginning what you're after, and then make your case. It works!

There's a saying that a cluttered desk is the sign of a cluttered mind. Here's how I keep my desk uncluttered, and, hopefully, my mind as well: If I'm on the opposite end of a memo, as the reader instead of as the writer, my motto is, "Be quick!" That philosophy should apply not only to memos but to letters, reports, articles, and anything else you receive in writing. Mail doesn't stay on my desk for more than one day. It never has, and it never will.

Pritchett's Personal Requirements for Leadership.

- Leadership must always be "we," never "me." Real leaders know intuitively when to critique, when to broadcast, when to listen, when to share, when to care, when to remember, when to forget, when to praise.

- Real leaders recognize that their role is a rare and refined one and must always be handled with great care and respect for others.
- True leaders know that they and they alone must align individual goals with corporate goals and that nothing great can be achieved without this harmony.
- The best leaders have a seemingly uncanny ability to see around corners, anticipate the future, and respond before an event occurs. Some call this attribute "genius"; I define it as "applied experience," and I maintain that it can be learned.
- The true leader understands the difference between overmanaging and underleading.
- In the words of one of my old bosses, the secret of leadership is "to comfort the afflicted and afflict the comfortable."
- Leadership also means "looking out for number two." That means that the leader helps the employee achieve all he or she possibly can accomplish instead of accepting anything less than their best. Bringing the people who work for you to their full potential is the most important job of a leader.
- Dedicate yourself to the tenet that people are your most important resource, and set out to create a work environment that stimulates, nurtures, and challenges instead of one that inspects, audits, and controls.
- Forge a psychological contract with your people. The more they care about the enterprise, the more they will invest all their energies and abilities into it.
- Create an atmosphere of trust. Trust your customers, trust your suppliers, trust your people, trust your peers, trust your superiors, trust your company, and trust each other. Remember, if you trust people, they will trust you. And the opposite is true—in spades.
- Be receptive to feedback—from above, below, and laterally.
- Believe in something and stand for something, anything— live the role!
- Believe in yourself—believe that *you* can make a difference.
- Decentralize decision making and reduce unnecessary layers of bureaucracy.

- Believe in the people you work with, too, and try to involve them in your cause and delegate authority along with responsibility. Encourage them to express their new ideas and approaches.
- Encourage challenges to the conventional wisdom. Excitement produces opportunity, which in turn produces change. Reduce your reliance on rules and policies, and view them as flexible guidelines rather than ironclad requirements.
- Remember that enthusiasm is contagious. So is apathy.
- Motivate your people by rallying them around a shared vision—not *your* vision, but a collective vision.
- Build a more sensitive culture where power and influence are derived from ability and commitment, not from title or rank.
- Be willing to take risks in order to make things happen.
- Remember that making new things happen is more important than reporting what old things have happened.
- Instill an "I can make it happen" attitude in all your people. Encourage a culture of pride.
- Recognize that when your organization's internal rate of change is slower than the external rate of change, disaster is just around the corner.
- Focus on doing the right things instead of just doing things right.
- Remember that the effective leader works every bit as hard at teaching as he does at training. He understands that teaching is a much more complex art than just supervising. Teaching requires patience, sensitivity, preparation, consistency, and commitment.
- Focus on *per*formance, not *con*formance.
- Always diagnose before you prescribe.
- Instead of looking inward, stimulate change by looking outward for new opportunities.
- Expand your limits. Never rest on your laurels; no matter how successful you have been in the past, strive to be even more successful in the future.
- Make that commitment to excellence.
- Be like and act like what you ask others to be like and act like.
- Leaders are the union of pathfinder and pioneer: They not only find the way, they lead the way.

- True managers are always real leaders in that they cannot manage effectively without leadership skills. Few managers today realize that management is a mechanical, technical, learned behavior, while leadership is a human, intuitive, compassionate, spiritual gift.
- Managers command and control the physical person, while leaders free the human spirit.

The bottom line: Managers are valuable, but leaders are essential.

6
Translating Theory into Practice: My Experience Running Procter & Gamble's Operations in the Philippines

"An economist is a fellow who can describe a thousand ways to make love but doesn't know any girls."

I read nearly everything I can get my hands on, and somewhere I came across that bit of wisdom about economists, which columnist Roger Clawson of the *Billings Gazette* wrote on July 17, 1987. Mr. Clawson's message is that theory may be great, but all the wonderful sayings in the world aren't worth a damn if they have no practical application. I talk and write at length about management techniques, but the proof has to be in the pudding. So, while I don't want to sound like I'm tooting my own horn, I'd like to tell you about what I consider to be my most successful experience as a manager.

As I've mentioned, I am known outside of Procter & Gamble primarily for the partnership I helped forge with Sam Walton and Wal-Mart. Inside P&G itself, however, my stewardship of our subsidiary in the Philippines during the early 1980s ranks right up there with the Wal-Mart partnership.

P&G expanded into the Philippines in 1935 primarily to guarantee itself a source of coconut oil used in manufacturing toilet soap. The Philippines, then as now, accounted for approximately 60 percent of the world production of coconut oil, and the company decided that establishing a copra-buying and oil-milling operation "on the ground" would not only guarantee a steady supply of oil but would tend to flatten the peak and valley price swings for this indispensable commodity. So P&G purchased the Philippine Manufacturing Company (PMC), a producer of laundry soaps and edible cooking oils that also operated a rather large copra-crushing mill. Our sales and distribution operations in the Philippines changed little during the 1950–1980 period. Given the archipelago's geography of over 7,700 islands, low annual per capita income (about $600, even today), limited electrification, and resulting narrow penetration of television and refrigeration, this Third World country was unable to capitalize on either its rich natural or human resources, and thus was not viewed as a very desirable market.

Especially during the decade before I arrived in 1981, P&G managed its Philippine subsidiary on a rather conservative basis—for good reason, since the country was then under Ferdinand Marcos's martial law. Also, during this ten-year period, three different presidents and general managers led the PMC subsidiary, each with the understanding that their tour would last only three to four years—a practice that, in retrospect, most likely contributed to the short-term tactical approach to business building, as opposed to a longer-range strategic approach. Moreover, our two major competitors, Colgate and Lever, both had been in the Philippines and southeast Asia much longer than P&G and were extremely well entrenched in the region.

The situation bordered on tragedy for a proud company like Procter & Gamble, which was missing out on an opportunity to capture a major market—the Philippines has a population of some 60 million, which places it in the top fifteen nations in the world. I mean, if you're a company like Procter & Gamble, why expend your precious resources in a country halfway around the world if you're not going to capitalize on it?

Eroding volume and profit, declining market shares, increased working capital, heavier bank borrowing, and lengthening trade receivables combined to create a demoralized organization. We were in what I call the "quicksand syndrome": The harder we struggled, the deeper we sank.

PMC, in fact, was flirting with bankruptcy when I arrived on the scene. Some numbers caught my attention real fast. Marketing surveys revealed that Filipino consumers preferred two of P&G's bar soap brands, Camay and Safeguard, by about 70 percent to 30 percent. And yet those two brands ranked last and next-to-last in the market. How could that be? Our people were tearing their hair out, trying to come up with the answer.

What I discovered was that during the previous dozen years, the company's entire sales strategy had been to focus 100 percent on selling volume to the wholesalers and retailers. Period. There was little effort made to help them resell. Most Filipino businesspeople are descended from a culture that glorifies traders. Traders make profits by buying, not selling. So our Filipino customers bought our brands in huge quantity, which of course delighted our sales force.

The thing that nobody was taking into account was that most of those bars of soap weren't finding their way into the hands of the consumers. They were piling up in warehouses, and, to some extent, in stores, all over the Philippines—as much as twenty or thirty weeks' worth in the pipeline. Now the Philippines sit nine degrees north of the equator, and most of those warehouses and stores weren't air-conditioned. It wasn't unusual for temperatures inside those buildings to reach 120 or 140 degrees. So you had these soaps, Camay and Safeguard, that were made with coconut oil and other fats and oils. Coming off the production line, these bars of soap were fine, but after they sat out there in warehouses and baked under the hot sun for five months or so, they had deteriorated and lathered like slick rocks. In addition, they lost their perfume and began to smell like tallow.

Now that we knew what the problem was, the solution was obvious, too: stop selling and get inventories in balance. Of course, that was just slightly against company policy; after all, if you're in the business of manufacturing soap, your objective is to sell soap.

My boss, King Fletcher, had given me the authority to do whatever I needed to do to turn things around in the Philippines. So I sent him a telegram (these were the days before faxes), announcing, "I am declaring a moratorium on selling. To hell with the volume base." At first, I thought King was going to die. But he and the people above him—his boss, Brad Butler, and Ed Artzt and John Smale above them—had sent me out there with a mandate, and it would have been too embarrassing for them to fire me immediately and bring me back to the States.

So we stopped selling. The result: We missed our volume goals by over 40 percent my first year. I ordered my sales organization to make sure that no customer had more than a four-week supply of our products. This was also before the days of computerized systems; we had a manual system, and if you walked into a store and the owner had a five-week supply, you got rewarded for *not* selling him. It was like farmers in the United States who get paid by the government for *not* growing crops. It was incredible! But the plan worked beautifully, and we finally got the inventory problem under control and then started selling soap again.

And within eighteen months, Safeguard and Camay were one-two in the Philippine market. Meanwhile, total PMC volume and profits rose to new record levels; substantially higher dividends were submitted to the parent company; working capital was reduced from about three months of sales to less than one month; inventories were drastically reduced; bank borrowings were reduced by 20 percent; trade receivables were reduced by 33 percent; and the morale of company personnel soared. Specifically, one thing led to another: When you make accurate sales forecasts, you can tell the purchasing department how much to buy. As a result, purchasing got its buying in line, so we didn't have excess inventories of raw material stretched out all over the Pacific. Next, manufacturing knew how much to produce. And as a result of that, working capital, which was measured in terms of months of dollar sales, dropped from 3.3 months of sales to less than one month. By reducing the cash we had tied up in working capital, our cash flow was enhanced, helping to turn the entire business around.

This was a classic, real-life example of understanding how the system worked. We went to what is known as turnover selling, which meant listening to the customer and shipping him product when he needed it instead of ignoring the customer and simply selling him as much as we could get away with. We could now make accurate sales forecasts because we knew what was moving and what was not.

In order to do that, I had to enlist every employee in my cause. Historically, labor unions in the Philippines had been very active, very belligerent, and extremely leftist in their thinking, and had often used organized labor's atomic bomb—the strike—to enforce their demands. The unions had become somewhat more docile during the late 1970s, but PMC management had effectively ignored them and made little effort to enlist them as part of our team.

Soon after I arrived in Manila, my director of manufacturing, Lanky Langcauon, told me that if we treated our people right, there really wouldn't be any need for the unions. The union leaders would see that they had accomplished their goals and that we were treating the employees the way they wanted to be treated. But first we needed to convince the unions that in order for PMC to survive, we had to mutually agree to declare a moratorium on wage increases and other costs like fringe benefits, which threatened to make the company less competitive. I felt that the normal, lengthy negotiation process, under which one party always had to lose in order for the other to win, would lead to even greater polarization of labor and management. So Lanky and I sat down with the union leaders and obtained their input in hopes of saving the company by working on a win-win basis versus the historical win-lose one, and making one plus one equal three. We agreed that above all we had to trust each other, recognizing that the only way we could weather the crisis was to substitute cooperation for confrontation.

We started inviting the union reps to company meetings for the first time in PMC history. Lanky and I used to have dinner with the union leaders and ask them what they wanted, what are we doing right, what are we doing wrong. We let them participate in the process—and they became part of the process, part of our team, as a result. One of the union leaders at PMC observed in 1981 that "this is the first time we [union representatives] were invited to the [PMC] State-of-the-Business meeting [at which I gave my annual address to PMC employees]. That's a real breakthrough—for us to feel that we are a part of this corporate family." And so we were able to forge a unique partnership with the labor unions there, one that has lasted for over ten years now.

When I left Manila in 1984, PMC was back in the number one position in volume, profit, and share of the Philippine market. Afterwards, people said to me, "Boy, you went out there and did an absolutely marvelous job. You worked magic." In fact, in June 1984, when I got ready to move from the

Philippines back to Cincinnati as general manager of sales for the United States, Ed Artzt, who was one of my strongest supporters, wrote me a letter expressing his gratitude "for a brilliant performance in a terribly important job." Coming from Ed, that meant a lot to me.

But my answer to all the praise was that I simply went out there, provided leadership and new direction, and helped the organization think differently about how the business ought to operate. I helped create an environment that allowed the organization to do what it was capable of doing. It was that basic. You thought about the total system and the principles of selling and business; you focused on the customer; you moved away from the narrow, parochial concept of sell, sell, sell at any cost to viewing the customers as partners and selling them only what they needed.

All I did was manage the Philippine Manufacturing Company with a strong customer and employee focus, the way any business should be managed, in my opinion. What I did in the Philippines wasn't attributable to genius; common sense was the root of it all. I didn't invent the wheel; all I did was capitalize on the rich talent of the Philippine workforce, which some who ran PMC previously had neglected to do. My people and I learned to diagnose before we prescribed and to apply people principles and customer principles that had worked well elsewhere.

Let's face it—there aren't that many original ideas running around, but there *are* plenty of great ideas that aren't being used. Some people, and I like to think that I'm one of them, are able to more or less see the real world and to realize that oftentimes the most simple or basic approach is what works best. I've always tried to spend a lot of my time thinking the business through instead of just thinking *about* it. And once I thought through the situation in the Philippines, it seemed obvious to me why it wasn't working.

One thing I did out there was to junk the stovepipe system under which each function—sales, advertising, manufacturing, finance, and so on—did its own thing but didn't worry about communicating with the other divisions. I always thought that was like wearing blinders; you're not allowed to look right and you're not allowed to look left. Blind obedience to functional and specialized jobs simply doesn't work, and hasn't for years, although a lot of companies haven't caught on yet. Functional managers tend to measure their performance and that of their subordinates entirely by what their function is doing instead of measuring their contribution to the entire enterprise.

What I did was organize PMC into multifunctional teams, what I call the team-within-a-team approach. And every week a different multifunctional team would report to me and the directors on what was happening in one of the major areas of the business. The directors and I listened to what these teams told us and thought a lot about what they were saying, and then, instead of telling them what to do, we questioned them and challenged them and stimulated them, and let them work with us to make the key decisions. Then, when I got back to the United States, I tried to apply the same system to the entire Procter & Gamble company. And that turned out to be not quite as easy as it had been for me in the Philippines, because, unlike PMC, Lou Pritchett was not in command of P&G.

Elevate Your Desk—and Lower Everyone's Opinion of You.

When I arrived in the Philippines, P&G's standing as one of the major American companies in the islands and as one of the U.S. corporations that had been operating there the longest (since 1935) instantly conferred VIP rank on me out there. That's how I happened to get a firsthand view of how one of the worst managers of this era—Philippine president Ferdinand Marcos—operated.

By virtue of being P&G's point man in the Philippines, I served on the board of directors of the American Chamber of Commerce, which is a very important and influential organization there. My company and I may have been big fish in a small pond, but big fish we—P&G and I—were. As a result, I had several "up close and personal" meetings with Marcos, who had been in power for sixteen years when I got to Manila. I was in the Philippines at the time of the 1983 assassination of Marcos's archrival, Benigno Aquino (whose wife, Corazon, wound up succeeding Marcos), one of the key events that led to Marcos's being overthrown and exiled to Hawaii in 1986, two years after

I returned to the States. (In fact, I was at the Manila airport where Aquino was murdered just two hours before he was shot and two gates from the scene.) So I really had an opportunity to witness not only appalling mismanagement in action but also its net results.

The leadership of the American Chamber of Commerce went out periodically and had meetings with Marcos at the famous/infamous Malacanang Palace, which afforded me an opportunity to learn precisely how *not* to exert power. You might say that Mr. Marcos was the opposite of Sam Walton in just about every way.

One of the first things I noticed about Marcos was that he sat up on a raised platform. It was an eight- or ten-inch-high riser at one end of the room. That meant that when you stood in front of him, he was almost at eye level with you—the message he was trying to get across was that the king is always above the subjects, physically and every other way. (I understand that J. Edgar Hoover—another classic case of an executive who misused authority—I won't dignify Hoover or Marcos with the title "leader"—had a similar type of arrangement with his desk at FBI headquarters in order to make himself appear taller.)

Something else I noticed immediately about Marcos was that he always had a glass of water sitting at his left hand with a coaster not only under the glass but also completely covering the top. The coaster covering the glass was almost certainly there to prevent anyone from dropping poison or any other foreign substance into his glass. When Marcos was thirsty, he would remove the cover, drink from the glass, and replace the cover. I found that fascinating, because I've never seen anybody else do that; because Marcos was a dictator, he couldn't trust anyone. And there were always guards around him, even inside the palace.

At our meetings with Marcos, the other American business leaders and I presented our thoughts about the situation in the Philippines as it affected us. The American Chamber's main purpose was to defend American business interests by maintaining a dialogue with Marcos and keeping him abreast of what was going on, as we saw it. And I must say he was always very attentive; our conversations took place in English, without an interpreter to filter our comments, and he was usually animated and seemed to be candid and to want us to be candid, although no hard decisions were made during these sessions. He was quite an actor, but I always felt that he was listening and hearing and responding.

One of our major complaints to Marcos about the problems American corporations encountered while trying to do business in the Philippines concerned cronyism, which was rampant throughout the country. Before long, my company became one of the principal victims of one of Marcos's henchmen.

This individual, among Marcos's most trusted associates, was in charge of the country's coconut industry. The Philippines produce something like 60 percent of the world's coconut oil, which is used in making cosmetics and soaps, among other things; that's why Procter & Gamble started building a business in the Philippines back in the 1930s, to make sure we would have a reliable supply of coconut oil.

Well, in September 1982, while Marcos was over in the United States meeting with President Reagan, his crony announced that he was for all intents and purposes nationalizing the country's coconut industry. What he did was stop us from of exporting our coconut oil. We had to sell it to a government monopoly, the Philippine Coconut Authority. My reaction was, "This is ridiculous. I'm not going to sit here and take this. I'm going to sue Marcos and the son of a bitch" who had issued the order that the government was taking over the coconut mills.

I hired a lawyer named William Quasha, a man who had been on MacArthur's staff and had stayed in Manila after the war. Quasha was very close to Marcos, and in November he and I requested and were granted a private meeting with Marcos at the palace to discuss the situation. Again, Marcos at least gave the appearance of being open to my point of view. "Well, tell me the whole story," he said to me, and after I finished, his response was, "I promised your president that relations with U.S. business are going to stay on an even keel, that American businesses are going to be able to repatriate their earnings." (American businessmen were growing concerned that we were sort of under siege in the Philippines.)

With that, Marcos turned to one of his assistants and, using the nickname of his crony who had nationalized the coconut industry, asked if the man was in the building. Yes, Marcos's assistant replied, the man was right outside the room where we were talking. So they summoned him in and Marcos turned to him and said, "Mr. Pritchett informs me that we have started a process of depriving him of his mill. Is that true?" The man answered, "Yes"—as if Marcos didn't know exactly what had happened, although I'm certain he did.

Marcos appeared to ponder the situation briefly, and then he declared, "I want to rescind that order. I don't want to do that. I want to give Mr. Pritchett back his mill." At that moment, a palace photographer snapped a picture of Marcos and me smiling at each other, and it ran the next day in one of the Manila newspapers. But instead of saying anything about the government's taking over our mill or that this meeting had resulted in our getting the mill back, all the caption said was that Lou Pritchett, the president of Procter's operation in the Philippines, and President Marcos had met to discuss the bright future of the coconut industry in the Philippines. What was reported in the newspaper had *absolutely nothing* to do with the actual circumstances.

That was the end of that particular crisis, but you might say that I was never again completely at ease in the Philippines. The Philippines have one of the great rumor mills in the world. And in those islands, rumors have a way of taking on a life of their own. From that day forward, there was a rumor that I had embarrassed Marcos's crony, the one who had seized control of the coconut industry. According to the local gossip, instead of going to Marcos's sidekick on this, I had gone straight to the President, and Marcos had called the man in and humiliated him in front of everyone, causing the man to lose face, or *hiya*, as they call it. When you lose *hiya* in the Philippines, it's like being castrated; you've lost everything. This individual was not someone you wanted to cross; he was very, very powerful. For a couple of months I was looking over my shoulder. Much as I loved the Philippines, I have to admit that I breathed a sigh of relief when I left the islands and returned to the United States a year or so after this incident.

My Ringside Seat, Watching How a King—and His Queen—Alienated Their Subjects.

During my years in the Philippines I had personal contact with both Ferdinand and Imelda Marcos on a number of occasions. One of the exciting parts of living in a small country and having a big job (president of an important company) is that you are indeed a big fish in a small pond, which may present you with opportunities that you never would have living back in the United States.

In 1982 the board of directors of the American Chamber of Commerce, including me, accompanied President and Mrs. Marcos to the city of Tacloban in the province of Leyte to celebrate the thirty-seventh anniversary of General MacArthur's famous wartime return to the Philippines. A thirty-seventh anniversary may sound like a strange time to stage a huge celebration, but Marcos had just gotten back from a trip to the States and a high-profile meeting with President Reagan. Being the shrewd politician he was, Marcos wanted to capitalize back home on his meeting with Reagan. So, celebrating MacArthur's liberation of the Philippines seemed to Marcos like a smart thing to do that year—and it no doubt was. Several groups of American veterans came to Tacloban for the festivities, as did many local businesspeople. A lavish feast was laid out on one of the landing beaches, and then Marcos and his first lady each spoke. Especially in view of subsequent events, it seems significant that both Marcoses were seated on "thrones" on a raised platform under a large awning. The couple always carried these thrones along for visits to the provinces. The thrones were large wooden chairs with the seats and backs made of red velvet and the exposed legs and arms covered with gold paint or gold leaf. These thrones were symbols of the Marcoses' authority and control over the country—they were indeed fit for a king and queen.

I always found it fascinating to watch Mrs. Marcos in action. It appeared to me that she controlled or dominated President Marcos. Imelda was always "onstage," while the demeanor of Marcos himself usually was low-key. She would frequently whisper in his ear as they sat before the throngs, and he would smile and nod approvingly. I concluded from witnessing the interaction between the two of them numerous times that she was telling him what to think and what to do.

Mrs. Marcos was very impressed with herself, and she never forgot it or let anyone else forget it. She was addicted to attention, and whether she was before groups of three or groups of three hundred thousand, she invariably played her role to the hilt. Once, when Barbara and I were among a group of twelve visiting a museum Mrs. Marcos had built in her city of birth, Tacloban, Imelda spent almost two hours leading us through the building and telling us about everything in it. She had boundless energy and seemed to get more animated as the tour proceeded. It may have been my imagination, but when she stopped us at the bottom of a huge and impressive staircase and pointed upward to a large (at least ten by twenty feet) mural of herself ascending from clouds and surrounded by cherubs, she was almost in a trance.

Barbara and I are convinced that Mrs. Marcos actually believed she was divine and had been put in her position by a supreme power. I could not help compare the relationship between Ferdinand and Imelda Marcos to my marriage to Barbara, who has always been the rock by my side and has taken this rough stone, polished it, and helped it reach its full potential. Barbara brought out the tender side of me, and the love, trust, and understanding that are the foundations of our marriage transformed me from the win-at-all-costs charger I may have been into a caring individual in business as well as in life. As far as I am concerned, Imelda's influence on her husband was 180 degrees opposite.

Ferdinand Marcos has been accused of many things, and no doubt is guilty on a lot of those charges. Nevertheless, it must be remembered that he was a product of his culture just as much as every other person is, be they Filipino, American, or any other nationality. From my vantage point it appeared that Marcos elevated the ancient art of cronyism to an art form. His wife was only the most notorious of the Marcos crowd. The skills and intelligence of his cronies seemingly did not matter much to Marcos because, again, he was simply playing out a cultural bias that was as strong as blood. In Tagalog this is called *utang na loob*—or "debt of gratitude." To a Filipino, whoever does one a favor must be repaid with some greater favor. For example, if someone helps you financially when you are down on your luck, not only will you repay your debt but you will work diligently to repay that person in other ways. If you help someone's child, you and your children will be repaid in kind or better. Or if you help someone gain political office, you can rest assured you will be repaid by that person in some special way. During the early stages of his political career, when Marcos was a local functionary in his home province of Ilocos Norte, both the powerful and the not so powerful did many favors for him. Marcos never forgot any of his benefactors. Over the years, his henchmen would become notorious for looting millions of dollars from the national treasury through every scheme imaginable—all the product of *utang na loob*.

None of this excuses the terrible abuses of power by Marcos and his cronies, but I believe it is important to understand how this type of thing can and does happen.

My experience with Marcos taught me a number of lessons:

First, when a manager is faced with any kind of threatening situation, you don't run for cover. What you do is try to address it to the best of your ability. In the instance when P&G's mill was nationalized, of course, I was very naive and very careless and did a very dangerous thing. But my company had been wronged; Marcos's buddy had violated the most basic law of the land by confiscating our mill, and I was determined to reverse his order.

Second, my impression, based on my own observation, was that Marcos, because of illness or for whatever other reason, had lost contact with his own administration. He had become isolated and was being taken advantage of by many of the people around him. Any manager who allows himself to lose control of his organization, whether it's a corporation or a government, makes himself extremely vulnerable. Things—usually, bad things—start happening, things that probably wouldn't happen if the manager were still in control. Losing control, taking your hand off the switch, not being involved in the daily business, and not knowing what's going on is a serious problem.

Finally, Marcos's failure to surround himself with honest, capable people caused terrible suffering for the people he ruled, and ultimately led to his own demise. The men he put in power were basically a bunch of sycophants. Had he placed real quality people in the top jobs, the country would have been better off. And, who knows, Marcos might have gone down in Philippine history as the hero he pictured himself as being. Instead, his people ran him right out of town—all the way out of the country, in fact.

Save Face, Save Your Voice, Maybe Even Help Save Yourself.

Due to P&G's role in the coconut oil business, I became closely involved with the Philippine Coconut Authority (PCA). The managing director of the PCA was an officer in the Philippine army, Colonel Dondo Dueaños, a bright, good-natured individual. Even though he was a political appointee, he took his job very seriously. In addition to his military skills, Colonel Dueaños was also a qualified aircraft pilot; I was frequently invited to fly with him to remote oil mills or coconut agricultural stations throughout the islands. I always enjoyed these trips, which gave me an opportunity to work with the PCA and see parts of the country I never would have seen otherwise.

On one of our trips, Colonel Dueaños and I flew from Manila to the city of Legazpi in the coconut-rich region of Bicol, about an hour and a half from Manila by small plane. We took off early on a beautiful morning and flew for the scheduled ninety minutes or so. Suddenly, huge thunderheads began building up, blocking the ground from our view. The colonel didn't utter a word, but I noticed beads of perspiration forming on his upper lip. It was obvious that he was growing increasingly apprehensive. We flew around for another half hour before I concluded that we were lost and that Dueaños couldn't locate the Legazpi airport. Since there were no navigational aids, all small-plane flying was done by sight, and the clouds had obscured the land. To make matters worse, one of the tallest volcanoes in the world, Mount Mayon, is located in the Bicol region near Legazpi. The situation was tense, to say the least.

Here was the head of the PCA, a very important institution, lost above Legazpi with the president of one of the country's largest foreign companies. Our situation was perilous, and I was scared, but I felt it would be wrong to express my fears, which might have caused Dueaños to "lose face," and, perhaps, to lose control of the plane. At last, the colonel reached into his flight bag and pulled out a map—which must have been a moment of supreme embarrassment for him. We changed direction and headed for another airport. As luck would have it, the clouds dissipated at that instant, and we saw not only the ground but the Legazpi airport. We landed immediately. Colonel Dueaños's flight suit was soaking with sweat and my knees felt like rubber. If I had been in the States, I might have cried out in terror, but knowing the Filipino customs, I kept my mouth shut—which helped the pilot. My panic would only have distracted Dueaños, who was under enough strain and didn't need any grief from his passenger. Sometimes you just have to go with the flow, and the flow can be a lot smoother in another culture.

Don't Ask Your Troops to Do Anything You Wouldn't Do Yourself— Even If It Exposes You to Danger.

Within thirty days after my arrival in Manila in 1981, I had been recognized by my employees as a "field manager." As president of P&G's subsidiary in the Philippines, I loved getting out into the field where the action was. I was one of those managers who "managed by walking around" as early as the 1950s, long before Tom Peters coined that phrase. To me, management by walking around is simply commonsense management. Your employees do not come to the workplace and check their brains at the door. So if you really want to find out what's happening, you go to your employees on the shop floor. They know where all the problems are. They know where the opportunities for improvement are. They know where the shortcuts are. If someone had gone and talked to the employees on the assembly line at General Motors years ago, they could have found out that the company was making shoddy products—that the doors rattled and the handles fell off and the plastic peeled. The rank-

and-file workers knew that long before the Japanese ate their lunch, but nobody ever asked them.

For some unknown reason, this style of management comes naturally to me, but it was different from the habits and practices of some of my predecessors who had headed P&G's operations in the Philippines. The impact of my style was so positive that I decided not only to accelerate it but also to visit areas of the country where few if any previous P&G presidents had set foot.

At this time, there were areas in the countryside that were considered unsafe due to heavy concentrations of "NPA" (the New People's Army, Maoist revolutionaries dedicated to overthrowing the Marcos regime). Both the Philippine government and the American embassy issued frequent warnings to expats to avoid these rebel-controlled areas, where pitched battles often occurred between rebel forces and government troops, and being kidnapped or murdered by the insurgents was a real danger. I was so comfortable in the country and among the people, however, that I took these warnings with a grain of salt. I would not travel by design into a known NPA stronghold, but I was not afraid to range widely around the country.

Moreover, I was convinced that if I assigned and allowed our salespeople to work these areas, it was not fair for me to avoid them myself. I felt it essential to demonstrate that I was willing to do whatever I asked my people to do.

My national sales manager in the Philippines, Vic Herrera, was an outstanding man and manager about my age. Vic had grown up in the rich delta province of Pampanga in central Luzon. As a young boy in the town of San Fernando he had watched as streams of Japanese invaders herded captive American and Filipino soldiers from the battlefields of Bataan and Corregidor to their prison camp in Capas—what would become known as the infamous Bataan Death March.

Vic was a sales manager's sales manager, probably the best I ever encountered in my entire career. One day he and I decided to inspect our operations in the city of Legazpi, about three hundred miles from Manila. As planned, we flew there on Philippine Airlines early one morning and spent the day working in Legazpi. *Not* as planned, however, a violent late-afternoon storm closed the Legazpi airport and caused our return flight to Manila to be canceled.

That put me in a bad spot. My boss from Cincinnati, Kingston Fletcher, was due to arrive the next day for one of his quarterly visits. Knowing that I desperately needed to get back to Manila, Vic Herrera decided to ask the local P&G district manager to drive us to the capital via the only road between Legazpi and Manila, one that passed through some of the strongest NPA areas, the provinces of Camarines Norte and Camarines Sur. The trip took eight hours in broad daylight; who knew how long it would take at night?

The three of us set out at six o'clock in the evening for what would be one of the most memorable and hair-raising experiences of my life. The road was not lit, and there was nothing to mark the shoulders of the highway. The potholes were big enough to shatter bones and axles. Occasionally, carabao, the basic Philippine work animal on the farms, would loom up on the road in front of us, looking like hippos in the night. After a few hours we ran into a torrential downpour (the same storm that had grounded our return flight), and what had been poor visibility deteriorated into zero visibility. Vic and the district manager switched off at the wheel; the trip took twelve hours, and not once did we see another car going in either direction. Finally, at six o'clock the next morning, we rolled into my driveway in Manila, exhausted and looking like we hadn't slept for a week, but no worse for wear.

Now all I had to do was face Alex Lacson. Alex, as our corporate affairs director in the Philippines, was responsible for security, among other things. Alex, another wonderful employee, liked to say that one of his biggest challenges was guaranteeing the safety of "our crazy president," as he described yours truly. Alex was determined that the P&G president would not be assassinated or kidnapped on his watch, and when I walked into his office at ten o'clock that morning, he was in a rage. He was mad at me, mad at Vic, mad at the district manager, mad at Philippine Airlines, and mad at the weather. In fact, he was as upset as any human being I had ever run into. Not only had we not returned as scheduled, we had driven twelve hours through NPA country—without bothering to phone in and tell anybody what we were doing. (I later learned from Vic Herrera that the reason he had not phoned Lacson to tell him we planned to drive from Legazpi was because Vic knew that Alex would say no; Vic was determined to get me home in time to meet with Kingston Fletcher. I also found out that Vic was Jesuit trained and believed in the maxim that it is always easier to obtain forgiveness than permission.)

This was a classic case of several of us completing a dangerous mission successfully through sheer determination—mine to get back to Manila and Vic's to get me there. Making this trip in the first place was also a manifestation of two of my basic rules of management—get out of your office, and do what you ask your people to do.

Let Sleeping Guards Lie, Particularly When They're Carrying Guns.

During my years in the Philippines, I became accustomed to having armed guards at both my office and my home. I never really felt unsafe or threatened, but during the recent turbulent years before President Marcos had cracked down and instituted "law and order," it was advisable for expats to have at least a semblance of protection. Those not-so-long-ago Wild West days in the Philippines had seen the security-guard industry grow like wildfire. Thousands of armed guards were trained and issued uniforms. The need for these services declined in the late '70s and early '80s, but companies like mine were slow to reduce their level of protection. As a result, when I arrived in Manila in 1981, uniformed, gun-toting guards were still the norm for major foreign-based companies.

These guards worked around the clock at our executive offices on the fifteenth floor of a bank building. On Sundays, when in theory the offices were closed, the guards would shut down three of the four elevators serving our floor by opening the doors and jamming the elevators about one foot above floor level. That prevented those elevators from moving and in effect secured the fifteenth floor.

One Sunday morning, I went to my office and instead of summoning the one elevator that was working, I decided to get some exercise by walking up the stairs. When I finally reached the fifteenth floor, the one guard on duty was scared witless. He had been sleeping on the sofa in the waiting room, and at the sight of me, he jumped up, and, still half asleep, put his shoes on the wrong feet. As he started to walk, he stumbled and fell, causing his pistol to drop out of his holster and slide silently across the tile floor directly toward the open elevator shaft.

I can remember the scene as though it happened in slow motion. There was the guard sprawled across the floor with his shoes on the wrong feet, watching in terror as his pistol slowly slid out of reach toward the elevator shaft. The moan from the guard was a combination of Tagalog and English, and it translated roughly into "Holy shit! There goes my gun down the elevator shaft! I'm going to lose my job!" Sure enough, his weapon reached the opening and then fell fourteen stories to the ground floor. I never learned what happened to that guard. Nor did I ever see him again at the office, my home, or the Procter & Gamble manufacturing plant.

The Kathmandu Man Does.

While I was working in the Philippines, Barbara and I went on vacation to Nepal and traveled into the central valley outside Kathmandu, where we found a large settlement of Tibetans. These political refugees had left their homes on foot and crossed the mountains into the safety of Nepal. Many of them were selling their personal possessions—knives, blankets, rugs, and jewelry—to pay for food and shelter. We struck up a conversation with one man who was trying to sell a beautiful antique hand-woven saddle blanket. After negotiating with him, we agreed to buy the blanket for U.S. $100.

We had that amount in traveler's checks, but we didn't have that much cash. And this refugee wouldn't take anything but dollars; after all, how was he to cash a traveler's check? After a few minutes of deep thought, he agreed to ride with us in our car to our hotel in Kathmandu, approximately forty-five miles away. We arrived at our hotel and paid him in dollars, and he returned on foot to his tiny campsite in the valley.

There is no end, I thought to myself as I watched him trudge off, to the hardships and lengths people will endure when they absolutely have to sustain themselves and their families. All this man had between starvation for himself and his family were a few possessions to sell, including his blanket. And he was doing whatever he could to earn his keep. He wasn't worried about OSHA rules and regulations, and he didn't have a union steward to tell him what he could and could not do, that what he was doing wasn't included in his job description. He wasn't looking for any handouts or welfare. Nor was he on the streets of Kathmandu, begging or stealing for a living. All he wanted was to do some legitimate business. And that's exactly what he was able to do.

Some people are made of stronger stuff, perhaps because they haven't been softened by civilization. After living all my life in the United States, I had forgotten how much a lone individual can do if he puts his mind to it, without the government or a big company or a labor union telling him what he can and cannot do.

Through Rain, Snow, Sleet, Hail—or Even a Revolution.

Among the many extremely dedicated and motivated people I encountered was Bob Hayden, a longtime Procter & Gamble executive. Bob is one of those people who regards duty as one of the highest callings in life and allows nothing to prevent him from carrying out his responsibilities.

It was in 1989, while Bob was living in Manila as P&G's manager of sales training for the Asia-Pacific-Japan division, that yet another coup attempt erupted in the Philippines. This particular revolt was led by a renegade former Philippine army officer, Gringo Honasan. Honasan and his rebels marched into the central business district of Makati, where Bob Hayden's office was located and where troops from the regular army battled the insurgents.

On that very same day, by coincidence, Bob's boss in Hong Kong, Fred Caswell, needed some very important information from Bob. With a war of sorts raging around him, Bob, lying on the floor of his office, phoned Caswell and began relaying the requested data. About ten minutes into the conversation, Caswell said, "What is all that noise, Bob? Why don't you close the door so I can hear you better?"

"Fred," Bob replied, "you'll just have to endure the noise. Those sounds you hear are machine guns firing over and into our office."

Nevertheless, Bob provided Fred with all the information he needed. Bob Hayden wasn't about to let anything like a little revolution keep him from doing his job.

Romance the Culture . . .

When I urge people to "romance the culture," what I really mean is that they should try to fit in. When in Rome, be a Roman, as I mentioned earlier. In the Philippines, for instance, I learned that to get the best results, you never give direct orders; you make suggestions. "Those orchids would look nice around the pool," you say to the gardener instead of ordering him, "Put them around the pool." This way of dealing with people works very smoothly and effectively. It's simply a nonconfrontational way of getting the point across. A lot of Americans arrived there with the attitude, "I'm not going to tolerate that bullshit. If I want something done, by God, I'll tell 'em to do it!" With that attitude, though, these aliens—aliens in the literal sense of the word—didn't get the results they sought. I think a similar system would work well in our society. I know that I personally use that method to this day, and I certainly did when I was at P&G. I was not known for issuing orders. I was known for presenting suggestions.

Something else they do in the Philippines that I'd like to see more of here in the States is that Filipinos avoid direct confrontations. They offer criticism through third parties, which has a lot of merit; it lowers the hostility level.

The fact is that not only will you do better by learning the rules of the foreign culture you find yourself in temporarily and living by those rules while you're abroad, you will also get better results back at home if you continue to live by such precepts here.

Living and working in the Philippines while I was running PMC was the best experience I ever had. My wife and I lived in a beautiful country filled with beautiful people. To me, my stay in the Philippines was like being on permanent vacation in an exotic land. The best part of all was the Filipino people themselves. I've traveled to dozens of foreign lands, and never have I seen an entire culture more willing to cooperate, get along, share, team up, collaborate, agree, and work like hell than the employees of the PMC Group and other Filipinos I was lucky enough to come in contact with.

Some Americans would make brief visits to the Philippines, and, noting that most Filipinos observed the tradition of an afternoon siesta (when nearly everyone takes a break from the heat and humidity), would conclude that the Filipinos were a lazy lot. This value judgment couldn't have been farther from the truth!

The Filipino dedication to the job at hand and commitment to hard work was exemplified once when Barbara and I were giving a dinner party for over a hundred people in honor of P&G's visiting CEO, John Smale, and international president Ed Artzt (who later succeeded Smale as CEO). About an hour before the guests were to arrive, one of the maids informed us that we had no water. The taps were bone dry and the toilets wouldn't flush. I quickly called our factory, which was located a dozen or more miles away, and explained the problem. Within a half hour, a young man from the factory was squatting over a concrete slab in the rear of our house, chipping away with a chisel and hammer. He had inspected the situation and determined that a pipe had broken under the concrete apron. With only two hand tools, he found the pipe, sealed it, and vanished over the garden wall. No one ever knew how close that dinner party had come to disaster. And it might well have but for this employee's efforts—which were typical of the Filipinos, but far above the norm I have experienced in many other countries, including our own.

. . . and in Turn, the Culture Will Romance You.

When I made my first speech to the PMC organization in Manila shortly after taking over in 1981, I walked to the center of the stage in the company auditorium. Some eight hundred people had been assembled to hear what the newly appointed president and general manager had to say to his 99.9 percent Filipino audience.

When I reached center stage, I found to my amazement not a podium or lectern, but a skinny, rickety, black metal music stand—like the ones used by orchestra conductors to hold musical scores. Not only was the stand flimsy and unstable for my heavy script and notes, but it didn't conceal my body. Unlike most podiums, this one offered me no opportunity to hide behind it, feel secure, put my hands in my pocket, shift the position of my feet—all the little things I do to put myself at ease when I'm speaking. The only thing between me and eight hundred of my new employees was a three-quarter-inch piece of tubular black metal.

I got through this ordeal somehow, but I was absolutely determined to avoid having it happen again. As soon as I finished delivering that speech, I went to our director of personnel, Pepito Fernandez, and asked him to make sure that from then on, whenever I spoke formally to any audience, there would be a suitable podium in front of me. Being a resourceful individual, Pepito took my request to the director of manufacturing, Lanky Langcauon, and asked for his help. Within twenty-four hours, my secretary informed me that two engineers from the PMC factory wanted to see me. These two men entered my office and asked if they could take my measurements, for they had just been assigned the task of building me a custom podium. I was making my weekly tour of our manufacturing facility several days later when Lanky called me into a warehouse and unveiled the most gorgeous podium I had ever seen. It was made of solid narra, a wood similar to mahogany that is considered the national wood of the Philippines. The podium was precisely the right height, the right width, the right angle. Except for the giant, pizza-size P&G man-in-the-moon emblem on the front, it would have looked perfect in any church sanctuary or boardroom in the world.

My new podium also weighed about eighty pounds and required at least two people to handle it. Lanky designated two of the plant people as "podium czars." With this title came the responsibility for being on call to transport the podium to the site where I was giving a speech and to make sure it was there at least an hour in advance. That could be at any of the major hotels in Manila, at the convention center down on Manila Bay, at our plant in Tondo, on the soccer field at the University of Santo Tomas, or at the headquarters of the American Chamber of Commerce.

For nearly four years and through hundreds of speeches, neither the podium nor the podium czars ever failed me. In certain cultures, doing whatever it takes to get the job done is all that counts. The fact that my requirements might seem silly or comical to some people made no difference to the Filipinos. All that mattered to them was meeting the needs of their president.

Don't Just Romance the Culture, Immerse Yourself in It if You Can.

My life had changed dramatically in 1942, when my brother, my uncles, and my cousins left to join the army or the navy and help rid the world of the likes of Hitler, Mussolini, and Tojo. Not quite eleven, I was of course too young to go, so, aside from my father, who was about fifty and too old to go to war, I was the only male left at home to comfort mothers, aunts, and sisters. I distinctly recall hearing sobs late into the night as these women worried themselves sick over their men who were off fighting somewhere in the South Pacific or North Africa.

I was fascinated during the war years to read censored letters from my soldier and sailor relatives to their families. I was convinced that each letter contained a code revealing where they were, what they were doing, and where they were going, and I spent hours trying to decipher their "coded messages." I learned later, of course, that it had never occurred to any of the men in my family to try to send secret messages. I eagerly awaited the day when I, too, would be old enough to sign up and join my relatives in far off places like Anzio, Saipan, Corregidor, and Normandy. The very sound of these names conjured up in my mind excitement, intrigue, action, and mystery. The romance of the war ended in late June 1944, when I watched my father turn ashen as he read a telegram from the War Department informing him that his son, my brother Joe, had been killed in action on Utah Beach in Normandy—a blow from which my father never recovered as he wasted away for the next year and then died.

The names of these battlegrounds give me chills whenever I hear them to this day, as they did in my youth. I am a card-carrying honorary member of my brother's old unit, the army's 531st Engineer Shore Regiment, and I attend annual meetings of the unit.

It was for these reasons that soon after I arrived in the Philippines almost forty years later the island of Corregidor, which lies at the mouth of Manila Bay in the South China Sea, became one of my favorite places. This hallowed spot is a special place for me because of all the stories I recall during the war years of 1941 to 1945: MacArthur's departure from the Philippines by PT boat; the fall of Bataan; the siege of Corregidor and its fall; the infamous Bataan Death March; the recapture of Corregidor by the American 503rd parachute regimental combat team; and MacArthur's fulfilling his fabled vow: "I shall return!"

In my young mind, Corregidor had become the symbol of everything good and brave about Americans during the war. Now, in 1981, forty years after the first battle on the island, I discovered when I actually visited Corregidor that almost nothing had changed. There I saw the bombed-out barracks, the concrete gun emplacements with the actual guns still pointing out to sea, the flagpole in front of MacArthur's headquarters, the old concrete dock from which MacArthur had been evacuated by PT boat. It was as if the soldiers had left just moments before I arrived, creating within me the most moving and haunting feelings I have ever experienced.

After a couple of visits to Corregidor, I noticed with surprise the absence of any type of memorial or museum to the Americans and Filipinos who fought and died there. In fact, the only memorials, ironically, were to the Japanese; several handsome granite monuments and literally thousands of small hand-lettered wooden shafts had been placed there by relatives of the Japanese soldiers who had visited the battlefield during the past ten to twenty years. There *was* one huge memorial and reflecting pool dedicated to all the combat victims of the war who lost their lives during the southeast Asia and Pacific campaigns, but none that were Corregidor-American-Filipino specific.

Barbara and I vowed to rectify the situation. I wrote a letter to members of the American Chamber of Commerce in Manila asking for their financial support to fund the creation of an American-Filipino museum. Additionally, I contacted the Filipino Veterans Association, several American veteran associations, the current Philippine military, and the Marcos government. The response from all was positive and enthusiastic. Since Corregidor is located nearly thirty nautical miles from Manila, getting there was a somewhat difficult journey. The Philippine army gave Barbara and me access to one of its helicopters, reducing the three-hour travel time by boat to about twenty-five minutes by air. For the opening and official dedication of the museum in 1983, we convinced the Marcos government to let us use one of the presidential yachts, *Mount Samat.* This hundred-foot, luxuriously appointed yacht carried seventy-five dignitaries from the Philippine government, the U.S. embassy, and the American Chamber of Commerce to Corregidor for a daylong celebration of the opening of the museum. What Barbara and I helped launch there in 1983 is today an incorporated organization called FAME (Filipino-American Memorial Endowment), which continues to collect and display material and remember the Americans and Filipinos who gave their lives there.

Meanwhile, after we had been in the Philippines for several months and had visited many of the historic sites, Barbara and I were invited to spend a weekend at the vast Del Monte Plantation in the village of Bukidnon, about forty-five minutes from the city of Cagayan de Oro on the northern coast of Mindanao. The president and general manager of the plantation was Paul Perrine, an American who had arrived in the Philippines in 1945 with the U.S. Army, had been mustered out of the service in Manila, and had decided to remain in the country. He soon joined a subsidiary of the Del Monte Corporation and stayed with Del Monte for forty years. Paul and I had become friends after meeting as fellow board members of the American Chamber of Commerce and as members of a small, low-profile, private organization that had been named "MESA," or Makati Eating and Singing Association, in an attempt to disguise what we were about: discussing politics and rules and regulations affecting American business interests in the Philippines. Members, all of us presidents and CEOs of our companies, felt a real need for a way to discuss what was going on in the country, given that the press at that time was strictly controlled by Marcos's cronies and apologists.

Our visit to Del Monte began with Paul giving several of us, including Barbara and me, a tour of the plantation where pineapples and bananas were growing on thousands of acres of perfectly manicured farmland. As we walked across a wide grassy field that separated the living quarters of Paul and his family from the tennis courts, Paul stopped and asked me to look sharply to my right and left. I saw what appeared to be two slight ruts stretching perhaps two hundred yards in each direction. Paul asked me what I thought these ruts were, and I replied that they looked like the remains of an old, long-abandoned one-lane road. Then, when Paul told me what I was standing in the middle of, the chills on my spine began to rise and fall. He explained that these slight depressions were the remnants of a small airfield that had been on the plantation during the late 1930s early 1940s. This very field, Paul continued, was where General MacArthur had been picked up by plane and flown to Australia after his escape by PT boat from Corregidor. I was standing on the exact spot where one of the great events in American military history had taken place! There were no markers, no monuments, no signs telling what had happened there. A soft breeze gently moved the short grass that had all but obscured the ruts in this beautiful grassy field where history had been made forty years earlier. This was another of the many unforgettable experiences I had in the Philippines as a result of making a conscious decision to immerse myself in the culture and make myself as much of a Filipino as I possibly could.

When I Say Immerse Yourself in a Foreign Culture, I Mean Immerse Yourself All the Way Up to Your Nose.

In March 1988, I spent a week in India working with the Richardson-Hindustan company. R-H was a subsidiary of the Richardson-Vicks Corporation that Procter & Gamble had purchased in 1985. One of my tasks while I was inspecting R-H was to assess the sales organization and personnel and to help begin the process of integrating R-H into P&G.

In order to gain a firsthand understanding of the exotic country I found myself in, I wanted to spend as much time as possible in the field with the sales force, calling on the various shops, stalls, and stores that sold the type of products R-H manufactured, such as cough drops, nasal sprays, and vapor rubs, and would be good retail outlets for the P&G brands that were soon to follow. Having spent the first half of the 1980s in Manila and southeast Asia, I was accustomed to working in the so-called Third World countries, where I found the sights, sounds, and smells of these strange (to a westerner) places to be truly enchanting. In fact, I have often said that I wish I had entered P&G's international division when I was thirty years old instead of when I was almost fifty.

I had worked in open-air markets, stepping over hobbled chickens and pigs; had stood in shops smaller than an elevator while being butted by visiting goats; had helped carry cases of P&G products through narrow alleyways crisscrossed by open sewers; and had done most of this when the temperature was 100 degrees and the humidity close to 90 percent, but nothing had quite prepared me for my first experience in India. One morning at seven-thirty I took my seat in the sidecar of a small motorbike and lurched into the stream of traffic in the outskirts of Bombay, heading for my first retail call of the trip.

The stiff breeze, a mixture of black diesel exhaust from the many road-crowding buses and the odor of animal dung that littered the roadway, blew my hair straight back and forced me to squint to protect my eyes. The R-H sales rep, who was driving the motorbike, was a master at avoiding the numerous potholes, many of which were filled with vile-looking black water. After about a mile of this we slowed and finally stopped for a major four-way intersection, where a lone policeman stood on a box in the center and directed traffic. At that moment I would have given a thousand dollars for a camera to take a picture of all the traffic that had come to a standstill. What a collection of traffic it was! There were two elephants chained together and pulling four huge logs, each perhaps forty feet long. There were two camels, one ridden by a driver and, following behind, a second fully loaded with bags of grain. There were two large buses carrying people of every color and description, wearing every form of attire—and sitting, standing, and clinging to the top and sides of the buses. And there were seven cows. Considered sacred in India, these cattle had the right of way. They just strolled along, oblivious to the din and confusion. Two huge oxen were pulling a two-wheeled cart stacked ten feet high with what appeared to be handmade chairs. Of course, there were dozens of small cars and hundreds of bicycles. Sitting at that intersection, I finally knew that I was the luckiest son of a bitch alive. Enjoying all these sights and getting paid for it. No! It just didn't get any better than this!

7
Companies: The Good, the Bad, the Best, and the Worst

Some Companies Are Created More Equal Than Others.

Each and every year, the San Francisco 49ers and my former hometown team, the Cincinnati Bengals, draft players from the same talent pool. In fact, the Bengals have a huge advantage every year because they draft at or near the beginning of every round in the draft, while the 49ers choose at or near the end of each round. Both teams have the same group of coaches from which to select. Both teams live under the same National Football League salary cap. And yet, year in and year out, the 49ers win or contend for the Super Bowl, while the Bengals win or contend for the first choice in the draft that goes to the team with the worst record in the entire NFL. Why is that?

Simple: Some companies are created more equal than others.

This is a vital lesson for businesses large and small. In the new global economy, the playing field will be level and resources will be available to everyone. Under NAFTA, GATT, and similar agreements, tariffs and other artificial barriers between countries are being reduced. As a result, everyone will have equal access to raw materials and to technology. Anyone in the global marketplace will be able to purchase those commodities. No one will have to say, "Well, we can't do XYZ because we can't obtain the technology or because we can't obtain the raw materials." Therefore, the only thing that is going to be unique in the system is going to be the people in that system; it is they who will make the difference.

Before, some companies and some entire countries had tremendous advantages. But now, anybody will be able to go anywhere in the world to purchase raw materials or technology.

And yet, some companies will thrive and some will fail. Just like the San Francisco 49ers and the Cincinnati Bengals. Each of those teams will continue to have equal access to players through the draft and through free agency, but the quality, the skills, the training, the scouting, the coaching, the entire workforce are still what will make the difference.

Relish Your Success, yet Sense the Winds of Necessary Change.

To me, organizations that have reached the top—ones such as Microsoft, Gillette, Coca-Cola, Campbell's soup, and McDonald's—must be ever vigilant against becoming complacent and allowing their very success to bring them down. Here are my top ten "watchouts" that companies that have reached the top must avoid:

1. Losing touch with the customer.
2. Losing touch with the employees.
3. Lacking a clear vision.
4. Trying to do too much too fast.
5. Confusing short-term motion with long-term progress.
6. Wasting too much energy trying to impress Wall Street.
7. Failing to integrate internal functions such as marketing, sales, production, and finance into high-performance teams.
8. Becoming management oriented instead of leadership oriented.
9. Focusing internally rather than externally.
10. Failing to understand that customer loyalty is the absence of something better.

Success Breeds Success—but It May Also Have Some Unwanted Side Effects.

An old adage about both business and life is that "Success breeds success." There is a lot of truth to that saying, but it's really people who breed success. Success can breed success, but it may also breed arrogance.

Oftentimes, success and arrogance go hand in hand. People mistakenly think that the reason they were successful is mostly because of what *they* did. When in fact, you can influence maybe a quarter or a third or half of what happens to you. You can't do it all alone. Much, if not most, of what happens to you depends on the actions of others. The real art of living is to get enough people on your team to help you win—people who may only influence you occasionally, or perhaps even only once in your life. But in that moment of truth, they do the thing that helps you because of the way you conduct yourself and the kind of character you have.

Not only can success breed arrogance, but arrogance breeds a lack of success; people love to see an arrogant person go down. There's nothing more fun than watching that happen.

Success can be a good news/bad news proposition in more ways than one. Don't get me wrong; it's a far, far better thing, of course, to be successful than to fail. Nevertheless, success also has the potential to produce complacency. Once a company gets up to the top of the mountain, part of its job automatically becomes to stay there. Staying there means you shift your emphasis to fighting off your rivals who are trying to climb the walls and get up to where you are. So success may cause a company to change from playing to win to playing not to lose. More on that later.

One of the best examples of a company that fell victim to its own success is Wang. Wang owned word processing in the early 1980s. For all intents and purposes, they were the only company in the business. Everyone else was still using typewriters made by IBM and Smith Corona. When old man Wang passed the business along to his son, the son apparently thought it would be more fun to be rich and powerful than to lead a business. He may have been right for himself, but not for the company. The result was that Wang was practically wiped off the face of the earth in less than five years. It was unbelievable! And they were a company that absolutely owned the business. They were so far ahead of everybody else, it was pitiful. And they had more than just a sexy product. They had great advertising. They had their whole act together. The Wang story shows the difference that one man can make. One man built the company into a masterpiece; it was straight out of a business-school textbook. And then he turned the company over to another man who fell victim to that success.

Some people, obviously, have what it takes to be successful, just as some don't. Sam Walton was a business visionary by intent. Ross Johnson of R. J. Reynolds was a business visionary by accident. Johnson did absolutely everything in the world correctly during his career at Standard Brands, during his career at Nabisco, and during his career at RJR. He maximized stockholder value in every single case. But in the biggest one, at RJR, I think it was by accident. Each of those men made fantastic amounts of money for both their stockholders and themselves. In the case of Sam Walton, he made so much that you can't count it. But those same stockholders revere Sam Walton and hate Ross Johnson. Why? Because Sam did it with intent, methodically, adroitly moving along, while Ross did it with great flamboyance and self-aggrandizement. Not to mention that he moved RJR's headquarters away from Winston-Salem. Little Bentonville was good enough for Sam Walton, but Winston-Salem was not up to Ross Johnson's standards. For moving out of Tobacco Road, a lot of the stockholders whom Johnson made very wealthy never forgave him. The lesson there is that just because you make money for someone and just because you pay them well, that doesn't mean they will love you and will follow you over the hill.

Unlike R. J. Reynolds—and for that matter Brown-Williamson—one tobacco company that is trying its best to make lemonade out of a lemon is Philip Morris and its new top management. Forget what you might think of smoking; that is, and always has been, Philip Morris's primary business. They're stuck with it, and while they *are* trying to diversify, they're also aggressively playing to win the tobacco wars. They're saying it's everybody's right to smoke and smokers have got a constitutional right to pollute the air a little bit. And they're also insisting that the cigarette business is going to be there for a long time and they're going to be a big part of it.

Or, take Lee Iacocca and John DeLorean. DeLorean was a visionary, the kind of individual I prize above all others. I'm not sure you could classify Iacocca as a visionary. If motor companies were football teams and you were trying to draft a franchise player, you might very well pick DeLorean before Iacocca. But DeLorean was an iconoclast, very difficult to work with. Iacocca may not have been the easiest man in the world to get along with, but he knew he needed to go along to get along. When Chrysler nearly went bankrupt in 1979, was Iacocca able to save the company? Most definitely! Could DeLorean have saved Chrysler? Probably not. If Chrysler's board of directors had handed the reins over to DeLorean instead of Iacocca, Chrysler would have produced the most futuristic, imaginative, ingenious collection of automobiles of any company that ever went bankrupt. Great leaders have to be able to seek and accept input from others. If you try to do it all yourself, the way I think DeLorean did, you probably will fail. Just as he did, for all his marvelous talents.

Easy Come, Easy Go.

When a company finds it too easy to make a buck and hard not to make a buck, it's natural for it to lose the discipline that hard times develop. To me, the American automobile industry during the postwar years and into the early 1970s is the perfect example. Detroit's attitude was, "This is going to go on forever. So we can give the consumer whatever we decide we want to sell them." There was very little research into what kind of cars people actually wanted. General Motors was the classic case; their attitude was that quality wasn't that important, while style was all-important. GM's approach was predicated on the assumption that the consumer would trade up every two or two and a half years and that gasoline would continue being cheap and abundant forever. You can't look back and fault General Motors for coming to that conclusion, because Ford and Chrysler operated the same way in those days. Nor was that arrogance confined just to those who worked for GM, Ford, Chrysler, et al. Consider this 1968 observation from *Business Week*: "With over fifteen types of foreign cars already on sale here, the Japanese auto industry isn't likely to carve out a big share of the market for itself."

What I do fault the Big Three for is not nurturing the dreamers and the poets—the people who might have informed them that nothing goes on forever and that one of these days all this almost certainly will end. As a result, the U.S. automobile industry had a sharp comeuppance at the hands of the Japanese. More accurately, the American automobile industry was not done in so much by the Japanese as by itself. Detroit gave the Japanese an opening that the Japanese were smart enough to take advantage of.

Don't Allow Your Company to Start Resting on Its Laurels.

The great lesson we can learn from the American car manufacturers' allowing the Japanese to become so strong here is that it isn't the outsiders who are going to come in and take your business away, it's your internal lack of vigilance that is going to make you vulnerable in the marketplace and allow competitors to come in. Just like in the automobile industry, IBM's lack of vigilance to what those sandaled, bearded guys out in Silicon Valley were up to is what hurt Big Blue. IBM holds more patents than any other institution in the world, which proves that it isn't what you've done that's as important as what you're doing and what you're going to do. All of IBM's inventions won't mean a damn if Apple and other companies come up with concepts that are more applicable to the present and the future. Both IBM and GM are textbook examples of success being the greatest enemy of innovation.

It's the outsiders who revolutionize most industries, and the automobile industry is no exception. Even today, when Saturn's sales methods are dramatically changing the way cars are sold, the primary impetus for the Saturn strategy comes from the Japanese. Traditionally, when people walked out of an automobile showroom, even if they had gotten a great price, they still were in a bad mood because the experience was so unpleasant. It's too bad they didn't apply the Saturn concept years ago at General Motors. The Saturn people became aware immediately that the whole process of selling a car had to be overhauled. It's interesting to me that in order to do this, they moved the whole operation out of Detroit. They weren't wedded to doing business in Automobile Heaven. They worked with customers, with suppliers, and with their own people and put together a program that has been immensely successful. It's a classic example in a very labor-intensive, capital-intensive industry that shows that if you have customer focus and deal fairly with your suppliers and your customers and you listen to your own internal people, miracles can happen. Saturn is making quality products at a very competitive price and delivering to the customer what the customer wants in a way that the customer wants to buy it. And the suppliers are lining up at Saturn's doors because instead of being hammered into submission, they are being allowed to make a living wage, which allows them to be on the cutting edge of improving quality.

It's too bad all this didn't start at home, but it probably wouldn't have worked at home. They were carrying too much baggage in Detroit to tear up the whole system and institute a new one.

I hate to pick on GM, but the way they went from world dominance to the equivalent of a prizefighter hanging on to the ropes for dear life is inexcusable. After losing an incredible $1.8 billion in a single year, 1980, Ford turned its whole company upside down. As a result, Ford got out of the blocks way ahead of GM, implemented total quality control, and got real about who they're building cars for, which is real live customers. Even though Henry Ford once said, "Give them any color they want as long as it's black," I think Ford's learning curve in response to the Japanese car invasion started much earlier than GM's. In fact, during Ford's darkest days, when the company's annual losses were being measured in billions of dollars, Ford had the courage to invest $3.5 billion to develop the Taurus—which has become the best-selling car in America. And while Ford was inventing the Taurus (and its twin, the Mercury Sable), the company even did something that was virtually unheard of in Detroit: The Taurus development team actually paid for several marketing surveys to find out what the consumer wanted in a car. Ford has even gone so far as to do something about one of the decisive elements responsible for loss of sales: labor costs. It has been widely reported that Ford's cost per car (as well as Chrysler's) is much lower than GM's.

Ironically, GM had an in-house visionary whose talents they succeeded in wasting entirely. I believe that General Motors would have taken a quantum leap forward ten years ago if they had listened—at least listened—to what Ross Perot had to say.

Forget Ross Perot the politician and whether you like him politically or not. The man is a business visionary, and he was part of GM until they ran him off. If they had taken one of their car divisions and let it operate the way Perot said, that division could have pulled the entire company along. And they could have rotated managers through it to learn a different way and a better way of doing things. Instead, GM actually paid a premium price for Perot's EDS subsidiary in order to get rid of him.

It's interesting to compare Harley-Davidson, the leading U.S. manufacturer of motorcycles, with what happened to the American automobile industry. Honda and Kawasaki and other Japanese producers had for all intents and purposes destroyed the American motorcycle manufacturers and become dominant in the U.S. market. But then new, progressive management came in at Harley-Davidson, and they reorganized themselves with tremendous customer focus, encouraged the workers to participate in the decision-making process, and turned the whole thing around. Today, Harley-Davidson is stronger than ever and has recaptured a large share of the American motorcycle business. Detroit is finally on the right track, but the automotive industry needs to keep on trying to get better. And Harley-Davidson is a hell of a starting point for GM, Ford, and Chrysler.

Trailblazers Don't Get Caught in Ruts Because They Aren't Following Any Herd.

By the mid- to late 1980s, I had been predicting that Sears Roebuck was on its way down. Again, it wasn't a case of Wal-Mart or anyone else doing it to Sears; Sears was doing it to themselves. The Sears model was: "We're the leader. We're on top. We're number one. Doing what we've always done, just doing it better—that's the solution."

I didn't believe that was the solution. I'm paraphrasing here, but former Sears CEO Edward A. Brennan apparently said something to the effect that "All we have to do is keep doing what we're doing, just do it better." Wrong!!! I became convinced long ago that just doing the same thing better, as Brennan proposed, is not the answer. As long ago as 1989, when I was about to retire from Procter & Gamble, I sat down with the company archivist for several hours and expressed my feelings on P&G and on business in general. And I said at the time, "I think that Sears is in deep trouble. I think the record in the next five years will prove this."

My conversation with the P&G archivist, during which I discussed the Sears situation, took place several months after I had read a December 1988 article about Sears in *Fortune*. "Can we retain our position as the world's premier retailer?" Mr. Brennan was asked in that story, going on to answer his own question: "Absolutely." When a *Fortune* reporter asked Brennan what he saw as the biggest problem facing Sears, Mr. Brennan's response was, "I don't see any huge problems. I feel very good about how we're positioned strategically." Incredible! I mean, if Mr. Brennan had been Custer at the Little Bighorn, he probably would have declared, "I feel very confident about how we're positioned strategically." Ed Brennan apparently did not have a clue!

"Sears claims that all you have to do in the future to be successful is continue to do what you've done in the past, just do it better," I told the Procter & Gamble archivist in 1989. "I happen to think that the 'just do it better' [philosophy], as opposed to 'do it different,' is the prescription for disaster."

As I said at that time, you have to do things differently if you're going to stay even, much less get ahead. Circumstances are always changing, so you have to change with them. Otherwise, you go the way of the dinosaur.

Kmart is another example of a company that once was a visionary organization, but is no longer. Back in the 1950s one of Kmart's vice-presidents helped develop the interstate highway system in America. Kmart got involved in that because the company wanted to find out where all the people were going to live twenty years later so that Kmart could buy up options on land near those important interstate interchanges. Which they did. That was brilliant! Unfortunately, they forgot that what's important isn't just where your store is. It's what's inside your store once the customers get there. That's been Kmart's problem for quite a while.

As a matter of fact, during the mid-1980s I proposed my concept of a partnering relationship to Joe Antonini, then Kmart's chairman and CEO, *before* I contacted Sam Walton. Antonini's response was that he would rather deal with a "thread salesman" (i.e., someone who sold clothing and other soft goods) than with a "soap salesman." It was after that that I approached Sam; since then, Wal-Mart has kept on hammering Kmart, virtually day by day and year by year.

The choice is between transforming and reforming: Reforming means you go down the same path more efficiently. You may repave the old cowpaths, the same winding roads—and pride yourself because you're more efficient at it than you've ever been before. Transforming means saying, "Hey, is the cowpath the right path? It looks like it has lots of twists, lots of turns, maybe what we ought to do is create a totally new road to travel instead of the old road." If you drive down the same country road at night and it's pitch black and you know that 3.6 miles down the road there's a hole that's going to break your axle, after you do that a couple of times, you're going to say, "Hey! Either I'm not going to drive it at night, I'm going to fill the hole, or I'm going to make the road go around it." You don't continue to do it. We seem to do the same thing over and over; we don't seem to realize the dangers and the pitfalls that can occur to us.

A lot of internal measurements ask, "How have you improved your efficiency?" when the question should be, "What are you doing differently today than you were doing yesterday that's going to make you better overall?" I just don't understand how people can fail to get out of a particular mode, a particular mindset, a particular style of management, the way GM, Sears, and IBM have.

Yesterday's Tools Won't Solve Tomorrow's Problems.

And speaking of the road, yeah, keep an eye on the road. But one eye only. With your other eye, keep a lookout for what's going on around you. If you look only where you're going, you will go only where you're looking. You can't focus solely on where you're headed; you have to have some vision, some sense of the future. Above all else, make sure you're looking ahead instead of in your rearview mirror. The past may be prologue, but the past is also history. Too many CEOs know where they've been, but they have no idea where they're going or where they want to get to.

Why did Sears fail and Wal-Mart gain? It's like the fall of the Roman Empire. There seems to be a lifespan or a time span for nations as well as for institutions like corporations. It's a self-fulfilling prophecy. But it doesn't have to be that way if managers are aware that they cannot use yesterday's tools to solve tomorrow's problems, that if you always do what you've always done, you will always get what you've always gotten.

You can't find a more successful retailer than Sears was. They had these brick-and-mortar monuments, these huge stores. They had the best selection in the world, and it was quality merchandise. They had outstanding prices. They practically owned the suppliers—they had joint ventures and all sorts of relationships with them. It was utopia. What they did, in my opinion, is they simply went to sleep. They became complacent. You tell a Sears story and you tell an IBM story, and you can swap the names back and forth. It's the same case. Same with GM. The thing that wounded Sears wasn't Wal-Mart. The thing that wounded IBM was not Apple or any of the other computer companies. The thing that wounded General Motors was not the Japanese. It was internal complacency. They did it to themselves.

A Wasted Effort: Trying to Defend a Fallen Fortress.

What can happen when a whale of a retailer fails to pay attention to a potential rival that's only a minnow? A friend of mine who used to manage a Sears store related to me an anecdote that shows exactly how Sears leaders allowed the Sears Tower to turn into an Ivory Tower and "managed" to let Wal-Mart beat them. Here's his story:

In 1982, during a meeting between the managers of several Sears stores in the Midwest and their boss, one of the company's three senior vice-presidents, the store managers expressed concern about the inroads Wal-Mart was making and their belief that Sears wasn't taking the threat seriously. After hearing them out for a little while, this senior VP stood up and ended the discussion by stating, "Gentlemen, have you forgotten that we're *Sears Roebuck*? As far as we're concerned, Wal-Mart and Kmart combined don't amount to a pimple on an elephant's ass!" My friend adds, "It became obvious that day that we were doomed, because the VP's statement confirmed our worst fears—that the Sears Tower in Chicago was filled with executives who suffered from a severe lack of oxygen, resulting in acute brainlock."

Soon after that meeting, my friend was ordered to shut down the highly profitable automobile repair service department at his store, where they worked on transmissions, engines, and valves and performed tune-ups. Headquarters decreed that the store would shift to a "replacement operation" for cars, which meant selling tires, batteries, and shock absorbers, but doing hardly any repairs. Headquarters' rationale was that automobile mechanics cost too much and that there was too much potential for customer problems. By shifting from repair to replacement, the store could substitute low- or no-skill employees for the mechanics. Before long, the store's total annual sales volume dropped from a respectable $28 million to $15 million. Not long after that, the store went out of business.

To me, Sears is the prototype of a company that became product focused instead of customer and supplier focused. Sears also became an organization of conformists. It was the perfect pyramid structure, just like Napoleon's army, where the top was telling the middle to do it to the bottom. I believe that virtually all of the communication inside Sears was from the top down, not reciprocal. And I don't think there was much horizontal communication, either. What Sam Walton did, conversely, was encourage two-way communication; he was as interested in what the employee on the store floor had to report as he was in what his top aides were saying.

Unlike Custer at the Little Bighorn, in Business You May Get a Second Chance.

One of the beauties of business is that, in contrast to war, you're not in a life-and-death struggle. If things go against you,

you may get a second chance. If you find yourself in that position, try to make the most of it.

Recently, I'm glad to say, GM and IBM seem to have reversed their fortunes—in a positive sense. Neither of these companies is out of the woods yet, because they face ferocious competition, but at least they're on the right track.

At GM, under the guidance of board chairman John Smale, my former boss at Procter & Gamble, 1994 profits doubled to $4.9 billion, the most in the company's eighty-seven-year history. GM sold 5 million vehicles in the United States during 1994, its best record in this country since 1989.

IBM reported profits of $3 billion for 1994, compared to a loss of $96 million in 1993.

Meanwhile, at Sears, Ed Brennan had begun the process of transforming the company. His designated successor, Arthur C. Martinez, has the reputation of being both a visionary and a hero to his employees, just as Sam Walton was. Several years ago, Martinez was faced with the choice between saving the catalogue business or saving the stores. He did his diagnostic and then gave Brennan some very bad news: "We either have to get out of the catalogue business or get out of the stores. We can't do both at the same time." The problem was that Brennan had been trying to save the entire operation, so he was failing to save anything.

One of the main problems facing Sears was logistics, so they brought in a man I think very highly of, General William "Gus" Pagonis, who was in charge of logistics for Desert Storm. That's really outside-the-box thinking. Pagonis has some challenges, because in business, everybody doesn't report to you the same way they do in the military, but he also had some fresh thoughts on logistics that the business world in general and Sears in particular can benefit from.

Making the Most of a Catastrophe: Coca-Cola.

A textbook example of how to capitalize on mistakes is the Coca-Cola Company. During the 1940s and 1950s, Coke was so fat and happy that the company became complacent. Back in the '40s, Coke could have bought out Pepsi-Cola for peanuts. But

Pepsi was nothing to Coke in those days, and Coke wouldn't pay a dime to absorb Pepsi. By the 1960s and 1970s, Coke had awakened and come to realize that Pepsi presented a serious threat.

So Coke came out of hibernation and reinvented itself as a bottler that was a take-no-prisoners battler. By the 1980s, Coke had changed 180 degrees, from being completely self-satisfied and nonchalant to going out too far on a limb. Yes, I'm talking about New Coke. With the introduction of New Coke in 1985, Coca-Cola really shot itself in the foot. And it wasn't because the Coca-Cola people hadn't done a tremendous amount of market research. New Coke was an archetypal case of reading all the numbers and all the stats in a vacuum inside the corporation. You can interpret those figures to tell you whatever the hell you want them to mean. W. Edwards Deming, the visionary "total quality control" genius who taught the Japanese how to rebuild their economy after World War II, always warned against placing too much faith in numbers. I had the opportunity to attend a seminar Deming conducted at Procter & Gamble; it was one of the most valuable learning experiences I ever had.

I don't fault Coca-Cola for trying to develop innovative products such as New Coke. I think that what must have happened is that Coca-Cola misread the numbers from its own marketing surveys when it started thinking about tinkering with its very basic, precious franchise. Either that, or those numbers weren't worth a damn.

However, the New Coke fiasco had a happy ending. In Chapter Two, Coca-Cola admitted its mistake, brought back Coke Classic, and snatched up even more of the market with New Coke. New Coke now has its own market share, even though it's a small one, but that share increases the total market penetration of the entire Coca-Cola line. Coca-Cola recovered beautifully from that catastrophe when a lot of companies would have thrown up their hands and said, "Oh, my God! Scrap it!" And would have written off a loss of millions and millions.

Coca-Cola executives, under the direction of CEO Roberto Goizueta (whose son, Jay, worked for me at P&G), have done what all brilliant managers do: They admitted they had a problem. If you fail to admit that you have a problem, that's when you really have a problem. The second thing they did was put a task force together to figure out the dimensions of the problem and how bad the hurt was going to be. And the third thing they did was say, "How can we take this disaster and capitalize on it and turn it into a victory?" They built something out of the ashes.

How did Coca-Cola do it? As far as I'm concerned, there are three major ingredients in Coke's secret formula for success: leadership, leadership, and leadership. And that leadership begins with Goizueta, who is doing such a good job at Coke that the board of directors waived the mandatory retirement and told him, "We want you here leading us for as long as you want to lead us."

Coca-Cola's archrival, PepsiCo, is also an extremely well-managed outfit. And, again, success breeds success; Pepsi's reputation for excellence is widely recognized throughout the business world, and that attracts other capable employees and executives. As my friend and former Procter & Gamble colleague John Bissell has observed, Pepsi has emerged as "a favorite cross-training camp among marketing's rising stars. Pepsi's primary pull is its emphasis on tactical marketing and its involvement in the full spectrum of distribution channels, not just supermarkets." Early on, one of Pepsi's prime innovations in the sales area was to equip its sales reps with handheld computers, which allowed them to fire orders back to headquarters almost instantly.

Everyone I know who has worked for Pepsi or been recruited by the company says the same thing. They talk about how Pepsi very definitely has a command structure, but at the same time there is a tremendous amount of freedom within the corporation to not only exercise influence from the bottom all the way up to the top but also to make things happen.

Whether You're Number One, Number Two, or Number Forty-two, Keep Trying Harder.

What it all comes down to, in my opinion, is how you play the game. If you play to win, you will dramatically increase your chances of winning. If you play not to lose, you will dramatically increase your chances of losing. Let's look at football again: The teams that go into the "prevent" defense late in the game to protect a slim lead, the teams that throw away their offensive plans, go into a shell, and try to run out the clock, the teams that kick the field goal on fourth and goal at the one yard line instead of going for the touchdown—those are the teams that often lose games they should have won. The same is true in the real world. Let's look at a few examples:

Wal-Mart plays to win, and it has succeeded because its rivals, like Sears and Kmart, play not to lose. The difference is the culture and the leadership, which is such a strength at Wal-Mart and such a weakness at its competition.

Management and labor unions. Labor has outlived its usefulness in most industries, so its primary focus has turned to just trying not to lose membership.

The difference is that champions often play not to lose, but the challengers *have* to play to win. The famous Avis slogan, "We're number two, so we have to try harder"—does that ring any bells? Fifteen years or so ago, the Chrysler folks were so far behind at halftime, it looked like they were just about dead. They had nothing to lose, so they pulled out all the stops, looked for new, untapped markets, like the minivan market, and, lo and behold, rose from the ashes, just like the mythical phoenix.

One of the worst situations a company can get itself into is to be in effect half pregnant. Part of the organization is playing to win and part is playing not to lose. When you do that, the employees who are playing to win are on the bleeding edge.

The people who are playing to win, in the good sense of the term, are playing for the entire company to win. But when you have people who are playing not to lose, that translates into more of a personal, selfish positioning, which is, "I don't want to lose my status. I don't want to lose my power within the organization." And that's a serious problem. Management must be ever vigilant for these "gatekeepers," who contribute little as they maintain the status quo in order to cover their ass.

Virtually without exception, the leaders of the companies I address tell me they're playing to win. Virtually without exception, the employees of those companies, in my informal meetings with them before and after my speeches, tell me that their leaders are playing not to lose instead of to win. The employees feel management's approach is conservative: "Don't make any mistakes; above all, there's a don't-screw-up mentality." Employees pick up on that real fast.

Again, if you're a CEO or in top management, step back and look at yourself and your company objectively. Are you playing to win or playing not to lose? Are you, yourself, part of the solution or part of the problem? The answers might surprise you. They also might help you turn things around.

Pritchett's Examples of Some Winners and Losers.

Like Wal-Mart, L.L. Bean is a wonderfully consumer-oriented company. If the sole falls off your boot, they'll replace it, no matter how old or worn the shoe is. But at the same time they're fixing your shoe, they say, "By the way, based on our records of your business with us, we noticed that it has been fourteen years since you bought your last fly rod. Do you need a new fly rod?" That's sheer brilliance—taking the best care of the customer and capitalizing on the opportunity to sell him something else at the same time.

And look at Nordstrom. Its corporate culture is legendary; employees of that department store chain are so committed to superior customer service and the highest standards of performance that most new recruits immediately fit into the mold, and those who don't quickly fall by the wayside without harming the company.

Another nonvisionary outfit that once was a visionary is A&P. The Great A&P Tea Company was one of the top corporations in America in 1950. They had twenty-two thousand supermarkets. Today they have fewer than fifteen hundred. Their problem is that at the time they built their business, people lived in cities. But as people moved out of cities, A&P failed to move with the people. They also forgot that they were in the retailing business and spent much too much time manufacturing Jane Parker and Ann Page products, to the point where the stores became outlets for their manufacturing business. A&P

began selling more and more to people of what A&P wanted to sell rather than what people wanted to buy. A&P is a classic example of how to do it all wrong.

By contrast, one of A&P's rivals in the Midwest, Schnuck's of St. Louis, is a classic example of how to do everything right. Schnuck's was the first big supermarket chain, starting in the late 1970s, to put in scanners at all its cash registers, which gave it the kind of information Wal-Mart and Procter & Gamble were getting from our arrangement. At that same time, Schnuck's installed highly automated warehouse systems to speed the flow of goods. While A&P was turning itself into a loser, Schnuck's was one of the winners. A member of the Schnuck family was quoted in the trade press as saying, "I make more money selling my data than I make selling groceries." That's when he was one of the only guys who had this sort of information.

Today, I go around the world speaking to and consulting with various companies. I don't mean this to sound immodest, but I think the fact that they call on me or someone like me to look over their operations and talk to their managers and leaders is a good sign; it shows that they care and that they are trying to change and improve. While most of the companies I've worked with have impressed me, a few of those companies, and some of their leaders, have impressed me more than others. Among the companies that have really impressed me, ones that I have worked with directly or those that have otherwise come to my attention, are:

• Qualex, a film-processing division of Kodak located in Durham, North Carolina. Under the leadership of CEO Peter Fitzgerald, Qualex has created a national quality board, made up of both its customers and its suppliers, to direct it toward achieving unequaled quality in the imaging industry.
• Ralston-Purina, which has reorganized from top to bottom and literally transformed itself into almost a new company in response to direct threats from its competitors, as well as broad-based change in the food products industry.
• Ambassador Cards of Kansas City, a division of Hallmark Cards. Ambassador is striving to be recognized by its cus-

tomers as the industry performance leader in the marketing of quality greeting cards. Ambassador's major focus is to remain the lowest-cost producer by building profitable and productive partnerships with its retailers.

• Manugistics of Rockville, Maryland. William M. Gibson, president and CEO, is positioning Manugistics to be the global leader in supply chain management (SCM). SCM is a concept for reengineering business that works by tying a company's supply chain together, linking decision-support systems to transaction systems to provide visibility and control throughout the supply chain. For the past decade, Manugistics has been the leading supplier of supply chain management systems that help companies make better, more informed operational decisions in the areas of demand, distribution, manufacturing, and transportation planning. Now the company has taken the next logical step of enabling companies to share planning information with their suppliers and customers.

• Paws, Incorporated, of Albany, Indiana, which, in less than fifteen years since it was formed in 1981, has built an empire to market a *cartoon feline!*—Garfield the cat, the 1978 brainchild of company founder Jim Davis.

• Rock-Tenn Corporation of Norcross, Georgia, which recycles paper and cardboard. Chairman A. Worley Brown and CEO Bradley Currey Jr., have led this recycling firm to the very edge of tomorrow. Their mission is to develop innovative, cost-effective solutions to customers' needs.

• Tilley Endurables of Don Mills, Ontario, one of the world's leading manufacturers of travel and adventure wear. Alex Tilley, the founder and owner of the company, is my kind of guy—irreverent, fun, and self-deprecating. He bills himself as "Canada's Glad Hatter" and claims to hold a Canadian scholastic record: "Six years at university; passed three." (Reminds me of the great John Belushi line in *Animal House* after the dean of the university threatened to expel the Belushi character—something like, "There goes eight years of college down the drain.") Tilley was an avid sailor who, as a sideline, designed the finest sailing shorts and a water-repellent hat that would float. He built his hobby into a business that makes 250,000 hats a year, and he insists on keeping "a watchful eye" on every aspect of his operation, which assures quality.

• Another example of a visionary company is a small, relatively unknown company called Road Show International of McLean, Virginia, the leading technology company in the world for routing big trucks. Road Show uses a very complicated computer program to determine exactly the right way to structure your delivery schedule each day so that you optimize the use and cost of your vehicles and run the fewest miles. Right now the company has about 50 percent penetration in its industry, even though it has some twenty competitors out there. What Road Show has done is take a very well defined segment of the operations part of the distribution business and created a tool that is a big time and cost saver and enables the user to produce a much higher level of customer service. Keep an eye on Road Show International. If you're a CEO, don't just keep an eye on Road Show; do what it's doing.

Individuals in progressive companies seem to have the liberty and freedom that individuals in the more traditional corporations do not. Every employee in these companies seemingly has the chance to participate in the decision-making process, to speak up and speak out, to really be themselves.

What these companies prove is that the litmus test for well-managed companies today is *not* pay and benefits, it's corporate culture and flexibility. What we as managers need to do is spend twenty minutes or so by ourselves, writing down the conditions that bring out the best in us, and then treating our employees the same way. When our list is completed and compared with a thousand other lists, all of them will be damned near identical.

How to Tell a Winner from a Loser.

As clearly as if it happened yesterday, I can see my Boy Scout scoutmaster, Buddy Irwin, reading the following rules from some unknown book to me and hundreds of other boys who never forgot these truisms:

1. A winner says, "Let's find out"; a loser says, "Nobody knows."

2. When a winner makes a mistake, he says, "I was wrong"; when a loser makes a mistake, he says, "It wasn't my fault."

3. A winner goes through a problem; a loser goes around it and never actually gets to it.

4. A winner makes commitments; a loser makes promises.

5. A winner says, "I'm good, but not as good as I ought to be"; a loser says, "I'm not as bad as a lot of other people."

6. A winner tries to learn from those who are superior to him; a loser tries to tear down those who are inferior to him.

7. A winner says, "These are yesterday's tools. There must be a better way to do this job"; a loser says, "Who needs new tools? This is the way it's always been done here."

8. A winner keeps his eyes on the road in front of him; a loser concentrates on his rearview mirror.

8
How to Be a Good Employee, Too

Screwing Up Can Be a Great Learning Experience.

During my college years I spent the summers working as a counselor at the Boy Scouts' Kamp Kia Kima in Hardy, Arkansas.

During these summers my jobs ranged from mess hall steward, where I was responsible for working with the professional cook and feeding the campers three meals a day, to waterfront director, where I taught lifesaving, rowing, canoeing, and swimming, to activities director, where, among other things, I taught Indian lore.

Teaching Indian lore was my favorite assignment. All week, everyone looked forward to the Friday-night campfires, when all the campers and staff would assemble for stories, singing, and the highlight of the evening—Indian ceremonies and Indian dancing. An added attraction was that our camp director normally invited the girls from the two camps just down the river to attend—Kiwani, a Girl Scout camp, and Mirameechi, a YWCA camp.

One Friday we decided that we would start the campfire ceremony in truly spectacular fashion by having our archery instructor, Harry Estes, cover an arrow with a kerosene-soaked cotton rag and fire it into the air over the river. This "fire arrow" would serve as the signal to light the campfire and begin the ceremony. That night, Harry took his position in a natural depression behind a large rock on the edge of the river. From there, the campers couldn't see Harry, but they would be able to see the magical fire arrow as it rose up and out over the river. Harry's signal to shoot the fire arrow was when I started pounding an Indian tom-tom.

Promptly at dusk, with nearly a hundred boys and girls seated around the circle, I started the drumbeat. Nothing happened. I continued to beat the tom-tom. Still no sign of a fire arrow. After about five minutes we heard a commotion behind the rock where Harry was located. Then there was a loud shriek, followed by Harry jumping up and running toward the river. It turned out that when Harry fired the arrow with the flaming rag on it, the arrow flew far up and out over the river, but the flaming rag fell off and dropped back into Harry's lap. Harry was dressed in his Indian costume, including a breech cloth, and the burning rag on his crotch scared the hell out of him. After unsuccessfully trying to beat out the flames, he decided to make a run for the river. The water did douse the fire before Harry was turned into a eunuch, but from that night on, we never attempted the flaming arrow ceremony again.

I have to say that I've met a whole lot of people who would have kept trying. "Lightning never strikes twice," they would have insisted. Or, "It's Harry's hide, not mine." But Harry and I had learned our lesson; we knew better than to try such a dangerous stunt over again.

Then there was the time—the one time—my car ran out of gas. I guess everyone lets their car run out of gas at least once in their life. It isn't that big a deal. But what happened to me in 1968 could have been a big deal—a big, bad deal.

One night, after attending a movie in Cincinnati with Barbara and our best friends, A. C. and Lou Ann Rolen, I was driving all of us back to our home in the suburbs. Then, to my embarrassment, I ran out of gas on an interstate expressway. Trying to look completely in control, I jumped out and flagged down the next car I saw. To my great relief, it turned out to be a police patrol car occupied by two officers. They were glad to help, offering to drive me to a nearby service station to buy a container of gas. I bought three gallons, placed it in the trunk of the police car, and we headed back to where my car, my wife, and my friends sat waiting on the expressway. We were about one mile from my car when the police radio came alive, announcing that a small neighborhood store had just been robbed. The patrol car I was riding in was the closest one to the scene of the crime, and my guys had to give chase. The driver hit the accelerator, and I was forced back against the backseat as if I were riding a rocket. With siren screaming and lights flashing we sped out I-71, passing my parked car; Barbara and the Rolens later estimated that we were traveling at least a hundred miles an hour when we flew by them. Three minutes or so into our "hot pursuit," the news came over the radio that the robber had lost control of his car, crashed, and been apprehended. The officers were able to break off their chase and return me to my car.

For me, this harrowing experience got my attention, like hitting a mule over the head with a two-by-four. It taught me an invaluable lesson: that you can get caught up in a situation, and before you know it, you might be in over your head. Suffice it to say that I have not run out of gasoline since 1968.

An old friend of mine from Cincinnati, Bob Jones, who was an IBM executive for many years, once had a similar learning experience. Bob spent a lot of time giving speeches to groups of IBM employees and to IBM's customers. In 1975, while preparing to drive from Cincinnati to Louisville, where he was to make a major presentation before a gathering of several hundred, Bob forgot to pack his black wing-tip shoes. His wife went with him, and the night before his speech, as they were walking back to their hotel in Louisville, Bob looked down at his feet and said, "Oh, my God, Joyice! I forgot my good shoes!" The event was early the next morning, and Bob had no choice but to wear the only shoes he had brought with him, a pair of white patent-leather ones, with his dark blue pinstripe suit. It was either that or go barefoot. To this day, many IBMers still refer to him as Bob "White Shoes" Jones. You can be sure that from then on, the first things Bob packed before he set out on an important trip were his dress shoes.

The moral of these stories is that in business, and in life itself, you can learn lessons under the most improbable circumstances and then apply that knowledge to any situation that arises later on.

If You're Up Against Someone Who Is Resourceful, Be Twice as Resourceful Yourself.

As I mentioned, Barbara and I were married on December 19, 1954, in her hometown, Lula, Mississippi. Lula is a small town even by Mississippi standards, and as is true in most small towns, everybody knew everybody and everybody else's secrets. After the wedding, Barbara and I planned to drive in my company car (the one that came complete with the P&G man-in-the-moon decal on both doors) the sixty miles to Memphis, before leaving the next day for New Orleans and a brief honeymoon.

In those days, hazing a newlywed couple was considered absolutely obligatory, and nearly everyone in town felt a duty to join in. The wedding took place at seven-thirty in the evening, and by nine o'clock or so, following the reception at the American Legion hut, we were ready to set out for Memphis—or, so we hoped! But some of my mischievous friends had placed a piece of cardboard inside the carburetor to stop the air flow, so my car wouldn't start. It took us a half hour to find the problem and fix it, and then we were off.

Almost immediately, we discovered that a friend of Barbara's family, a fellow who was a trooper in the Mississippi Highway Patrol, had set up roadblocks on the main highway to Memphis to further delay us. By then, Barbara and I were tired of the pranks; all we wanted to do was get to Memphis and begin our honeymoon. She and I had spent a lot of time hunting for arrowheads around Lula and I had often gone dove hunting in the same area with Barbara's father, so we knew the region quite well. From Lula to the next town, Tunica, there was a back road made of dirt that we had driven many times. So, on this, our wedding night, we set off down this dark, unmarked dirt road, driving with our lights off to avoid detection, passing thousands of acres of cotton farms, huge barns, hundreds of mules, several cotton gins, and many sharecropper houses.

We finally arrived at our hotel in Memphis shortly after midnight, exhausted and feeling like two escaped convicts. But we had outwitted the posse! To this day, the former highway patrol officer continues asking us how the hell we eluded all his road-blocks. Until now, we have always refused to tell him.

Knowledge Is Power, Part II—for the Troops as Well as for the Commanders.

After I graduated from Memphis State in 1953 I joined an army MASH reserve unit. Four years later, I was called for six months' active duty. For basic training I was sent to Fort Jackson, South Carolina, an outpost distinguished for its sand, heat, and seemingly endless downpours. The drill instructors? Well, they were combat-hardened veterans of the Korean War who looked down on us "six-monthers" as freaks who needed to be yelled at twice as loud and worked twice as hard as ordinary enlistees.

Two weeks or so before we finished our training, some members of our unit were singled out for weekend guard duty. Five soldiers in each group were picked at random and subjected to the most intensive inspection of uniform, boots, rifle, and haircut and then to a quiz about topics pertaining to the U.S. government or the military. The deal was that whoever scored the highest would get the weekend off, while the other four members of each group would have to stand guard.

I was one of those selected by lot, and I left no stone unturned, in hopes that I would win a free weekend. I had a crease in my pants that could cut beef, a shine on my boots that would have blinded a dog, and my M-1 rifle was so clean it looked like it had just come from the manufacturer. The only thing that worried me was passing the oral quiz. The physical inspection was a breeze for me, and then came the question that would leave us with one lucky winner and four brand-new guards.

I held my breath, and then the drill instructor asked his question: "Who has President Eisenhower just named as secretary of defense?"

I couldn't believe it; my guardian angel must have been smiling down on me. And I immediately shouted:

"Neil McElroy, the former chief executive officer of the Procter & Gamble Company, SIR!"

With that, the drill sergeant yelled back, "You're excused for the weekend, soldier!"

None of us in that training unit had had any time to read a newspaper, and there were no radios or TVs allowed in basic training. As far as we were concerned, the outside world didn't exist. Except for mail call. By pure luck, I had received a letter only two days earlier from one of my salesmen in Memphis, and he had mentioned that our CEO, Mr. McElroy, had just been named secretary of defense. My friend had added that with both McElroy and Pritchett on active duty protecting the nation, he and his family would sleep much more soundly.

Right then, I knew for sure that knowledge is power and that no matter the source of your knowledge, the more you had, the more powerful you were. This lesson, of course, applies not only to employees but even more so to managers.

A Good Attitude Can Compensate for a Multitude of Sins, Including Gross Ignorance.

Fast-forward six years from my experience in basic training. By 1963 I not only knew very well who Neil McElroy was but had become personally acquainted with him. After serving for two years in the Eisenhower administration, McElroy returned to Procter as chairman of the board. He visited Memphis at least once a year to inspect the Buckeye plant, and, as manager of P&G's Memphis district, it was my duty to be McElroy's host whenever he came to town.

On McElroy's 1963 trip, I was assigned to meet the company plane and escort him to his hotel. When we arrived at the hotel, he asked me to come up to his room while he made a few phone calls and changed for dinner. This was a huge honor for me, a thirty-one-year-old midlevel manager, to spend private time alone with a man who had served as secretary of defense of the United States, who was now the top executive of my company, and who had even been briefly considered a presidential candidate in 1960.

The great man—and I mean that sincerely—excused himself to go into his bedroom and change his clothes. He told me to make myself comfortable, and I did, enjoying the view over the

Mississippi River and reveling in this heady moment. A few minutes later the phone rang, and from the bedroom Mr. McElroy called out, "Lou, will you please answer it for me!"

I picked up the phone, said hello, and heard a voice that sounded vaguely familiar say, "Neil, is that you?"

"No," I answered, "this is Lou Pritchett of Procter & Gamble. Mr. McElroy is getting dressed."

"Please tell him Dwight is on the line," the caller said, adding, "I will hang on for a few minutes."

"Dwight who?" I inquired.

At that moment, McElroy walked into the room, and, overhearing my question to "Dwight," smiled widely and said, "Thank you, Lou. I'll take this call."

"Hello, Mr. President," McElroy said into the phone, laughing.

I was indeed among the gods that afternoon, but I was too dumb to realize it. At that stage of my life, I was completely innocent of how the power game was played, and I was just being me. I made no attempt to be something I was not or to pretend to know something I didn't. Neil McElroy saw my naïveté as a virtue, and saw me as someone worth keeping an eye on and pushing ahead.

Honesty and enthusiasm, I mused the countless times I recalled that episode, were definitely the best policies.

When You Begin to Think You're Hot S—, Oftentimes You're Half Right.

I was tickled pink one day in 1963, during my time as a district manager in Memphis, when I learned that Dutch Janney, P&G's vice-president of sales, was going to spend a day observing me on my calls. Janney, a man in his mid-fifties, was idolized by many of us in the sales force. Not only was he a wonderful man and leader, but he had been a hero of sorts while fighting in Europe during World War II. For a young sales guy to have Dutch Janney actually work with you in the field was similar to having God do the same.

Mr. Janney flew in to Memphis early one morning on the company plane, a DC-3, and he and I spent most of that cold, windy, overcast day visiting stores and talking about selling. Throughout the day, Mr. Janney took abundant notes on small pieces of paper, hanging on my every word and writing down practically everything I said and every answer I gave. After writing his notes on these small pieces of paper, he would stuff each one into the pocket of his trench coat. After several hours, I became convinced that I was going to be promoted very soon, given his intense interest in what I had to say. I was all set to go home and tell Barbara, "We're on our way! This guy loves me! He was hanging on my every word!" Yeah, I was thinking that Janney undoubtedly was planning to incorporate the fruits of my wisdom into the company sales manual. A senior officer of the company simply did not write down virtually every word a young district manager uttered unless that district manager really had something valuable to say. There was no doubt in my mind that I had passed muster and impressed "the Dutchman," as we often referred to him.

About three o'clock in the afternoon, Mr. Janney said he needed to get back to the company plane and return to Cincinnati. En route to the airport, he was very supportive, and our conversation turned to personal as well as business matters. Our camaraderie was further proof to me that I had impressed the big guy, and my head was in the clouds. At the airport, I drove out onto the tarmac near the big silver company DC-3, with its nose pointing up in the air and the tailskid down, much like the airport scene at the end of *Casablanca*. I got out of the car and walked over toward the plane with Mr. Janney.

As he and I stood talking at the bottom of the steps leading up to the plane, the right engine was already running. That, coupled with the windy weather, was whipping our coats and our hair rather vigorously. As Mr. Janney put his foot on the first step, he turned to me one last time, stuck out his right hand, and said it had been a great visit. Simultaneously, he stuck his left hand into the pocket of his trench coat (it looked just like the one that TV detective, Columbo, wears). With a rather surprised look on his face, Janney pulled out about two dozen little pieces of paper, upon which he had written all the wisdom I had shared with him during the day. And with one nonstop motion he raised his left hand and let all his notes go fluttering into the wind and prop wash, mumbling under his breath, "What the hell is all this paper?"

Janney ran on up the steps and disappeared into the plane while I stood there dumbfounded, watching this record of my "wisdom" be blown toward the cyclone fence two hundred feet behind the aircraft. Once those bits of paper reached the fence, they were immediately mixed in with all the old brown grass and bits of paper and potato chip bags and other debris that had accumulated along that fence and in the deep grass there.

Never again have my spirits fallen so far and so fast as they did on that cold, damp day while I stood on the tarmac at the Memphis airport and watched Dutch Janney's plane taxi away.

Several years later, one of my employees in the sales division had a comeuppance like mine. Procter & Gamble field managers were always required to phone the district office once or twice a day to see if the district manager needed them or if they had received any phone calls from customers. Late one afternoon, Jacksonville sales manager Gene Ellerbee called in and was told that his boss, district manager Bill Evans (who reported directly to me), needed to talk to Gene and that it was urgent. Evans came on the line and asked Ellerbee to report to his office *immediately*. Ellerbee, being a smart, aggressive junior sales executive, was certain that something big was in the works, undoubtedly something involving him and his career. Why else would the district manager want to see him not only in person but right away? The more Ellerbee thought about it during his forty-minute drive to the office, the more convinced he became that he was on the verge of either being promoted or transferred to another office. Thoughts about selling his house and preparing to move occupied his mind.

A onetime football star at the University of Colorado, Ellerbee bounded up the steps of the district office three at a time and charged back to Evans's office. The secretary greeted him with a big smile and said, "Gene, Mr. Evans has been pacing the floor, just hoping you would get here before four o'clock. Please go right in." Ellerbee was still reaching for the doorknob when Evans hurried out of his office, carrying his coat, and declared, "You made it. Let's go!"

With that, the two of them returned to Ellerbee's car on the run. As Gene cranked the engine, Evans turned to him and said, "Gene, Publix has an unbelievable sale on Hellmann's mayonnaise, and it's Mrs. Evans's favorite brand. Unfortunately, they have a 'one per customer' limit and I need you to go with me so I can buy two jars instead of one." (Evans's frugality was legendary within the company, and many of us still joke about it with each other, as we did with Bill up until his death in late 1993. He always smiled tolerantly at our making fun of his habits, but until the day he died he considered most of us frivolous because we weren't as tight with a buck as he was.)

Today, Gene Ellerbee still chuckles over this episode, explaining that "Many times, life will fool you, just to test you. It will sometimes bring you back to earth by tempting you with something as basic as a jar of mayonnaise."

An Innocent "Abroad"—in the Big Apple.

Boy, did I ever wow the locals on my first trip to New York! This occurred in late 1964, as I was being transferred from Memphis, where I had been a district manager, to corporate headquarters in Cincinnati. Except for one eighteen-month stint in Columbus, Ohio, my entire career up until then—in fact, my entire life—had been spent in the South. Brad Butler, then the national sales manager, decided that I needed at least a taste of the retail selling experience in a tough eastern market, so he arranged for me to spend ten days selling to store owners in the Bedford-Stuyvesant section of New York City.

I arrived in New York both excited and apprehensive. Excited because of the challenge and because I knew the company did not waste time and money giving someone special sales experience unless the executives felt you were a likely prospect for upper management. Yet also apprehensive because of all the stories I had heard about how dangerous New York was and how bad the traffic was. Furthermore, I had no idea where my stores would be located or how I would find them, and map reading has never been one of my strong suits.

I spent most of my first day in New York with two local

managers, who gave me a map and a list of the stores I would be calling on for the next ten days. By taking a few stores here and there from several different sales territories, they had created a mini-section for me right smack in the heart of Bedford-Stuyvesant. Fortunately, or perhaps unfortunately, I had never heard of Bedford-Stuyvesant, so I didn't know what awaited me. Even if I had, I wouldn't have complained or let these two New Yorkers know that I had any apprehensions. After all, I was an experienced manager in my own right, now being moved to Cincinnati and marked as a rising star; nothing was supposed to bother me.

Toward midafternoon, my hosts drove me to a garage in Manhattan, handed me the keys to a company car, and pointed me in the right direction. Off I drove, as if I knew what I was doing, negotiating among the buses and the taxicabs and the rest of the New York City traffic. I proceeded according to my directions, arrived at my first call about three o'clock, and found a metered parking space a block or so from the store. I was walking toward the store, wearing my Procter & Gamble "uniform"—a dark blue three-piece suit, black wing-tip shoes, and a hat. About halfway to the store I walked past a couple of young men who mumbled something, possibly about my shoes. But I just kept walking.

When I reached the store, I was surprised to find all its windows covered with plywood. My first thought was that the store had closed and the information I had been given was outdated. Just in case it was still in business, I tried the door and it swung open. Inside, the owner, all three hundred pounds of him, was sitting behind a counter that was covered with small racks of candy and gum and a couple of five-gallon jars of pickles and pickled pigs' feet. In front of him was a bronze and chrome antique cash register that gleamed like old gold in the bright fluorescent lights. Then I noticed something else: Cradled in his arms across his massive stomach was the most evil-looking shotgun I had ever seen. It had been sawed off to maybe one-third of its former length, and the twin short barrels that were pointed straight at me looked large enough to roll tennis balls down.

Not wanting to be taken for a hick from the sticks, I introduced myself as a P&G salesman who was pinch-hitting for the regular guy and asked the owner if I could check his P&G stock. He pointed to the stockroom, which was in a basement that was entered from outside the front door, and handed me a key. I surveyed his stock, wrote out an order plan, went back to the counter, and gave him one of my finest sales pitches. Without glancing at my order form, he just looked at me and said, "Son, don't you have any idea where you are?" I laughed and said I thought I did, but maybe he knew something I didn't. Yeah, he said, he had just been held up at gunpoint a little while earlier, and it was his third robbery in four days. (Upon hearing that, I felt certain that the two men I had passed on my way to his store were the robbers. I was thankful I had encountered them in broad daylight.) The store owner added that all the sales reps knew to be out of this area by three-thirty, and it was now four-fifteen. "Are you crazy," he inquired, "or just stupid?" I explained that I was from Memphis and had never heard of quitting at three-thirty in the afternoon, but I would take his advice, although I would appreciate it if he would sign the order I had planned for him. Shaking his head in amazement, he put his shotgun on the counter and signed the order. As I started to leave, he asked me where I was parked. I told him where my car was, and he insisted on locking up his store and escorting me to the car, his sawed-off shotgun in hand.

I got in the car and waved good-bye as he started walking slowly back to his store. I decided I had had enough adventure for one day; now all I had to do was find my way back to my hotel, the Lexington, at Lexington Avenue and Forty-eighth Street. It was now about quarter of five and starting to get dark—and I realized that I had no idea how to get to the hotel. I drove up one street and down another for a while. Just as I was beginning to think that I might spend the next ten days looking for my hotel, I spotted a guy standing on a street corner. I put on my brakes and rolled down the window, intending to ask the fellow for directions. I pulled to a complete stop, and just then he jumped like a gazelle, leaping from the curb onto my car and spread-eagling himself on my hood. Then he started yelling for me to give him my money. By now I was scared practically witless; first the shotgun incident and now this maniac on my hood. I hit the accelerator and drove off at maybe forty miles an hour, with this guy still hanging on to my hood. His predicament apparently scared him as much as his presence terrified me, and he pressed his face to the windshield and began screaming, "Stop! Stop!" I was hell-bent to get rid of him, but there was no way I was going to stop. Instead, I slowed to fifteen miles an hour, executed a hard right into an alley, and watched as he slowly slid off the left side of my car and rolled to the gutter like a bowling ball. I got out of there as fast as I could, drove around for several more hours, never seeing a policeman and too frightened to ask anyone else for directions, and finally reached my hotel about nine o'clock that night.

The next nine days, I'm happy to say, passed uneventfully, and I fulfilled my sales quota. At Procter & Gamble, just like in the army, you were trained to carry out your mission and do what the company expected of you. And, after a little trouble getting started, I had succeeded. I left New York convinced that if I could survive that experience, I could survive almost anything.

When in Doubt, Wing It.

During the late 1960s a small group of P&G managers formed a pheasant-hunting club, "Sugar Hill," a few miles east of Cincinnati. The club's purpose was to develop camaraderie among people who enjoyed the thrill of the hunt, the barking of the dogs, the taste of bourbon, and the opportunity to return to nature and get away from business on the weekends. It was a real change of pace from the soap business, offering an excellent opportunity for younger managers to gain nonbusiness exposure to senior management.

My first opportunity to hunt at the club came in 1968, when I was a sales manager in the soap division. Jack Hanley, a company vice-president and one of my mentors, invited me to meet him there one cold Saturday in December. Not being a hunter, I arrived wearing remnants of my old army fatigues, a field jacket, and combat boots. I was cradling a borrowed 16-gauge shotgun and trying my best to look like I knew what I was doing. We warmed ourselves in the clubhouse and swapped a few stories with others who were hunting that day, and then Hanley and I headed for the field, where the full-time caretaker, who managed the lodge, raised the birds, and trained the dogs, had released a few pheasants that morning.

Jack Hanley was working the two dogs, yelling at them as they ran back and forth in front of us while we walked slowly across the frozen field. I had never hunted with dogs before, and I was a nervous wreck. I had no idea what I was supposed to do, much less what the dogs were trained to do, but I didn't want to embarrass myself in front of my big boss by asking stupid questions. So I kept my mouth shut and faked it as best I could, vowing to do whatever Hanley did.

Suddenly, right in front of me, a huge pheasant started running along the ground through the thick brush. The dogs were a couple of hundred yards away, too far removed to help me with this bird. I ran after the pheasant for about thirty yards, when all at once it took to the air, flying away from me about eight or ten feet off the ground. There was only one thing to do: I raised my shotgun, closed my eyes, and pulled the trigger. Practically deafened by the blast, I could barely hear Hanley shouting, "Great shot, Lou! You got him!"

Afraid that I might have just wounded my prey, I dashed ahead to where the bird was lying, picked it up, and started back toward where Hanley was standing. Eyeing me with a tremendous grin, he uttered words I will never forget: "Well, you just demonstrated that you can shoot like a pro and outpoint, outflush, and outretrieve the damned dogs. I think there is a glimmer of hope for you in this company."

Some people might have found Jack's words insulting, but to my ears they were better than a raise in pay. I had demonstrated to the man I regarded as the epitome of everything Procter & Gamble stood for that I could perform, even if my methods were a bit unorthodox. Jack Hanley's words of approval on that cold Ohio Saturday reassured me that I was on my way up in the company. And if anything went wrong, I knew I could always land a job as a bird dog. The lesson, I thought to myself, was, when in doubt, just wing it and hope for the best.

To Get Ahead, Get Yourself a Claim to Fame.

During the mid-1970s, when my protégé Tom Quinn was a district field rep, which was a training position for the first level of management, Tom's first manager, John Seelander, pulled him aside one evening about eight o'clock. Tom had a wife and two young children, and Seelander ordered him to go home to them, or else, Seelander threatened, he would fire Tom. Seelander asked Tom why he was there so late, and Tom said he wanted to do a good job so he would get promoted.

"You want to be promoted?" Seelander responded. "There are three ways you can get promoted here at Procter. One is to deserve it, which covers about 5 percent of the people who get promoted. You can almost deserve it, but you have so many people pulling for you that you get it anyway, which is how about 90 percent of our people get promoted. Or you can have a claim to fame, which covers the last 5 percent. They've done something absolutely no one else has ever done. They're known by that deed. If you've got two of those three, you're a shoo-in. You can't miss."

That always stuck with Tom. A couple of years later, a young sales rep named Kevin Mulrain was working under Tom, who was then a unit manager in the bar soap department. Young Mulrain came up with the idea that he would attempt to set a Guinness world record for a sales marathon, which would become his claim to fame both inside and outside the company. He and Tom went out one morning at seven o'clock and worked thirty-six hours straight. They didn't even know that Guinness allows you to rest for five minutes every hour, so they just worked straight through. They say it was a wonderfully liberating feeling to go into a store and know that you didn't have to leave until everything was perfect. They called on thirty-six customers in thirty-six hours, made thirty-six sales, and Mulrain sold 20 percent of his annual sales quota. The next morning they showed up at work unshaven and bleary-eyed. The other sales reps asked Mulrain and Tom what was going on, and these two schemers claimed they were undergoing a test everyone had to go through. The other sales reps took this seriously at first, and all of them were just about ready to quit.

Mulrain did get promoted about three months later; no one ever forgot that episode. The division managers were shaking their heads and saying, "Anybody's who's that committed and that crazy, we want him leading more people."

A Go-getter Gets to the Top.

During my tenure as national sales manager of the paper-products division from 1975 to 1980 the sales organization was at the top of its game and our business was excellent. I had always believed in the old adage, "When the business is bad, nothing is good and when the business is good, nothing is bad." During those five years in the paper division, nothing was bad and management pretty much left the sales department alone. One of the many reasons the business was so good was the exceptional quality of individual sales reps and sales managers. The paper-division sales force had an "attitude"—we felt invincible.

One example was provided by Seattle district manager Bill Driessen. Along about 1977 we started calling the paper division the "flagship" division of the company and expressing our belief that nothing could stop our upward spiral of sales. This air of confidence sparked Bill Driessen to personally demonstrate his commitment to our goals and ourselves. One Saturday, Bill climbed Mount Rainier outside of Seattle, carrying with him a life-size cardboard cutout of "Mr. Whipple," the store-manager character in our television commercials who always refused to let his customers "squeeze the Charmin." Bill climbed Mount Rainier, all 14,410 feet of it, with the cardboard Mr. Whipple in tow, placed that totem on the summit, had his picture taken standing beside it, and then climbed back down the mountain, still hauling Mr. Whipple.

To me, Bill Driessen's initiative was a perfect example of the wonderful human spirit. Individuals who truly believe in something and are committed to a goal will go to extraordinary lengths to stand above the crowd and to demonstrate that they are winners. It's fairly easy to think of something like this happening in war or in time of family crisis, but it can also occur in the corporate world when the environment is right. Yes, intelligent men and women will rally around something as mundane as toilet paper—if they are properly motivated.

Two Ears and One Mouth Mean Man Was Intended to Do More Listening Than Talking.

Being impulsive has been a lifelong problem of mine. Sometimes I ask myself why I don't learn more and faster from my mistakes than I do. It seems that periodically I step in the same stuff I've stepped in before, making life a lot tougher than it should be. This is a propensity that can be harmful in daily life as well as in the business world. I refer here to my occasional outbursts of temper and outrage, most recently on display at the Savannah airport on Christmas night, 1994.

Barbara, our son Brad, and I arrived at the airport three days before Christmas to fly to Dallas for a holiday visit with our youngest son Joe and his family. The parking lot at the Savannah airport was full, and the rain was coming down in sheets. Suddenly, a policeman appeared out of the rain and directed me to turn right and follow the signs to where cars were being parked on an overflow area of grass near the parking-lot toll booth. He added that a van would pick me up and deliver me to the terminal, which turned out to be true.

Fast-forward to midnight on Christmas. We had just returned from three highly enjoyable but stressful days with our son and his wife and three children under the age of five, who terrorized their poor old grandfather for much of our visit. All of us were exhausted, and we certainly were not looking forward to the hour's drive home. First, though, I had to retrieve my car.

While we were away, Savannah had soaked up a lot more hours of rain. It wasn't raining, though, when our return flight landed, and I hoofed it the quarter mile to where I had parked my car in the "temporary grass lot." To my amazement, what had been a beautiful grass field when we left was now pure mud. The entire parking area looked like a giant pigpen, with muddy ruts as deep as eighteen inches. I could feel the hair rising on the back of my neck and my face getting red. How in the world was I going to walk through that mess to where my car was? Nevertheless, at midnight on Christmas, I didn't have much choice. I put my brand-new Nike tennis shoes into the muck, first one and then the other. I started the car, shifted into reverse, backed up about twelve feet, and abruptly found myself stuck. The harder I tried to extricate myself, the deeper in I went. By now, I was ready to murder whoever had gotten me into this predicament. At last, with Barbara steering and Brad and me pushing, we managed to free the car. I drove up to the toll booth and screamed at the male attendant to go ahead and call the police, because I sure as hell wasn't about to pay him for ruining my new shoes, leaving me out in the mud, and then causing Brad and me to cover ourselves with mud from head to toe while we liberated our car.

I was yelling so loud and was so focused on making my point that I failed to notice that the green light was on and the toll gate had been raised. When I finally paused to catch my breath, the attendant said politely, "Sir, if you would only calm down, I could tell you that we are not charging anyone who had to park in the grass this week. Just give me your ticket and you can be on your way. And Merry Christmas!"

Fortunately, in the spirit of Christmas, Barbara refrained during the drive home from giving me a tongue-lashing about how acting impulsively always gets me into trouble (a lecture I richly deserved). Barbara and I have two sons, and one of my friends insists that Barbara actually raised three babies but only got credit for raising two. Who am I to argue?

What Pritchett Looks for in Good Employees.

I maintain that 90 percent of the typical workers in America are born with most of the traits they need to succeed in business. If they are put into a work slash job environment that allows them to become all they can become, to use all their talents, they will succeed and the company will prosper. The traits I look for include:

• *Attitude* is the key characteristic of the successful employee. And that, of course, is something that must come from within. Even when I was selling shoes at Bond's, which I never had any intention of making my career, my attitude was never, "Why should I care about this job? I can always find another one." I put as much effort and as much energy into learning the shoe business and selling shoes as I did later into learning the soap business and selling soap.

• Whatever you do, put your *best effort* into it. When you do that, there are a couple of winners. One winner is your employer. Which is a good thing because, let's not forget, if your employer isn't in business, you don't have a job. But the biggest winner is you. It's all part of becoming everything you're capable of becoming. I think one of the worst mistakes people can make on a job, whether it's a task within the job or the whole job itself, is to make the value judgment that "This is not very important" or that "This will not make a difference in my career. Instead of hitting at a full ten all the time, I can hit this at a six or a seven."

Don't misunderstand me. I am not saying that I've put out a full 100 percent every day for the past forty years that I've been in business. But that has always been my intent. Trying to put everything you have into your job, busting your butt to do the best you're capable of, regardless of whether you're carrying slop to the pigs or selling soap or designing jet aircraft, is what counts. Remember, there are no unimportant jobs. It doesn't matter whether you're hauling garbage or serving as the CEO. Take pride in your job, and do the best you can.

• An intense sense of *curiosity* is indispensable. Absolutely! Always be questioning and challenging. "What does this mean?" you must ask. "Why is this? Why did they build this building this way. Who invented the flying buttress? Why were these floors run this way?" Never lose sight of how vital a sense of curiosity is in business.

• Be *perpetually discontented* with the way things are. There's an old saying to the effect that "There are two kinds of discontent in the world. The first gets what it wants, and the second loses what it has. There's no cure for the first but success; and there's no cure at all for the second."

• *Believe in yourself*—otherwise, no one else will.

9
A Different Drummer: Lou's Primer on Win-Win Selling

Let me tell you a secret—too many business exec*utives t*oday think that corporate success is determined by the number of Ph.D's in the laboratories, the price of their stock on Wall Street, their impressive ROI *figures a*nd their state of the art information systems. They are dead wrong! Corporate success is determined solely by a company's expertise in continuously anticipating and exceeding its customer's expectations.

Customers Are Interested Only in Your Product and What It Does for Them—and Not in Your Problems.

One of my favorite sayings, which I came across at some point over the years, is, "The fact that we are a multidivisional, multifunctional, multiregional, multiplant, multiproduct company is not the customer's problem."

A second (also by an author unknown to me) is, "You can do almost anything wrong in business and still succeed if you serve the customer, and you can do almost everything right in business and still fail if you do not meet the customer's needs, desires, and expectations." In other words, as the old adage goes, "The customer is always right."

Those two statements really provide the secret of selling: Don't bore the customer with your problems, because that isn't what he or she is interested in. And always put your customer first. I can tell you a lot about sales and selling, but no other lessons will be as valuable as these two.

By the way, that second message, that the customer is always right, is not as universally practiced as you might think.

Throughout most of my career with Procter & Gamble, we couched our sales strategy as one of aligning ourselves "against" the customer. That meant that we deployed the members of our sales organization depending on our customers' needs, but the word "against" was certainly a Freudian slip of sorts. That mind-set was probably why some of our customers, such as Sam Walton and his people at Wal-Mart, were so suspicious of us before we decided to try to refashion our relationships with the customers.

The Art of Selling.

Selling is as much an art as singing, writing, dancing, acting, or painting. But it is also something that usually can be learned by observing, listening, reading, and practicing. Basically, selling requires an understanding of human nature and human emotions. Since each of us has firsthand experience in both of these areas, there's no reason why most of us can't learn to sell.

You know, everybody has to sell something at some time, even if it's only when you walk into the boss's office and try to sell yourself—by asking your boss to give you a raise in pay.

It's true that there is no such thing as a natural-born salesman. As far as I'm concerned, the only beings that are natural-born are babies. Nevertheless, almost anyone can learn or acquire the skills needed to be a good salesperson. I think my own career is proof positive.

All superior sales reps—that is, those sales specialists who have a deep, intuitive feeling about the art, who can empathize with their customers and think as their customers think, who can sense what a customer will like or dislike about a product before they present it—are a very rare breed. They should be protected under an endangered species law because they are the engines that propel thousands of enterprises, large and small, all around the globe.

Above all else, these sales masters understand that the key to sales success is not to yell louder and stir up more dust but to learn "before contact" if possible what the customer really needs and then to demonstrate how their product meets that need better than others. More often than not, these special sales reps will, through proper questioning, research, or intuition, figure out what a customer actually needs before the customer himself knows.

When I was selling shoes at Bond Clothes in Memphis during my college years, I always tried first to sell the models that had been classified as slow sellers. I found that doing this sharpened my selling skills because it enabled me to learn more about each of my potential customers. By finding out from them why they did not like a particular shoe, I discovered simultaneously what they really did like. After that, it was fairly easy for me to bring out the model that they had already convinced themselves to buy, as they were in the process of convincing me why they didn't want to buy the first models I had offered. I sold a lot of shoes using this technique. And, most important, I satisfied a hell of a lot of customers.

That's the formula I have used throughout my career: Whether I was trying to sell soap or shortening, I took my job as seriously as I took life in general.

I Learn About Selling from Some of the Best Shoe Salesmen in Memphis.

When I was seventeen and went on to college, I had to pay my way through Memphis State. As a state school, it cost only $28 per quarter. That isn't much money, but when you don't have any, it's a hell of a lot of money. So I had to have a job, and I went to work selling men's shoes at a national chain called Bond Clothes. As I mentioned, I didn't have a car until I joined Procter, so I would take the bus and ride downtown to Bond Clothes and sell shoes until they closed at six-thirty and on Thursday night until they closed at nine.

I worked for and with some interesting characters—men who were on their fifteenth job and hadn't advanced beyond selling shoes. Fortunately, most of the men that I worked with when I was in college made me feel like they had an interest in trying to help me. I think that in those days, maybe, older folks had a different kind of feeling about young people and were more willing to help them and show them how things were done. The other salesmen treated me as an adult and always praised me lavishly when I did well. Probably my biggest booster was the manager of the store, a man named Carlos Wilson. He made a point of introducing me with pride to the customers, to the sales reps from the shoe companies, and to everyone else. Mr. Wilson was proud of me because I was going to be the first shoe salesman at the Bond's in Memphis who had graduated from college. He was truly delighted that he had a young kid working for him who was probably going to do well in life and turn out to be much more than a career shoe salesman.

It was while working at Bond's that I first became sensitive, probably subliminally or subconsciously or however you want to describe it, to the fact that customers are the driving base for business. Back when I was working at Mr. Ugolini's grocery store I was too busy bagging and stocking shelves, and probably too young, to be all that aware of what was going on around me.

At Bond's, I quickly noticed that oftentimes, when a customer came into the store, some of the other salesmen had the attitude, "Oh, my God, here comes another one." Their body language expressed to the customer the idea that "I am doing you a favor by waddling over here and asking you what you want." Salesmen like that wouldn't hustle, even though they got an extra quarter or fifty cents for selling a pair of shoes.

I approached the customers differently—not because my intellect was such that I saw all this stuff so clearly—but to me, almost a common, internal, atavistic thing was, "Look! How would I want someone to treat me if I were coming in here to buy something?" I always felt that the customer was *entitled* to be treated the same way I would personally like to be treated. I am not very religious, believe me. Never have been. But the saying, "Do unto others as you would have them do unto you"—I have found that to be foolproof. That attitude came naturally to me; some people, I think, are more capable of grasping this than others. But almost anyone can learn it.

It later became a game with me and with the manager of my department, a man by the name of Bob Creamer, to see if I could make a sale. I would say, "I'll bet you anything that I can sell something to this guy." Now, it might not be the high-priced pair of shoes that you always wanted to sell. It might be the bargain shoes. But I was confident I could make the sale. In retrospect, whether I really understood that then, I don't know; I doubt it, because I wasn't looking at selling then as a science. But when the customers came in, whether they looked like they had money or looked like they were down to their last nickel, I treated them all the same. And the way I tried to treat them was as though they were the most important person in the world to me. In other words, I treated them almost like they had just walked into my house.

First thing I would do was stick out my hand, shake hands with them, and say, "Oh, I really appreciate your coming into our store, sir. I'm Lou Pritchett. I work here part-time and go to Memphis State." And then I'd ask them a series of questions: "What brought you in here?" "Did you see our ad?" "Was it our window display?" "What are you looking for?" "How can I help you?"

After I'd been there a little while, one of the other salesmen said to me, "The way you treat those people when they come in here, it's as though you've known 'em for years." But I found that that little personal touch of focusing in on "Hey, you are the only person in the world today who matters to me and I'm here to serve you" really helped me sell.

(Addressing people by name, incidentally, is something I do to this day in every aspect of my life, not just when I'm trying to sell. If someone is wearing a name tag, I'll read it and then call them by their name. Some cynics look at that and say, "You conniving son of a bitch! You're using people by doing that." But that isn't true at all; it's simply that I like people to address me by name and I try to do the same.)

So now the customer has walked into Bond's, and I've done my best to put this person at ease—nice and relaxed. The second thing I'd try to do is have him understand that he had a salesman there who was going to try his best to meet his needs. Now at that time I didn't think about exceeding expectations; I had had none of that training or experience. But I had an instinct for how to do it. And I was right. The proof: I quickly became the leading shoe salesman in that store. Bond's wanted me to stay on and sell shoes for them. Who knows—maybe I could have graduated to men's suits. But I had much bigger things in mind.

Make It Easy for the Customer to Buy.

When I was selling shoes at Bond's I quickly learned, or taught myself, something I've passed on to thousands of salespeople:

One of the first lessons in selling is, make it easy for the buyer to buy. Don't make it complex. Don't make 'em have to do a lot of things. Don't make 'em have to think. Don't make 'em have to make decisions. Always give them a choice between something and something. *Never* give them a choice between something and nothing. Because 50 percent of the time, they're going to take nothing. So I would say to my shoe customer, "I've got the $10 shoe or I've got the $14 shoe. I've got the wingtip or I've got the moccasin toe."

At that time, as I say, I had had no training, and I'm a very average guy. Almost anybody can learn this; it's just a matter of human, personal skills.

But not everybody does learn this lesson without some positive reinforcement (i.e., the proverbial two-by-four)—not even huge and hugely successful companies like Procter & Gamble. Several years ago, a large supermarket chain in New England was running a big promotion on Bounty towels. The day before the store's advertising campaign was to hit the newspapers, its shipment of Bounty towels still hadn't arrived. The head of the company was having a world-class headache: In many states, it's against the law to advertise a sale on a product unless you have the product in stock, and even if it's not illegal, not having a sale item in stock is the perfect way to alienate your customers.

Just as the CEO was about to go out of his mind, his secretary came running down the hall, yelling, "There's a Procter guy in the lobby!"

And the CEO was shouting, "Oh, I'm saved! I'm saved!"

He went flying out of his office and practically embraced the Procter salesman. "I have my big Bounty ad breaking tomorrow," the supermarket CEO explained. "And I don't have any Bounty yet. Whenever I call the Procter offices, all I get is a tape, because it's snowing or something out there in Cincinnati. Please call someone and get me those paper towels."

Well, our sales rep freed himself from the man's grasp, stepped back, and, without much interest, said, "Sorry, sir, I don't have anything to do with Bounty. I'm in the toilet goods division." The soap division sold soap; the food division sold food; the paper division sold paper; and the toilet goods division sold toothpaste.

I learned about the Bounty fiasco while I was out doing focus-group interviews with our customers, not an original practice but one I instituted at P&G for our retail customers. That supermarket executive was in one of my focus groups, and he told me that Procter had segmented itself and sectionalized itself into so many different divisions that he didn't know who the real Procter & Gamble was.

That's why, after I became vice-president of sales, I tried to reduce the sales force into a single entity. Bureaucracies may not kill, but they sure as hell wound, injure, and maim. It's a good thing that the politicians have finally gotten around to seriously trying to reduce the size of government. Let's hope that this time, they accomplish more than just talk.

Let Your Customers Help Sell Themselves.

When I was a young salesman, out there selling Tide and Camay and Ivory soap, Neil McElroy, the legendary CEO of Procter & Gamble, once told a group of us salespeople, "You know, women aren't really buying Tide. They're buying the end result: cleaner clothes. Women aren't really buying Camay beauty soap. They are buying softer skin."

Similarly, people aren't buying fax machines, they're buying the ability to communicate instantly. Now, some people might say, "Of course, you idiot, everybody knows that." Well, it may seem obvious to some folks, but, unfortunately, everyone *doesn't* know it. What Neil McElroy taught me that day was something very, very profound. It changed my approach and made me see that if you can just learn what the buyer is really interested in, that's the crucial bit of information you need to know.

By the same token, when I was working with Sam Walton, I came to understand early on that Sam had no interest in just selling more Tide. He was interested only in selling more goods, across the board. With detergents, for example, it didn't matter to Sam whether he was selling Procter detergent or Lever or Colgate or whatever. Going in and saying to Sam, "Hey, I want you to sell more of my stuff" would have been selfish and wouldn't have gotten me anywhere with him.

Anytime you're trying to make a sale, you must convince your customer that what you're selling him will be good for *his* business as well as for *yours*. And if you're a manufacturer and you're trying to sell a product to a retailer, you must show the dealer how he can sell more in the entire category, not only your product. Because unless they're expanding their total sales, selling more of yours means selling less of someone else's; why is that good for the retailer? That's an easy one: It isn't.

Never forget to ask yourself what it is that your customers really want. Look beyond the obvious and ask yourself the question, "What are they really doing?" For instance, the reason the American railroads got in trouble, in my opinion, was that they couldn't change their mind-set from "We're in the railroad business" to "We're in the transportation business." Had the railroads recognized forty years ago that they were in the transportation business—and not just the railroad business per se—they probably would have gotten into airplanes with American and Delta and all the rest. Instead, they left a huge opening in the transportation business that companies like Federal Express and UPS have gone on to fill. Nowadays, even FedEx and UPS and the like have their own aircraft fleets. If the railroads had asked the basic question, "What is it our customers want? What is it that we're really selling? Is it transportation by railroad, or is it simply the best, the fastest, the most cost-efficient transportation there is?" things would have been a lot different.

If you think about that individual customer—whether you're in there trying to sell a pair of shoes or a bar of soap or a fax machine—if you take a genuine interest in the customers, in their business, in their interests, in their price range, in why they need what you're selling, you will dramatically improve your chances of making the sale.

The successful sales organization is the one that exceeds its customers' expectations and adds value to the transaction and to the client's business.

Thrive on Rejection.

One of the biggest barriers that prohibits some people from succeeding at selling is the fear of rejection. If you cannot tolerate rejection, then you will never, in my opinion, be a good salesman. Rejection is the name of the game in selling; you may strike out ninety-nine times for every sale you make, particularly if you're trying to sell through cold calling. But that one "yes" mixed in with all the "nos" makes it worthwhile. If you thrive on rejection, if "No!" is the beginning for you, that's the first sign of a supersalesman. The name of the game in selling is to love combat, to have that "Do or die, never say never" attitude. You have to be driven by the feeling that "My challenge today in this store is I hope that buyer says he doesn't want what I'm selling, because the thrill of the chase for me is to convince him that my idea and my point of view, my product, whatever it may be, is for him." I have to tell you that as a salesman, I would have a boring job if everybody I called on said, "Okay, sign where?" That would be awful! No challenge.

Of course, it was always better in the final analysis for the customer to say yes rather than no, because my pay and my bonuses depended on it, to have the guy sign here. So I definitely did not seek out only those customers that I knew were going to say no just so that I could have the fun of the chase.

At the same time, I felt that the people who did say no, who rejected me, who were the toughest, were the best teachers that I had in the business. Because having to deal with them, learning how to overcome their resistance, made me so much better. I *love* to convince people, to make them change their minds, to move them, to get them to talk about themselves, to get them to open up, to make them relax, to make them laugh. It's like a game to me. To this day, I consider being a field salesperson one of the best jobs a person can have. You're out on your own instead of being confined to an office. Everything you accomplish is the direct result of how skilled you are. Every call, every day, presents a new challenge.

I mean, as a salesman out on the street, I was really primed. Back during the 1950s, before I went into management and when I was actually carrying the bag and selling, I could almost predict in the morning the volume of orders that I would write during that day. Because I knew everybody that I was going to call on. And I knew what turned them on and what didn't and I knew that I could come away with a certain volume. It was almost as though there were certain switches that you had to pull.

Speak the Customer's Language.

In 1955, when I was office head salesman in Procter & Gamble's Memphis district, I was assigned to spend a day in the field with the district's senior sales rep, Charlie "Soapy" Asbury. Charlie had been around for over twenty years and was a legend in the state of Mississippi, where he had always lived and worked. It seemed like virtually every retail store owner and retail clerk knew Soapy; these people would wait impatiently from month to month just to hear his tales, his jokes, and, of course, his spiel lauding P&G's soaps. Young sales reps who were assigned to work with Soapy considered it an honor as well as an invaluable learning experience.

That day in the Mississippi Delta country was an eye opener for me. To my surprise, Soapy did not use any of the proven techniques we had all been taught from the manual. He just walked in and took over a store by sheer force of personality. His arrival at any of these small mom-and-pop stores, which controlled the business in that area (there were no supermarkets in this territory in those days), was equivalent to a movie star making a grand entry. Everyone, including the customers, looked up to Charlie and treated him as somebody special.

One of my first stops with Charlie was at a very small store that was typical of the time and place. Out front was an antique gasoline pump; two hound dogs sat on the small porch. Waiting for Charlie inside were the Chinese couple who owned the store. They lived in a room just behind the selling area of this tiny store. And, as I quickly observed, their command of English was limited.

The first words out of Soapy's mouth were, "Is your bed soft or hard, Mr. Bing?"

Without a moment's hesitation, Mr. Bing replied, "Bed is hard!"

Hearing this, Soapy declared, "Thank you very much, Mr. Bing. I'll see you next trip."

As soon as we got outside, I asked Soapy what that had been all about. He explained that due to lack of storage space, Mr. Bing kept all the cases of his P&G products under his bed in the backroom. Therefore, when the bed was hard, he had ample inventory; but when the bed was soft, he needed to reorder from Soapy.

This episode made a very strong impression on me. Knowing everything about your customers and being able to communicate with them, on their terms, is what it takes if you are to own your market—which is what the successful sales rep does.

Never, Never, Never, Never, Never, Never, Never Give Up. And on Top of That, NEVER GIVE UP!

I often think back to one of my early experiences at Procter & Gamble. During the early 1960s, although I was a midlevel sales manager in Memphis, I had retained the Safeway division in Little Rock as one of my personal accounts. Over the course of twenty months, I called on Safeway no fewer than forty times, delivered wonderful presentations filled with precise details, and was shown the door without receiving a purchase order of any significance no fewer than forty times. But on my forty-first try, in September 1962, my persistence paid off—Safeway finally agreed to increase its P&G products distribution by over 35 percent. This was one of my proudest moment as a salesman, and my tenacity was brought to the attention of Vice-President Jack Hanley, which helped keep me on his mind and on tap for future promotions.

One of the famous stories that has been handed down from generation to generation of Procter & Gamble salespeople involves Art Glenn, a company unit manager several years ago. Back during the late 1930s or early 1940s, Art was in some little town in Texas, making a call on a dealer in a huge two-story wooden frame warehouse. While Art was in the midst of making his pitch, a tornado roared right down the center of town and destroyed this warehouse. First the glass blew out, then the roof flew off, and next all the walls exploded. The customer had grabbed his pen and was starting to sign the order when that tornado hit. As Art told the story, the tornado passed on and the two of them discovered that they were both still alive, although they both were down on their hands and knees under a heavy oak counter where they had taken refuge. The dust was still settling and the howl of the tornado was still fading, and Art looked at the dealer and said the only thing he could think of: "Now, tell me again, did you want twenty or twenty-five cases of Oxydol?"

As Winston Churchill said, "Never, never, never, never, never, never, never give up."

But Don't Forget There Can Always Be Too Much of a Good Thing.

A famous story within Procter & Gamble's sales division is about one of our managers who was making what were called "follow checks" back during the 1920s. A routine part of a manager's job then, given the great distances, the need to take the train in the days before the jet age, and the fact that most communications were conducted through the U.S. mail, was to periodically retrace a sales rep's route and see whether he was doing what he claimed he was on his reports. These checks were not announced in advance and were conducted by the manager, traveling alone.

On this particular follow check, the manager was suspicious because the salesman had been reporting sales of huge volumes of soap products to a relatively small store in a tiny Texas town. When the P&G manager inspected this store's stockroom, he found over 150 cases of company product, which would have equaled nearly a year's supply for this dealer. Returning to the front of the store, the sales manager took the owner aside and commented that he must sell an awful lot of soap.

"No, I don't," was the answer, "but your sales rep sure as hell does!"

This anecdote was handed down from generation to generation within the company as a reminder that moving product from our warehouses to the retailer didn't accomplish much if the retailer wasn't moving it out of his store, too. That sales rep was only doing his job—keeping his customers loaded down with our soap product. But, the truth is he was doing it a little too well.

If Your Customer's Just a Customer, He's Just a Customer, but If He's Your Partner, the Sky's the Limit.

When I got my first managerial job, as a unit manager in Memphis in 1955, I had a special relationship with Malone & Hyde, the largest wholesaler in the South then. My relationship was with the buyer, the merchandise manager, and with the old man, Joe Hyde Sr. What I did, which at that time was very, very unusual, I convinced them to let me come in every week to their card room, they called it, where they had an old punch-card computer, and count the inventory cards and write my own orders. That sounds very commonplace, but my objective was, "Why don't you let *me* be a part of your company? Why don't you let me come in and manage your inventory for you?" And they agreed to allow me to do just that. By trusting me and allowing me to do this, they also put some very, very tight self-imposed controls on me. Because I was not about to violate their trust; I knew that if I ever did, I would lose it. I was one of the few people who had that privilege. And I worked out the same arrangement with the Kroger Company and Liberty Cash Grocers—my three biggest personal accounts. I saw very early in my career that there was a better way to handle a customer than just to walk in and say, "Hey, I'm here to take your order today, what do you need?" I didn't use this term back then, but what I actually was doing was almost starting a partnering relationship. I felt that if I could genuinely show the managers of my three biggest accounts, my biggest customers, that I was adding value to the process and contributing ideas that would benefit their businesses instead of simply being an order taker, I could help both them and me.

Interestingly enough, several of my bosses—not including

my immediate boss, Ernie Baker—felt that I shouldn't be going out of my way to help my customers and win their confidence. These executives said, "Look, what you should be doing as a manager is making sure that your salesmen are making their fifteen calls a day. You have management duties. And by taking some of your time to go down and 'work for' these companies, you're taking time away from your real Procter & Gamble job. They pay buyers to do that; why the hell are you doing it?"

That was the mind-set then. And I had a very difficult time making some of those executives understand. "You can't *buy* this kind of relationship. You can't buy the ability to go in there and do your own managing of their business and write your own order."

There's No Substitute for Street Smarts.

To sell—whether it's by telephone, in person, or out on the street—one trait you must have above all is street smarts. I'm certainly not going to criticize the business schools and the marvelous education they provide. I wish I had had the opportunity to go to business school myself. But in addition to the book learning, a good manager must have intuition, like the safecracker's fingers. You know, the safecrackers who file their fingers so they can actually feel the tumblers move. It's plain street smarts.

Probably the most street-smart rivals I ever competed against were two men I encountered when I was in the Philippines during the early 1980s. One was the president of Colgate, Brian Bergan. And the other was the president of Lever in the Philippines, Clive Butler. They were very intelligent; yeah, that was a given. But they were also extremely street smart. Those guys had the sensitivity of a gang member. They really knew what was going on.

For example, we introduced Crest toothpaste in our standard way in the Philippines, with a huge advertising campaign and by blanketing the islands with free samples. Colgate had been the number one toothpaste out there; it had owned the market and made tons of money for years. But now, Crest was a threat to their cash cow. What Brian Bergan did, being so inventive, when we dispatched teams to pass out free samples of Crest, he sent his own teams right behind ours. His people paid five pesos (equal to about twenty-five cents in U.S. money) to the people we had just handed samples to and bought up most of our samples. Just imagine going down the street in Manila or in one of the provinces and you've got a guy wearing a Crest outfit and he's saying, "Here's a sample of our new toothpaste, madam. Try it." Right behind our man comes one of theirs, saying, "Somebody just gave you a sample, didn't they? We'll pay you five pesos for it." And, given the economy of the Philippines, most of these people took the money and handed over their sample of Crest. So the consumer never had a chance to try Crest and wound up staying with Colgate. That's street smart! That's genius! I can't help laughing at it today, nearly fifteen years later. At the time, though, it didn't seem so funny. We threatened to sue Colgate and made Brian stop what he was doing. But he damaged the hell out of our Crest introductory campaign and managed to delay it for about six months. I hated the bastard for doing it, but I had to admire him at the same time. They weren't playing not to lose, they were playing to win. I mean, these guys were playing hardball. And I think that what they did was brilliant. Absolutely brilliant!

To Sell, You Have to Listen to What People Say—the Phrases "Shoot" and "Don't Shoot" Both Have the Word "Shoot" in Them.

There's no telling how much mischief folks can get into when they don't pay the slightest attention to what's happening around them. Good communications are absolutely essential for success. So, too, are paying attention to detail and being a good listener. But many of us aren't good listeners. I think a lot of us are so busy either running our mouths or thinking about what we're going to say at the earliest moment we have a chance to run our mouths again that we fail to listen carefully to what the other person is saying to us. And that can cost us. A case in point:

Several years ago, my wife and I and another couple from Hilton Head were getting ready to take off for a vacation in Russia. There's this one taxicab company that I've used for years, and they've never let me down. Nevertheless, as someone who has been in sales for over forty years, I'm always sympathetic to people who take the initiative and try to sell me something new. One day not too long before our trip to Russia, I was at the Hilton Head airport when the owner of a new cab company walked up to me. "Which cab company do you use, mister?" he asked me. I told him, and he inquired, "Would you mind giving us a try?" I agreed, but I made it clear to him that I'm a real stickler for detail and that I won't tolerate mix-ups. We were leaving for Russia from the Savannah airport, which is about an hour's drive, and I told the man that we had to be picked up at least an hour and a half before we wanted to be at the airport. We wanted to be there at five o'clock in the afternoon, and to be safe, we wanted the cab to be at our house at three o'clock.

"Don't worry," this new entrepreneur answered. "If you give my company a try, I guarantee you'll be happy with us."

I carefully explained that I live on Bear Island Road, *not* Bear Creek Road, which is nearby. He promised to give explicit, unmistakable directions to his driver and vowed there would be no problem.

Just to make sure, I called the cab company the day before our trip to double-check. The dispatcher's reply was, "Oh, yes, Mr. Pritchett, we've got you down. We'll be there at three o'clock sharp."

Three o'clock came, and no cab. Three-fifteen, the same. At three-twenty I called the cab company and the dispatcher told me the driver was lost. The cab finally rolled up at three-thirty.

"I'm sorry," the driver explained, "but I got lost on Bear Creek Road."

Needless to say, I was not in a good mood, and I let him know it. "I told the owner and the dispatcher three different times that I live on Bear Island, not Bear Creek."

"Yes," the driver agreed, "but both streets have the word 'Bear' in them."

That's when I replied, "Buddy, the phrases 'Shoot' and 'Don't shoot' both have the word 'shoot' in them. But, by God, you had better be clear and understand whether you're supposed to shoot or not, because it could mean the difference between getting killed and surviving."

On top of that, the owner of the company had promised me that he would provide his largest, newest vehicle, and, in response to my demand for one with good air-conditioning, he promised that the cab would feel like we were at the North Pole if we wanted it to. Well, to make matters worse, the air-conditioning hardly worked at all, and it looked like someone had cleaned his windshield with a combination of buttermilk and peanut butter.

When I got back from my trip I called this fellow who had asked me to give him a chance. I said, "Listen, my friend, you're not going to like what I tell you. I gave you a chance because you came to me on a personal basis, supplier to customer, and asked me to give you a chance. I like to explore new companies like yours, so I did give you a chance. I had a few conditions: be on time, be air-conditioned, be clean. You were thirty minutes late, the air conditioner was inferior—it barely worked—and the car was filthy. So you have not only lost my business, you have lost any business I might ever recommend for you."

The guy wasn't the least bit apologetic, or even concerned. "Well, too bad," he commented. "You win a few and you lose a few."

Yeah, well, he lost a customer. And I doubt if this will surprise you; before long, he lost his business, too—the company went under.

Some people just have no concept of what selling and doing business are all about. And those people are doomed to fail. Don't let yourself be one of them! Don't walk when the sign says "Don't walk." Don't wind up on Bear Creek Road when you're looking for Bear Island Road. And, above all, don't shoot when you're out in the woods hunting game and someone yells, "Don't shoot!" The life you save may be your best friend's, if not your own.

The Customer Is Always Right—Especially If He Has a Gun.

Coupon fraud has always been a reality in the retailing business, just like shoplifting, employee theft, and bad checks. One of the most common methods of coupon fraud is for crooked retailers to buy coupons from the consumer for five cents or a dime apiece and then turn them in to the manufacturer for the face value—twenty-five cents, fifty cents, sometimes more. Another trick is for retailers to buy newspapers and have a kid in the back room clipping out all the coupons. Sometimes the coupons are in sequential number, so it's obvious that something funny is going on. Or they've been cut out of a newspaper with a cleaver or something. When the company receives suspicious coupons, it returns them to the sales rep and instructs him, "We're not going to redeem these. Take them back to the dealer and find out what's going on."

One of my jobs when I was a young sales manager was to guard against coupon fraud. In 1956 or 1957, a P&G sales rep and I stopped by a grocery store in south Memphis. We must have had ten pounds of coupons in a big sack. We walked in, greeted the owner, put the coupons on his desk, and said, "We've got something here we need to talk about. These coupons, we believe, were not redeemed legitimately."

He sat down behind the desk and said, "Why don't you boys tell me about it?"

We laid out the coupons and started telling him how we saw it, not necessarily in accusatory fashion, but just trying to explain to him why we were suspicious. The coupons were sequential, they looked as if they had all been cut with the same sharp instrument, they were all stacked together—they didn't even look like they had ever been handled; they were all like brand-new one-dollar bills straight from the U.S. mint.

We had been talking to him for a few minutes, a pleasant enough conversation under the circumstances, when he bent over and reached under his desk. I wasn't even paying any attention to what he was doing. But I started paying real close attention when he came back up from under the desk and I found myself looking down the business end of a pistol that looked like a German .88. Staring down the wrong end of the barrel, that weapon looked to me like the biggest thing I had ever seen in my life, like it was a shotgun.

The shopkeeper finally broke the dead silence: "Well, boys, let me tell you. We can talk about this for a while. But I don't think I like hearing what you're telling me. So perhaps you ought to leave my store." So I said, "Thank you very much. We'll take the coupons with us." I reached over and grabbed the coupons and my colleague and I very slowly backed out of the store.

We sent a note to Cincinnati, informing the home office that we had the coupons, that they indeed were fraudulent, that the store owner had pulled a gun on us, and that we were removing his page from our callbook. Which meant we never called on that son of a bitch again. He still was free to buy our products from a wholesaler, but we sure as hell weren't ever going to set foot in his store after that! Every time a bundle of coupons falls out of my Sunday newspaper, that incident comes to mind. I can't picture that store owner, but I sure do remember what his gun looked like. Just imagine—nearly getting shot over a bunch of discount coupons. That ain't the way it's done, babe!

Selling Will Never Be Obsolete, but the Way We've Sold in the Past Will Be.

In the future, will there be sales reps like me, men and women out there carrying the bag?

Well, yes and no.

The way I see it, salespeople should think of themselves right at this moment as trapeze artists, suspended between trapezes. We have to let go of the old trapeze—the old way of selling— and grab the new trapeze before it swings too far away from us to catch hold of.

There is always going to be a place for a sales organization. But I think the sales organization of the future is going to look quite different than it has in the past. In the past, what it basically did was perform the critical function in the distribution process.

It's always going to be necessary, regardless of information technology, to have salespeople. Some things will remain the same. Salespeople will still have to make things happen. They'll still have to get decision makers to respond, which is going to take more and more perseverance. To call on a customer with the situation at X, and, because of your ability, change that situation to Y—whether you're talking about getting a larger order

or a better position in the store or an order for new brands—
that's a tremendous thrill. That's what we salespeople live for.

But salespeople will have to be much better informed and
much better equipped, which is going to make the competitive-
ness of the game that much sharper. Still, organizations are
always going to have to have salespeople who are able to provide the linkage between the customer and the supplier. I compare the new role of the sales rep to that of an electrical wall
outlet that accepts two prongs and you've got an appliance
you're trying to plug in that has three prongs. So you need an
adapter. And the sales role in many cases in the future is going
to be that adapter. It isn't necessarily that this adapter is any
smarter than the customer or the balance of the supplier team,
it's that the real salespeople who have those very special skills
can play that role better than most.

The adapter is the one who can communicate with the supplier's people on one side and with the customer's people on the
other side, pull the whole thing together, and make everybody
feel good about it. Picture the communications gap between
seller and buyer as being a swamp and a quagmire of molasses
knee deep; the new-age sales rep will have to be able to lay a
concrete bridge across so that nobody gets mired in the muck.

Selling is a lot harder than it was when I joined P&G, and it's
getting harder all the time. It was phenomenally easy to sell
after World War II, from 1945 until around 1975. Basically, all
you had to do was put the merchandise in the pipeline.
Americans were relieved to be finished with the war and to
have won, and the postwar prosperity made practically everyone feel rich, or at least well off. There had been tremendous
advances in technology—for example, we started the war in
open cockpit fighters and ended it with the atomic bomb. And
everybody wanted a television, the latest version of the automobile, the most modern refrigerator, air-conditioning, and lots of
other consumer products. This combination of factors resulted
in tremendous consumer demand.

The post–World War II period was just part of the revolutionary changes in selling. Back in the early 1900s and the
1920s, guys who had my job were called drummers. They went
out and drummed up business, just like in *The Music Man*. And

on into the 1930s and 1940s, before there was the mass-media saturation that there is today, a sales organization's job was to be the manufacturer's representatives in the field. When I started with Procter & Gamble in 1953 in Tupelo, Mississippi, P&G was a company that produced soap and other products somewhere else. The only way we had to reach the retailers, the only way my customers knew what I had to offer, what my prices were, or what my promotions were, was for me to go out there and personally tell them. We had what we called total penetration. As we used to say, we called on every store that had a door. And this system worked beautifully. It's one of the foundations and underpinnings of a company like Procter. The salesman was very vital to perform that role of communication and to actually sell the product. Otherwise, the small store owner didn't have any contact with the producer. In those days, the sales reps were the walking ads, if you will. The retailers didn't have the expertise or the resources that they do today. I used to help write grocery ads for a lot of my retailers and help design their promotion programs. A lot of them simply didn't know how to do it themselves. So I would prepare ads for my customers the night before I called on them because I was making my fifteen calls every day and I didn't have time to do the ads while I was visiting their stores. I was like a consultant, sharing with my customers the benefit of big Procter's wisdom, its consumer data, all the advertising. We sales reps were a walking fountain of knowledge for the individual store owners.

Nevertheless, let's face it: At companies like mine, we weren't selling life-sustaining drugs or high-tech machinery; there's only a certain amount of knowledge you have to have about detergent. Product knowledge was not that important. Hell, the housewife or the store manager knew as much about the products as we did because they used them. What you really had to know was the marketing and the promotion of it.

Then, as the retailers began to add scanners at the front end of the store (which, by the way, they added for the wrong reason, to lower front-end cost—not to gain the valuable information scanners provide), that's when the retailers were able to start keeping track of inventory on their own, to know where it was going, what was selling and what wasn't. When the retailers began to get this data, they began to know more about our brands than we knew and they knew it faster.

The result is that today, the balance of power has shifted dramatically; the retail trade is much more in control of how the game is played. When I was out in the field, the balance of power was about ninety-nine to one in favor of the manufacturer. Then it slowly shifted to around fifty-fifty, and today it's more like sixty-forty or seventy-thirty, with the retailer holding the upper hand over the manufacturer.

What this means is that the manufacturer has to completely revamp the sales role. The sales reps must function as an information conduit back to the company, too, instead of just being a one-way street. The sales reps have to be out there finding out what the customer wants, what the customer needs, what the customer's expectations are, and explaining all those things to the company.

Marketing is changing at light speed today, in every country around the world. Core beliefs about the customer, which managers and marketers all took for granted as recently as five years ago, have suddenly been rendered obsolete. Customers have become more sophisticated and more demanding in what has become a world of choice for everyone. Today's customers are seeking products they trust—not just products that meet a need. As technology becomes a tool for the masses, customers have become free agents in the marketplace. They are confident of themselves, and they can no longer be manipulated. Today's customers want the supplier to help them conserve time. Therefore, the gift of time must become an integral part of the added value of the product or service. Yesterday, we marketed to segments of the masses; today, we must market to segments of one. To compete successfully in this new marketing environment, suppliers must not only change the way they have perceived and thought about their customers, they must change the way they have organized to serve them.

The unpleasant truth is that the computer—that is, technology—does a better job of selling than the sales rep used to. So the sales rep of the future is not going to be dinging around in retail. The days are over when a salesman walked into the store with his order book and asked, "What do you want today?"

and the retailer answered, "I'll have ten of these and fifty of those and a hundred of that." Sales reps don't go into warehouses now and count stocks and say, "Well, you had a hundred, you sold fifty, you need fifty more." That's all history. Instead, the retailer can look at his records and tell instantly what he needs, what's selling and what isn't, and order it all electronically. That whole industry of interacting and transactional selling, buyer-seller at the retail level, no longer exists. There's no reason for it any longer. It's been surpassed and become outdated, just like gaslights. Technology has changed the entire sales role. A lot of what sales reps used to do can now be performed by computers.

For all those reasons, the sales rep of the future is going to be working in teams with the decision-making teams of the buying company. The leverage point is not going to be in the retail stores; all of those decisions are going to be moved much higher up the scale. Is the sales role doomed? No. But it's going to be a totally different role in the future than it's been in the past.

Another big change in selling is that all markets have become local—just as Tip O'Neill said that all politics are local. At the beginning of my career we basically ran the same advertising all over the country. The entire USA really was a single mass market. The housewife in California wasn't all that different from the housewife in New York. And the salespeople performed in the same way all over the country. We had the same promotions from coast to coast. But the generic mass-market approach has become obsolete.

It really has been only during the last ten years or so that we have begun to realize that there is regional, niche marketing with targeted audiences. Today, we have hundreds of mini-markets, and vendors must adjust to this new system. The challenge is to figure out where these mini-markets are, how to treat them, how to market to them. Fortunately, with information technology being what it is today, that's a lot easier to do now, to identify those markets and reach them.

A P&G story from many years ago shows how different things were before the "all markets are local" concept began taking hold. One of my first bosses was E. E. "Ernie" Baker. Ernie used to describe how, years earlier, when he was a supervisor in the sales office in Dallas, a new sales rep kept sending in reports of huge orders for Ivory Flakes from his territory in west Texas. Ernie and everyone else in the district office were well aware that there was little demand for Ivory Flakes in west Texas because the water out there was iron hard and Ivory was a tallow-based soap chip that did not lather well in that water. The experienced sales reps, in fact, made only a minimal effort to sell Ivory Flakes in those locales, even though their job was to distribute as much of each brand as they could in every sales area.

Ernie questioned the young sales rep about how he could be selling so much Ivory Flakes. The answer was, "I'm sorry, Mr. Baker, I didn't know that Ivory Flakes wouldn't sell in west Texas."

Ernie cited this salesman's experience as a classic case of letting preconceived opinions and value judgments get in the way of doing business. Unburdened by these biases, not realizing that he supposedly *couldn't* make the sale, this novice sales rep went out and did what he was supposed to do: sell. Not knowing any better, he was able to turn the whole thing around. That sales rep did a marvelous job, but today a company would offer products that were better suited to the customers in the area where he worked.

The sales organization of the future, instead of being geographically specific and product focused, is going to have to be customer specific and service focused. At Procter, for instance, we would sometimes have as many as seven or eight salesmen calling on the stores of the same customer. There was no coordination. And we really weren't too interested in what the stores' overall marketing strategy was; all we were interested in was selling our products to them.

In short, the most valuable information for the sales force of the future is going to be customer knowledge: How do our customers operate? How do they charge for their products? What are their systems? How can their systems become compatible with our systems in ordering, billing, and everything else? How can we help them expand their category sales? Do we understand their marketing strategies and their product mix? After all, we are only a part of their total product mix.

Once you start achieving that, you will be on your way to becoming a twenty-first-century sales operation.

One Eternal Truth in Selling: The Best Product in the World Ain't Worth a Damn If the Consumer Doesn't Want It.

All the new technology, all the new ways of doing business, will tremendously help salespeople do their jobs. But one thing will never change: to make the sale, you have to be selling a product the customer wants.

For instance, I'll bet you've never heard of Fluffo. And there's a good reason why.

In 1954, not long after I joined P&G and while I was still working out of Tupelo, Mississippi, our company, with much fanfare, introduced a new brand of shortening. It was called Fluffo, to bring to mind the image of fluffy, perfect biscuits popping out of the oven. Procter had had a dominant product on the market for a half century or so—Crisco, a pure vegetable shortening. But Fluffo was considered a breakthrough because it combined both vegetable and animal fat and had a rich golden color. There are three major factors that usually determined a new brand's success: sheer volume, broad-based wholesale and retail distribution, and newspaper advertisements featuring the new product. And we had covered every base, dotted every *i* and crossed every *t* in those areas. All we had to do now was sit back and wait for Fluffo to go marching off the store shelves by the millions and millions.

It never happened! Unfortunately, the masterminds who had developed Fluffo had overlooked one crucial point: Housewives prided themselves on their ability to bake large, white biscuits—not large, yellow ones. Alerted by our introductory campaign, they tried Fluffo once, looked at their yucky yellow biscuits with horror, and went back to buying Crisco and similar products. The retailers were not pleased, and neither were we.

Three months into the glorious Fluffo crusade, I was promoted to district head salesman and reassigned to the Memphis office. I hoped that Fluffo would be my first success, and I helped plan a stepped-up effort that included discounts,

coupons, and ever- increasing purchases of radio time to advertise Fluffo. We were confident that only a fool would pass up
Fluffo, but the number of fools who could live without Fluffo
seemed to grow by the millions every week.

At last we received word that my idol, Southern division
sales manager Jack Hanley, was coming to Memphis to see
about these problems with Fluffo for himself. We compiled
every analysis, comparison, and chart we could think of in
preparation for our meeting with Mr. Hanley.

The day before our meeting, Hanley instructed me to buy
five three-pound cans of Fluffo and bring them with me. This I
did, which no doubt doubled Fluffo's sales in Memphis that
day. Hanley opened the meeting by handing a can to all five of
his managers who were present: Red Collins, Grady Collins,
me, and two others. Next, he told us to open the cans. Once
they were opened, Hanley ordered each of us to stick our fingers into the Fluffo, to feel its texture, to smell it, and finally, to
taste it. I can still see the look of horror on the face of Red
Collins, our nattily dressed, sophisticated senior district manager, as Red regarded the Fluffo on his finger. Most of us barely
put it in our mouths, but then Hanley shouted, "Goddamn it! I
said *taste* it!" All five of us stuck about three fingers down our
throats and swallowed the Fluffo as though it were the best
bourbon Kentucky could distill.

Jack Hanley, you see, was from the school that believed that
salespeople could sell any product as long as they loved it and
had an intimate knowledge of it. As far as Hanley was concerned, our job in the sales division was to sell. Not to do market research—that had already been done to a fare-thee-well
out of headquarters in Cincinnati. Not to complain about yellow biscuits. Not to make excuses. Just to sell. Part of our job
was to report retailer and consumer reaction, but we in the sales
force did not have the research tools that would allow us to
evaluate numbers or predict future buying patterns. As Al
Davis of the Los Angeles Raiders would say, "Just sell, baby."

So we sold and sold and sold. But no consumer bought and
bought and bought. And a few years later, Fluffo was quietly
withdrawn from the market.

Pritchett's Maxims to Help Maximize Your Sales.

Though P&G's consumer studies had failed to reveal that housewives didn't want yellow biscuits, dooming Fluffo to failure, I learned several valuable lessons from the Fluffo fiasco about challenging and motivating salespeople:

- Never accept no for an answer.
- Learn everything you can about your products, and believe in them with an abiding faith.
- You can sell anything if you put your mind to it.

And don't forget some other lessons I've learned about selling:

- Always offer a choice between something and something.
- Customers are interested only in what your product will do for them—not in your problems.
- Make it easy for the customer to buy.
- Let your customers help sell themselves.
- Thrive on rejection.
- Speak the customer's language.
- Never, never, never, never, never, never, never give up. And on top of that, *never* give up!
- If your customer's just a customer, he's just a customer, but if he's your partner, the sky's the limit.
- There's no substitute for street smarts.
- To become a great sales rep, you must first become a great listener.

10
Rocking the Boat

Over the years, they have been called movers, shakers, change agents, entrepreneurs, and, occasionally, just weird dudes. These are the men and women from all walks of life who are never satisfied with the status quo; who are always uncomfortable with treating their job as just a job; who are always asking, what if; and who find themselves deeply depressed during the lull between finishing one project and starting another.

These are the individuals who, if they aren't stretching the envelope and challenging the system and everybody in it, don't feel like they're earning their pay. These are the men and women who thoroughly enjoy taking on city hall or senior management because they, like Thomas Jefferson, are acutely aware that there *is* a better way—and they are driven to find it. These are the people who do not suffer fools lightly. These characters know intuitively that those with rank are often handicapped by that very rank, which may inhibit the brass from standing up and speaking out.

The people I'm talking about are the ones I laud with the title "boat rockers." Throughout history it has been they who have made the difference in politics, in education, in religion, in the military, in business, and in society in general.

Unfortunately, the boat rockers often make the boat paddlers uneasy. The boat rockers are always a threat to create unwanted motion, to make waves, to speed up events, and to change the course of the vessel. In the process, they make the paddlers, and especially the captains, seasick. Sadly, the captains of the ships in which the rockers are passengers tend to fall back on the old show tune, "Sit down! Sit down! Sit down! Sit down! Sit down! You're rocking the boat!" These captains want no conflict, no rough water, no counter to the speed and direction in which the ship is being steered. Few of these captains recognize that the very success of the ship may depend on the boat rockers they want to silence.

My prescription is that the captains must learn quickly to recognize and encourage the rockers to rock even harder. For, in the information- and knowledge-driven era we are now entering, it is the paddlers who pose a threat to the enterprise and the rockers who will rescue it.

Sending Wake-up Calls.

As I mentioned at the outset, when I told Sam Walton in the spring of 1989 that I was going to retire from Procter & Gamble, his response was, "Lou, I hope you will continue to be out there, giving wake-up calls to America. Because we need it. If we fail to drive costs out of this system, we're all going to wind up selling hamburgers to each other." Two and a half years later, shortly before Sam's death, he wrote me a letter that contained a similar theme: "I'm glad you're sending out those wake-up messages to folks throughout this country. It's an important message and one we're going to have to listen to in order to compete in a global way with what everybody is doing around the world."

Over the centuries a number of traditional, even establishment-oriented, tutors have handed down messages from which I derive my philosophy about change. Among these visionaries, and their messages, are:

- "There is nothing more difficult to take in hand, more perilous to conduct, or more uncertain in its success, than to take the lead in the introduction of a new order of things, because the innovator has for enemies all those who have done well under the old conditions, and lukewarm defenders in those who may do well under the new."

—Niccolò Machiavelli, *The Prince*
- "Great things have been effected by a few men well conducted."
—George Rogers Clark (1752–1818), a U.S. soldier and frontiersman, and the brother of William Clark, the co-commander of the Lewis and Clark expedition to Oregon

- "All men dream, but not equally. Those who dream by night in the dusty recesses of their minds wake in the day and find that it was Vanity. But the dreamers of the day are dangerous men, for they may act their dream with open eyes, to make it possible."

—T. E. Lawrence ("Lawrence of Arabia")
The Seven Pillars of Wisdom

- "All progress depends upon the unreasonable man."

—George Bernard Shaw

- "The world will go on somehow and more crises will follow. It will go on best, however, if among us there are men who have stood apart, who refused to be anxious or too much concerned, who were cool and inquiring and had their eyes on a longer past and a longer future."

—Walter Lippmann

I distilled these teachings into my own words, written in 1982:

"To do what everybody else has done for thirty years is not a challenge. To innovate, create, and redesign for tomorrow is my idea of what management is all about."

Yes, I, Lou Pritchett, definitely do believe in "sending out wake-up messages." I have to admit that Sam was just being nice to me with his choice of language; I'm a classic troublemaker, change agent, and boat rocker. And I'm looking for a lot more like me—and for a lot of companies that will not only tolerate us but encourage us, promote us, and follow us boat rockers into the future.

At the same time, though, I don't consider myself and other boat rockers to be rebels. You might think that since I *do* advocate change, not to mention that I came out of Memphis about the same time as a famous singer—fellow named Elvis—I am a rebel. Absolutely not! To me, "rebel" connotes smoking out back behind the barn, drinking beer when you're fourteen, skipping school, and dressing like James Dean. I did none of those. James Dean was a *Rebel Without a Cause*; I consider myself a *non*rebel *with* a cause. My message, unlike what Elvis's deteriorated into, is not "sex, drugs, and rock 'n' roll"—that is, anarchy.

Hold Loosely the Keys to Your Office.

As I have looked back over my career, one fundamental question I've asked myself again and again is, why did I take it upon myself to rock the boat, to try to change the way an ultrasuccessful multibillion-dollar corporation did business and dealt with its customers? Why didn't I simply settle down in my beautifully appointed office, enjoy the privilege of using the company's Gulfstream jet airplanes, and watch my profit sharing pile up?

My answer to that question is that I was driven by a conviction that this company, which was family to me, had reached the point where it had to adapt in order to continue being successful. I decided that I was not going to simply be a holder of the keys and keep the waters flat. Some corporate officers change when they reach the executive suite and start concentrating on agreeing with each other instead of getting things right. Their philosophy becomes, "I have arrived, and now I'm going to make sure that I don't do anything to screw it up."

My approach was somewhat different: "Now that I have arrived, I'm finally in a position to help the people who helped me get here." How could I do anything for my troops and my company, much less look myself in the eye, if my major motivation abruptly became covering my own ass? Neil McElroy's words—his command—to "do something" if the opportunity ever came my way were firmly etched in my brain, and I was determined to act on them.

In looking around for fellow believers, I found many who agreed with me, but only a few who were willing to pay the price or run the risk of suffering the penalties that come with going against the grain. I also found that some of those in positions to make things happen were unwilling to consider revolutionary change. They would tolerate only evolutionary change. I, however, was convinced that we needed to act quickly, take the high ground, and redesign the template for how to align with our customers in the future, which would leave our competitors far behind and with no choice but to follow our lead.

In an attempt, perhaps, to justify my course of action, I concluded that nothing moves very fast on a slick or smooth surface, and that the key to progress resides in someone or something providing the necessary friction. I chose to be that someone.

I was very confrontational, combative, and aggressive, and I have to admit that I enjoyed taking on city hall. I relished the thrill of the battle, the give-and-take, the duel of ideas. Most important of all, it was the very corporation to which I became in some ways a thorn in the side that afforded me the luxury of speaking out.

I never was afraid of being fired, and that's to the credit of the Procter & Gamble company. I came to work each day not seeking to be fired, but willing to be fired. That means I brought my best, wildest, most unconventional, maverick self to the shop floor. Visionaries have to come to work willing to be fired. That's part of the price you must pay. You've got to be willing to take chances, to speak up, to rattle cages, to challenge the basic premises, to suggest a better way of doing things. Be bold, be audacious, be brazen. That doesn't mean be obstructive. My counsel to management in today's environment is to create a work environment that not only allows but encourages employees to bring to work their outrageous attitudes on what's good/bad and what's right/wrong about the business, as well as their ideas on how to fix the problems.

As for myself and my situation, I was confident that if I did get fired, I could always find another job. That's why I was able to go out to the Philippines and do the right things, things that had never been done before, because I was sure that I wouldn't get fired, or that if I did, I would land on my feet. By the time I got there, I was almost fifty years old. I already had my career. I wasn't worried about being promoted or being fired. I had no pressure to prove myself, which allowed me to avoid doing dumb, short-term things to make myself look good.

New Rules, New Ways of Thinking and of Doing Things, Will Always Be Written Out at the Edge—Never in the Comfort of the Center.

Boat rockers, mavericks, change agents, plain old employees who try to tell management what it doesn't want to hear— they're rarely welcome within the corporate bosom. This is understandable, because it is human nature to want to maintain the status quo, to avoid discomfort, and to keep on doing what you've always done, to take the safe road, to avoid risks, to follow the proven formula for success.

So it can be scary out there all alone on the cutting edge, trying to be a reformer and a visionary and wondering how to create the future. Not long after I was promoted to vice-president in 1985, I began calling for changes in the way P&G sales operated. One of the first things I did that some executives found threatening was to suggest that we make an effort to find out what our customers were thinking and to work together with them, as partners, in order to reinvent ourselves and our business so that all of us could compete successfully in the new "information age." Too many managers, including me, had been making too many value judgments about what customers wanted and what they didn't want. Procter & Gamble was the best company in the world at doing focus groups with the ultimate consumers, the supermarket shoppers. There's absolutely nobody better in the business. But we had been less than proactive and successful in doing that with our direct customers, the retailers. I decided it *was* important to find out from our major customers what they thought of us and how they viewed us in comparison with the competition. As you might suspect, the reaction of some managers was, "Why do this? Don't rock the boat. You're just asking for trouble."

I did it anyway. And the fears that our customers would make huge demands on us proved unfounded. No one asked us for anything. Not only that, but the customers answered candidly and tried to help us. They reported that their biggest problem was that we had too many divisions calling on them. One of our major customers said, "I've got about seven different sales reps from Procter calling on me. And every one of them seems to be different for the sake of being different. I have to hire an extra person or two just to manage the Procter & Gamble business." He added, "I don't know who the real Procter is. You guys collectively have got tremendous strength and you represent a sizable slice of my total business. But you have fractionated this thing into six, seven, eight different divisions, all with different agendas, all with different approaches. It's gotten so confusing that I can't even figure out who the real

Procter is." That helped us understand that we had plenty of sales knowledge and plenty of product knowledge but very little internal knowledge of our customers. Before long, we started testing one integrated sales force in Florida. That system proved successful, and we phased it into the rest of our operations.

As my campaign of change proceeded, some of my colleagues started trying to entice me back into the fold—back into what you might call the conspiracy of silence that caused problems for companies like Sears, GM, and IBM. "Hey, guy," they would say, "forget about all this 'New Era' stuff. Stop trying to push water uphill. Come on back into the fold, be our friend, all is forgiven, we'll be nice to you." Plus, "You don't want to do these crazy things. Why don't you just worry about AM/FM radios and air-conditioning in the sales reps' cars? *That's* what a sales vice-president is supposed to be doing."

Then, when it became clear that I was determined to stay out on the outer fringes of the circle, the message from these same colleagues turned a little less friendly: "We don't want you back in this comfort zone with us. You're a maverick, and there's no room here, no need here, for mavericks."

Question Authority. And If You Are *in* Authority, Authorize Questions—and Those Who Ask Them.

Let me emphasize one point: I am not advocating a manifesto to get people fired. What I *am* talking about is constructive criticism from within, a *healthy* spirit of dissatisfaction with the status quo. I repeat, *healthy*. The people who establish for themselves and for their organizations new and higher goals, and do their best to achieve them, are the ones I'm talking to. Their philosophy is that no matter how great today's accomplishments are, tomorrow's must be better. There's a big difference between being critical for the sake of being critical—simply pointing your finger and blaming others—and offering constructive criticism in an attempt to improve things. I make no brief for malcontents who bitch merely for the sake of bitching. Furthermore, when I call for people to "rock the boat," I'm talking not only to the employees but even more so to management. What I'm really doing is looking at the situation from the opposite end of the telescope. I'm asking management to value and cherish and encourage boat rockers, which, in turn, provides the conditions that boat rockers and visionaries—the people I refer to as poets and dreamers—need in order to flourish.

Management needs to understand that mavericks and change agents speak out and speak up because they have strong positive feelings, admiration, and, yes—love—for the institution. That's why I did. Change agents are the ones who genuinely care for the entity, believe there is a better way, and commit themselves to help find it. Those who take the position that to speak out is to speak ill must be reminded that the road to bankruptcy is paved with self-muzzled nonparticipants.

Above all, I am not advocating anarchy. To me, an anarchist within a business or any other organization is one who practically wears a dark coat, has a hat pulled down over his eyes, and carries a bomb. Anarchy is the absence of a hierarchy. I'm 100 percent solidly in favor of a hierarchy, one in which everyone knows who the boss is; I just want to be sure that the boss nurtures the boat rockers and allows them to help improve the organization.

In Search of Industrial Priests.

One of my first acts as vice-president was to issue what you might call *Pritchett's Manifesto*—my vision for P&G's sales division. One of my more hostile colleagues started calling that my "little red book" and referring to me as "Chairman Mao." Remember, now, that I do happen to be quite conservative politically, and you can imagine how absurd it would be for anyone to compare me to Mao Zedong.

To compound matters, there were those who accused me of trying to create a "cult of personality," especially after an ill-fated boat trip my salespeople and I took on the Ohio River. (It's interesting that at an ultraconservative company like mine, if someone wanted to really tar your name they used Commie-speak terms such as "little red book," "Chairman Mao," and "cult of personality," which was one of the charges lodged against Nikita Khrushchev and used to oust him from his post as ruler of the USSR back in the 1960s.)

"Boat trip?" you say. "Another boat trip?" Yes, indeed. In fact, this trip preceded the famous 1987 canoe outing with Sam Walton, and this time I managed, quite inadvertently, to *literally* rock the boat. What happened was that every three years the sales organization held a worldwide management meeting in Cincinnati. My first year as vice-president of sales (1985) coincided with that meeting, so I decided to charter one of those paddle wheelers that operate out of Cincinnati. Nothing like this had ever been done at Procter & Gamble before, and I wanted to set the stage from the moment the party began, alerting the sales force that a new era was being launched in sales. Business would no longer be done as it had been done in sales in the past, and I intended to outline my vision for sales when I gave the main address to several hundred sales managers who were present.

My plan was that we would go for a nice boat ride up to Coney Island, an amusement park on the river north of Cincinnati, where the banquet would be held. The boat trip takes about fifty minutes, and then we'd have our glorious dinner and ride the boat back home.

What I had not counted on was that two days before my Big Event, the biggest deluge in recent history would hit about 110 miles upstream, completely flooding the river downstream where we were. What was to have been a less-than-an-hour-long cocktail party on the boat turned into three hours of drinking on empty stomachs.

By the time we finally arrived at Coney Island, a number of my followers were in a party mood, all right. Some of them could barely stagger off the boat, and we had one hell of a dinner, highlighted by a couple hundred sales managers chanting, "Lou! Lou! Lou! Lou!" To add an exclamation point to the revelries, this event happened to coincide with my birthday, November 5, and on the way back to Cincinnati, my crew surprised me by setting off fireworks from the boat to celebrate. By then it was after midnight, and it's true that we woke up a number of people who lived along the river.

When word of the evening's festivities reached the executive suite back at headquarters, some executives, believe it or not, were not amused. And that's the true story of how I came to be accused of trying to establish my own "cult of personality" within Procter & Gamble.

I wasn't trying to create a personality cult. But I *was* attempting to show my colleagues that what we need—not just in the company I worked for but throughout the business world—are more of what I call "industrial priests." These are committed individuals who deeply believe that there is a better way, who are emotionally committed to finding that better way, and who are willing to stick their necks out and search for new paths and take those paths. If you have people like that, encourage them. If you don't have any—recruit some.

No Room for Heroes

Procter & Gamble is and always has been a conservative corporation. I made some of my fellow executives uncomfortable, but at least they tolerated me. Unfortunately, tolerating mavericks is still the exception, not the rule, in American business. And actually encouraging them—well, that's truly rare.

After the Coney Island incident, I was accused of trying to establish my own cult of personality, and some of my superiors lectured me that "Here at Procter & Gamble, we do not have heroes." What they seemed to forget is that from time to time, everyone needs heroes. Even in the executive suite at Procter & Gamble, they have portraits hanging there of William Cooper Procter, Harley Procter, Neil McElroy, and other company leaders. Every year someone gives a speech about the people who have gone before us and the great things they've done. I guess what they were really saying to me was, "We don't have any heroes before their time. We don't have any current heroes. You can only become a hero or a cult figure once you're exiled, retired, or dead."

Again, human beings *want* heroes; moreover, they *demand* heroes. You don't have to take courses in sociology or psychology to recognize that one of the things human beings need is leadership—that is, heroes—people who will set an example, people who make you say, "I want to be like her! I want to follow him!" How do you think baseball, football, politics, the military, would get along without heroes? Take your heroes away from your company or your culture and you take away the culture itself.

I have to admit that I met resistance from below as well as from above. As one of my associates during that period observed recently, "The P&G sales organization before Lou took over was like a bunch of people in prison banging their tin cups against the bars. And then Lou came along and unlocked the cell doors and said, 'Okay, you're free!' Some said, 'Uh-oh! If I'd known you were going to open the door, I wouldn't have pounded my cup on these bars. I kind of like it here in my cell. I get three square meals a day, I don't have too many demands on me. You mean I have to go out there and participate in this revolution? No thanks!' So when push came to shove, some of the people in that army Lou was leading weren't willing to come out of their cells. It wasn't that they were bad people; they were just typical victims of the system. They had been in their cells for so long they just didn't want to come out."

The Great Pretenders.

Some managers *pretend* to want mavericks in their companies, but they really don't. In practice, they treat change agents like a fighter who's getting the hell beaten out of him and then gets knocked out of the ring. They'll put alcohol on your cuts and fan your face, help revive you, and then push you back up into the ring so you can continue getting beaten up, but there's no support beyond that.

It has been my experience that most corporations are run as tight ships. Management expects everybody to be at the oars doing their job; there's no room for anybody simply strolling along the decks with his hands behind his back, gazing up at the stars. If you aren't doing a prescribed job, you're not working. If you're not doing what they think as work, you're useless overhead. If you're a prophet, you're creating problems, not solving them.

These companies don't understand that the organization of the future is going to have to value ideas and make room for the dreamers and poets and prophets. One reason corporations with rigid structures do not value prophets is because prophets generally are singing a song of doom about the corporation. And management doesn't want to hear that. As the song from *The Wiz* goes, "Don't nobody bring me no bad news." Most top executives don't want to hear the very words that they should be hearing.

While a close associate of mine was in his first few months on a new job with a large company, he saw some things that he thought maybe should be done differently. So he told management. The response was, "You answer the telephones and attend to your work and your customers. And we'll answer the questions and do the thinking." Needless to say, that certainly made an impression on him. Management's feeling was, if somebody bailed out, or got fired, "So what?" There were a hundred lined up to replace them. All this fellow was doing was trying to improve the company, but management had no interest in hearing him out.

A Welcome and Unexpected Source of "Boat Rockers"—New Employees Who Have Clean Slates.

My own philosophy of dealing with new employees is 180 degrees opposite that of the company this individual worked for. With new people you have a tremendous opportunity for diversity of personalities and perspectives. They're innocent in the ways of "The Organization." They say and do things that are natural and instinctive. There is no facade, no deception, no ass-covering or game playing. I used to say to new hires and people who had just been promoted to new jobs, "One of the most marvelous periods of your business career is going to be the next six to twelve months. The first six to twelve months you're on this job, the thing that you are going to enjoy most is a period of objectivity. You're carrying no baggage, you have a fresh perspective. So what I want you to do, before you become part of the problem, is to keep a diary. Observe everything you think we're doing right. Everything you think we're doing wrong. Everything you think needs to be improved. And let's discuss this periodically." And I've had many people tell me,

"Lou, you were right. After eight months or ten months or whatever, I had indeed become part of the problem."

A classic mistake is for companies to bring in new people with new ideas, with curiosity, with questioning minds, and immediately start the process of making them walk like, talk like, act like, behave like, dress like, perform like, think like everybody else in the organization. It's amazing! I visualize a tunnel. At one end of the tunnel you've got people coming out of college, dressed in T-shirts or sport jackets or uniforms or whatever. It's a mixture of all kinds of dress. Coming out the other end of that tunnel, everyone is wearing a hat, three-piece suit, and wing-tip shoes, and carrying a briefcase. One temptation any company anywhere in the world must try to avoid is taking the greatest strength it has, the human resource, and attempting to mold everyone into cookie-cutter shape and make all the employees be alike. We have got to be able to tolerate diversity and differences within the organization, beyond the cultural diversity. Diversity of the human spirit, if you will. I don't think we in corporate America do this now. We say, "Hey, we've got a formula for success. It has worked for us for umpteen years. It's going to continue to work. No mavericks allowed."

When you think, really think, about this it will start to make you crazy! Consider your own behavior. You go onto campus to recruit, or else your human resources department sends you a bright new person, and your immediate reaction—your challenge—is to transform this person into a "corporate robot." The corporate drill, and your own standard, is, how fast and how well can you shape this person into "one of us"?

If I were running a company today, before I hired someone I would say to them, "I want to tell you something. This is not a place where you're going to come in and put in your eight hours a day and go home and get your paycheck. I want you at least once a day to challenge something that I'm doing or that someone else in the organization is doing. You may be dead wrong, but I want you to bring us three good ideas a week, even if we discard all of them. Because sooner or later, you're going to knock one out of the park. Just like in baseball, if you give me ten and we only accept three, that's pretty darned good.

I want you to think about this business. And I'm not going to keep score, tally how many pitches you hit and how many times you miss. All I'm going to do is insist that you bring me new ideas and keep presenting them and keep challenging the system and challenging the basic assumptions. I want you to act as if you own the company, you manage it, you run it, you lead this organization with the same authority, the same ability, the same sense of dedication that I do. If all of us do that together, we'll haul in so much money we won't be able to count it."

The standard operating procedure of leaving all the thinking to management is nonsense. Of course, this is partially the result of corporate arrogance. But more often, it's due to what some postwar German apologists ascribed to "following orders." Most of us know that to hire bright people and then not capitalize on their free spirits is grossly wrong. But, then again, we're all victims of the ever-controlling internal reward/recognition system.

Throughout my career, recognizing that the best time for people to be objective is during their first six to ten months on the job, I challenged every new hire with whom I came in contact to question all the basic premises—before they, too, became "part of the problem."

If we do not or cannot fix this very basic flaw, we are destined to always do what we have always done, to make the same mistakes over and over and over, and to get the same results we've always gotten.

Homogenize Milk, Not People.

Back when I was growing up, before milk was systematically homogenized, the milk was delivered to our door with about four inches of cream on the top. You had to shake it up in order to homogenize it yourself. Of course, you can't even buy milk like that today, because machines homogenize it automatically. By the same token, most corporations today try to automatically homogenize all their people. And that's not good. We need to find a way to really allow individuals to be themselves.

I used to have customers tell me that they could spot Procter guys a mile away, just like IBM guys, by the way we dressed, the way we talked, the way we were. Because we were homogenized, we were expected to perform pretty much like everybody else on the scene. When you saw one of us, you saw all of us.

Now that I am retired and on my own, I finally have the opportunity to be myself. I never before had the freedom to just be Lou Pritchett. Now I am doing what I never had the luxury of doing when I was under the corporate umbrella, bound by all the rules and regulations and all the control mechanisms. Corporation management needs to figure out a way to allow employees to feel free, to be themselves, while they're *still working* for the company. I think miracles would happen. It's sad that people feel that they can be themselves only after they've left the company or when they're away from the job—in other words, only once they've broken the shackles of corporate control. Most people are not themselves while they're at work because of the demands of the corporate culture, the reward/recognition system, and the bias on the part of many bosses who have very rigid feelings about how people should behave. Oftentimes, as the corporate culture tells you not only how to behave but what to say and what not to say, it degenerates into almost total mind control. That's not the best way to run a corporation today, whether it be American or foreign. "Cultural diversity" has become a buzzword these days, but maybe what we really need is a trait I'll call "personality diversity." Most people will stick their necks out and try to be a maverick only once or twice during their careers. After they get their wrist slapped a couple of times for pushing the envelope or breaking the rules, they're not going to do it again. Their attitude is going to be, "Burn me once, shame on you; burn me twice, shame on me." The tragedy is that some of the best ideas will never be presented because people will keep those ideas to themselves for fear of breaking the rules and getting chopped down by the boss.

I wonder how many people understood for years what was wrong with the IBMs of the world, the General Motors of the world, the Sears of this world. I'd be willing to bet that hundreds, if not thousands, of employees at each of those companies knew they were headed for disaster, that they had taken their eyes off the customer and become more concerned internally than externally. But, given the regimen of the organization, given the rule that you weren't supposed to speak unless spoken to, no one spoke up.

When workers are allowed to be themselves and to enjoy themselves on the job, to act like they do at home, everyone benefits—the corporation most of all. There is absolutely no reason why American business cannot create a work culture in which employees come to work feeling just like San Francisco 49er fans do on a Sunday afternoon at Candlestick Park. I've often wondered why a sports competition like football or baseball or even the Olympics usually seems to bring out the best in both the participants and the spectators, while so many companies bring out the worst in their people.

How do we go about creating corporations where human beings can be themselves and enjoy themselves on the job? I think the answer is corporate leadership. I think the person at the top has to recognize that by not allowing freedom, he or she is not drawing a full 100 percent from each employee. CEOs don't establish a rigid control structure out of malice or anything; it's just part of a very ancient, very outdated organizational structure that's been in place for too long. CEOs need to give every employee, from the one who sweeps up the shop to the CEO himself, the freedom to be themselves, to bring to every single job the real individual.

Conforming Versus Performing

What it all comes down to is that in the future it isn't going to be the big eating the little, it's going to be the fast eating the slow. And those organizations that are fast are the ones that will value and cherish and even turn themselves over to, and be led by, the poets and the dreamers, the boat rockers and the mavericks.

The world is changing. It's not changing by itself, it's being changed by people. So why can't you or I help change it, help capitalize on those changes? We can! Practically every human being is qualified to change things. It's not as if there are just some magical 8.65 percent who are qualified to do this. Almost everybody, to varying degrees, is qualified. But there are a lot of tight-ass, control-oriented organizations that don't allow it.

Those organizations that do allow it, they are the ones that will go to glory.

I hate to sound like a preacher, but for a moment I need to maybe do a little pontificating. I want to point out that everything begins with our educational system. That's where kids are first taught to play the game a certain way, and that if they do, they'll move from point to point and class to class and probably do well on the achievement tests. The trouble is that our schools—that is, most of our teachers—don't teach the kids to think or to problem-solve. But go to kids and ask them who their favorite teacher is and it's always the one who's outside the box, the one who made biology or chemistry or English come to life in a unique way. And in college, professors are rewarded with tenure, without anyone asking, "What does the business world want the universities to be producing? What's their need? And, two, what's the need of the student who has to learn skills that will enable him to get a good job after he earns his degree?" But academia, too, has a recognition and reward system that to a large extent ignores these issues.

In sum, all organizations need both conformists and nonconformists. People must change from a mind-set of *con*formance to *per*formance. I've seen many companies that were conformance driven, where everyone was expected to behave the company way. Without a doubt, that was a very successful formula that was appropriate at one time.

As I've gotten older, however, I've come to see that there is a place for both conformance and nonconformance or rebels and mavericks—poets and dreamers. To me, the corporations that will make out the best in the future are those with a balance between conformists and nonconformists. These companies will have the ability, the skills, the foresight, the wisdom, to know on which issues there should be conformance and on which issues the opinions of rebels should be solicited. There should always be a small cadre of poets and dreamers in order to keep the CEO and the rest of senior management in line. What companies need to do with poets and dreamers is find an office, lock them in, let them dream or write poems or sing their songs. For every ten poems they write, maybe only one will be worth a damn. But I'll guarantee you, that will be one that will really advance the organization's cause.

Managers must be on guard against closing their minds and saying, "Hey, there's only one way to do something, to perform a particular act, whether it's your way or not." They need to always be aware that there is a better way, and to try to find it. This cannot be done by surrounding themselves with yes-men but by keeping their minds open to suggestions and being able to weigh all the different points of view.

One final word: What I am saying may sound contradictory or illogical when we look at our foremost rivals for world business leadership, the Japanese. The Japanese discourage nonconformity; their saying is, "The nail that stands up must be hammered down." And yet they are immensely successful. It all goes back to cultural differences, to "romancing the culture." To be successful when you're in Greece, you must be a Greek; when you're in France, you must be French; and when you're in Japan, you must be a Japanese and do things the way the Japanese do.

The Japanese philosophy is that the individual wins only when the team wins. That is a cultural bias of theirs that probably won't work here. The Japanese system of conformity works well because, culturally, the homogeneous Japanese people are inherently conformists. I'm sure there are and have been many nonconformists, even in Japan. Mr. Toyoda, the man who founded Toyota, had to have been a visionary. Nonconformists simply aren't as prevalent in Japan because, again, it's a different culture. And my message is intended primarily for America and Americans.

In the words of San Francisco's grand old longshoreman-philosopher Eric Hoffer: "In this time of dramatic change, it's the *learners* who will inherit the future. The *learned* will find themselves equipped to live in a world that no longer exists."

My take is that we must unlearn as well as learn! We must *non*conform as well as conform! We must be shapers of what might be instead of servants of what already is! We, or at least some of us, must stop paddling and start rocking the boat!

11
Into the Twenty-first Century

"If we are to achieve results never before accomplished, we must expect to employ methods never before attempted."
—Francis Bacon

That four-hundred-year-old bit of timeless wisdom from Francis Bacon, the English philosopher, still applies today. For instance, progress means devising an entirely new concept rather than tinkering with an existing system or product. Thomas Edison did not invent the light bulb by tinkering with the candle. Nor did the Wright brothers get their airplane off the ground that day in Kitty Hawk by trying to figure out how to make trains go faster.

And speaking of making trains go faster, look at the Japanese bullet train. If you want to increase the speed by 10 percent, you start working on the engines and the horsepower. But if you want to double the speed of the train, what you do is throw away the design of the train as it has existed, assemble a group of talented people, and start over with a clean sheet of paper. You have to forget the current version and totally redesign and reinvent in order to make a quantum leap into the future. That's the approach the Japanese took when they designed the bullet train.

Earlier, I touched on how the ATM—dispensing money from an unattended vending machine—is a revolutionary new idea. But there's a corollary of ATMs and EFTs (electronic fund transfers): Banks won't need as many brick-and-mortar branches. So, if you're running a bank, you'll have to factor that into your planning—you won't be building as many branch offices as you did in the past. And if you fail to make this adjustment to new circumstances, you'll be saddling your bank with satellite offices you don't need and wasting money.

Right now, IBM is developing a radical new way of selling computer software that should be both popular and cost-efficient. Traditionally—and traditionally means for just the past few years, because that's how fast technology is changing in the computer industry—we've walked into a store and purchased our software on floppy disks wrapped in preprinted boxes. But IBM, working with Hughes Network Systems, plans to put kiosks in shopping centers and retail stores where customers can try out computer games and other programs. A customer who wants to buy the product will press a couple of buttons, and the program will be delivered to the kiosk via satellite, encoded on a disk and handed to the consumer.

The lesson of this for companies is: Those that will succeed in the rest of the 1990s and into the twenty-first century are the ones that use their poets and dreamers, their boat rockers, to provide them with new ideas. You can't reenergize an obsolete business, like manufacturing adding machines. But you can *convert* an obsolete business into something worthwhile and energize your employees at the same time. Instead of producing manual typewriters, you can start manufacturing personal computers. No demand for those beautiful old polished brass cash registers? Then start producing computerized ones. They may not look as nice, but they're functional.

Just remember: In the twenty-first century, the source of corporate strength will be change—not stability. As the Greek philosopher Heraclitus observed in the sixth century B.C., the only thing that's permanent is change itself. Some twenty-five hundred years later, that's still true!

Not willing to make a quantum change? You're history, baby. Reinventing yourself, redesigning your organizational structure, that's what must be done immediately if you are to succeed in the future. Doing these things now is essential, before it's too late. Doing nothing, standing pat, is asking to have history pass you by. You're not going to have a future otherwise. My concern is that a lot of managers are saying, "I know a lot of things are happening around me. But I'll get to it when I get to it." Which will be too late.

They're *People*, Not a Pile of Human Capital.

We all agree that a sports team is no better than the people who make it up. Why, then, do we think a company or a business enterprise is any different?

Until management understands and embraces the concept that the ultimate success of the enterprise depends upon skilled and committed people working together in a positive and enlightened environment, management will continue to obtain mediocre results. By the year 2000, raw materials and technology will be available to most companies in most countries around the world. Therefore, all that will separate the winners from the losers will be the quality, the training, the commitment, and the dedication of the workforce. The major corporate players in the next century will be those that understand that the individual, not the corporation, will be the source of competitive advantage. Those successful corporate leaders will make sure that the individual is appropriately cared for and that the individual and the corporate mission are properly in tune.

Stop Focusing Entirely on the Bottom Line Before You Hit Rock Bottom.

NEWS ITEM: New York, NY (December 1, 1994)—Best Buy Company, a Minneapolis-based retailer, today disclosed that its earnings for the third quarter of 1994 will rise more than 50 percent per share from the same period a year ago and that same-store sales had climbed by a dramatic 17 percent this November over November of 1993. However, since "Wall Street analysts" had expected an even larger increase in earnings, the stock *lost 28 percent of its value today*, dropping from $45.25 to $32.50 per share. Investors stampeded to sell, and the company's volume on the New York Stock Exchange was more than twenty times its normal level. There was a simple explanation, according to one "expert": "If you don't hit [Wall] Street expectations, the stocks plummet," said John Hughes, an analyst with Piper Jaffray in Minneapolis.

NEWS ITEM: New York, NY (December 28, 1994)—Stock in Toys "Я" Us lost 9 percent of its value today, dropping $3 a share, from $33 ⅛ to $30 ⅛. With 4.6 million shares traded, Toys "Я" Us was the second most active stock on the New York Stock Exchange.

What had happened to Toys "Я" Us? Had a natural catastrophe destroyed 9 percent of its stores? No. Had the company lost money investing in derivatives? No. Had it reported lower earnings? No.

What had happened, what caused Toys "Я" Us stock to fall 9 percent in one day, was that "Wertheim Schroder analyst Robert Schweich trimmed his 1994 earnings estimate by 10 cents a share." In other words, Toys "Я" Us didn't do anything notable, good or bad, on December 28, 1994. The stock would have fallen 9 percent even if all of the toy company's executives had decided to call in sick that day.

According to reports out of New York, "Toys "Я" Us declined comment." But I, Lou Pritchett, will not decline comment: "Way to go, Robert Schweich—whoever you are."

NEWS ITEM: New York, NY (January 3, 1995)—Chemical Banking Corporation revealed today that a foreign currency trader's bad bets on the Mexican peso resulted in a $70 million pretax loss in the fourth quarter.

An analyst at Salomon Brothers Inc., Diane Glossman, declared, "We believe that such announcements serve to diminish the credibility of management discussions about procedures and control with regard to their risk-management-trading businesses."

Sounds like terrible news, doesn't it? Chemical Bank lost $70 million in currency speculation, and a stock expert said the situation would "diminish the credibility of management."

Maybe that's why stock in Chemical Bank went *up* 37 ½ cents that day, to $36.25 a share!! Investors were reported to have "shrugged off the bad news."

Okay, I'm not John Maynard Keynes or Adam Smith. So please explain to me why this news would cause Chemical Bank's stock to *rise*. Better yet, show me why *any* company should pay attention to Wall Street and what the Street's "analysts" have to say.

NEWS ITEM: New York, NY (January 23, 1995)—IBM's profits in the fourth quarter of 1994 more than tripled over the same period in 1993, from $362 million to $1.2 billion. In fact, Big Blue's quarterly earnings, equal to $2.06 a share, far surpassed the $1.40 to $1.93 per share that "industry experts" had expected.

Nevertheless, the company's stock closed *down* $1.125, at $74.25, on the New York Stock Exchange.

What accounts for that? Well, this is a good one. This time, in spite of all the good news about IBM, the "analysts" were concerned that sales of personal computers *might* (I emphasize "might") be weak in the future!

NEWS ITEM: New York, NY (January 25, 1995)—Stock in the Compaq Computer Corporation lost 12 percent of its value today, dropping $5 a share from $42.38 to $37.38, and Compaq was the most active stock on the New York Stock Exchange, with nearly 20 million shares traded.

The action came exactly two days after industry reports showed that Houston-based Compaq sold more personal computers than any other company in the world during 1994. Compaq shipped 4.8 million PCs in 1994, up 53 percent from 1993, and Compaq now has 10.3 percent of the global market. IBM ranked second in 1994, followed by Apple. Moreover, Compaq also announced on January 25 that its 1994 fourth-quarter profits surged 61 percent, to $243 million, and that during all of 1994 it earned $867 million, twice its 1993 earnings.

In spite of all the good news, Compaq's situation "fell short of Wall Street's expectations." Becoming number one and having its profits skyrocket did not satisfy "the analysts"! "The experts'" unfavorable impression of Compaq's news also caused a drop in the stock value of other computer makers, including IBM, Hewlett-Packard, and Dell.

NEWS ITEM: New York, NY (February 1, 1995)—Ford *dropped* 12½ cents a share, to $25⅛, and Ford was the second most heavily traded stock on the New York Stock Exchange (nearly 10 million shares changed hands)—today, the *same day* the company announced that soaring sales of cars and trucks helped it more than double its 1994 earnings, to a record $5.31 billion, up from $2.5 billion in 1993. Profits for the fourth quarter of 1994 also more than doubled, to $1.57 billion, up from $719 million during the last quarter of 1993.

NEWS ITEM: New York, NY (February 7, 1995)—Sears Roebuck reported its best retail performance in a decade, along with profits of $685 million in the fourth quarter of 1994, up 26 percent from 1993. Wall Street didn't seem impressed; on the New York Stock Exchange, Sears was the sixth most heavily traded stock, with the value of a share *dropping* 37½ cents to $45.75 a share.

Many times, it seems, the stock market moves regardless of—if not contrary to—what a corporation is actually doing. This being the case, why do CEOs give a damn what the Street thinks? The sad truth is that most CEOs do care, but they shouldn't. We American businessmen are hamstrung by having Wall Street looking over our shoulders all the time and constantly checking the numbers, the bottom line. So nobody wants to be vulnerable; everybody wants to keep those numbers looking good. The system in which we operate forces us to make most of our decisions short term. That's why I'm grateful that I had the wonderful advantage in the Philippines, or I seized the advantage, of doing something that a CEO in the States could not do—ignoring the bottom line for a while.

Too many stock market insiders simply don't know what they're doing. Successful CEOs won't place so much emphasis on them in the future. Instead, twenty-first-century CEOs should, and will, I hope, worry about the market less and tend to their own businesses, without paying so much attention to what Wall Street thinks.

No Matter What Else You Do, Make Sure You Don't Throw Your Company to the Wolves.

For the record, *Webster's* defines a market as "the area of economic activity in which buyers and sellers come together and the forces of supply and demand affect prices."

But one of my mentors and former bosses at Procter & Gamble, A. M. Wood, describes the present situation succinctly: "There is no market today. The hustlers and the pseudoexperts, with their computers, have destroyed it." Quite an astute observation, especially from someone who will soon turn one hundred! Sadly, we've become a scorecard economy, and the only measure that counts is the bottom line.

Today, with program buying and selling schemes, all made possible by computer technology, what was once a market has turned into the world's most sophisticated gaming arena. Where there is prey, there are wolves, and the wolves are now running the stock market. The wolves know a good thing when they see it. And one of the good things the wolves see is "volatility." Translated by the wolves, volatility means making money on both the upward and downward moves of the so-called market.

Unfortunately, the wolves have changed the market from being supply and demand driven to perception driven. That is, the market moves today more on perception than on reality. So the pseudoexperts do their trading based on differing perceptions of reality, but always based on short-term perceptions of reality. That leaves corporate managers at the mercy of the wolves; the captains of industry can respond only by attempting to manage by expectation instead of by doing what's best for their companies. And when results fall short of expectations, the price of their stock tumbles. It's chilling to think that America's corporations are for all intents and purposes being run by the type of high rollers you would expect to find in Las Vegas or Atlantic City or the off-track betting parlor.

The net effect is that in the stock market wars, one wolf with a computer and a big mouth is equal to two airborne divisions on the battlefield. Maybe I should have been a wolf. Then I'd be really, really rich. But being a wolf is not my style.

Nevertheless, corporate managers who know better continue to throw money at problems, trying to make things look good short term. They continue to do things that they know full well they will either have to undo or explain away or pay off, long term.

There's an old proverb, "Man can only serve one master." Trying to serve half a dozen masters is a big mistake. All these external circumstances can make bad managers or mediocre managers. The pressure of external forces, if you will, causes every captain of industry to do things that shouldn't be done. One of the biggest downsides to this is the costs that are added into the system. You take short-term corrective or short-term reactive steps in order to avoid getting bad reports that could devalue your stock, affect your public image, and permanently damage you. But what you're really doing is increasing your cost of doing business, in most cases. And that's a tragedy, that's one of the real problems American business faces.

Lou Pritchett's Rx for American Business.

The answer, as I say, is for business not to be so driven by the immediate pressures from Wall Street. But who is going to buy into that when we've got a two-hundred-year-old system that drives us? Who's going to convince the stockholders and the boards of directors that "we aren't going to worry about Wall Street anymore"? I hope *you* will be the one to do that, my friend.

This much I can tell you: If I started my own business, the last thing I would ever do is take it public and bring the "Wall Street analysts" into the picture. That's the great advantage of being a private business. My experience has been that the owners of privately held companies are much less fearful of creativity. They know that no matter what new methods are put into effect, they're still going to have a job; they aren't going to fire themselves. Look at some of the big privately held companies and how they operate, such as Hallmark. You can see that creativity and outrageous thinking *is* Hallmark. And it's permissible there, because Don Hall is not going to fire himself. But the more you get into a business-as-usual situation, with a board of directors and management that has a fairly high rate of turnover, the more you see creativity stifled.

The privately held companies I deal with, like Rock-Tenn, which recycles paper, and Lykes, the Florida-based orange juice producer, seem to do more things right because they don't have to worry about the immediate bottom line. Not long ago, I was doing some private consulting work for the CEO of a private company, and he said to me, "We make decisions that are right for this company. We do not make decisions to appease stockholders, to appease board members, or to appease Wall Street." And his company is very successful. Of course, some of the largest American businesses, such as the Mars Candy operation, are privately held and don't have to answer to anyone else.

If I did find myself running a public company, I'll tell you how I'd fix the Wall Street problem. I'd spend most of my time cultivating the stock market experts and analysts—and I'd paint the bleakest possible picture of my company and its prospects that I legally could under SEC regulations. That way, no matter how bad my earnings turned out each quarter, they would exceed the experts' expectations, and the price of my stock would rise. Why bother spending your time trying to manufacture a good product when you can make money so much more easily this way? It's the same as Lou Holtz always poormouthing his football team. If Holtz were playing the Little Sisters of the Poor, he could make a convincing argument that Notre Dame didn't stand a chance.

A few investors do take the long-term view, but the majority of the high rollers insist, "Hey, we want the stock to increase 10 or 15 percent a year, so make the stock look good, make sure the earnings go up." But if you look at it from a practical standpoint, *nothing* can go up forever. The risk of this attitude, that every year you have to show the same growth percentage or better, is that you're not simply asking for trouble; you're virtually assuring it.

"Smart Technology"—an Oxymoron?

Computers and the rest of the new technology are said to be intelligent; we talk about "smart offices" and "smart homes" and the like. In fact, computers are simply dumb machines. They're only as smart as the human beings who operate them.

All this new data that is becoming available won't mean anything unless you know what to do with it. All the computer does is give you the information at light speed. But if you don't know how to use it, so what? In fact, in many instances, the new information technology is falsely touted as a saving. If you don't know how to use all this information to make better decisions, all the new gizmos become an increased cost. You may wind up with more information than you know what to do with, or too many bells and whistles for your own good.

Not long ago, my wife and I were planning a trip to South America, using a travel agency that specializes in the kind of tours that interest us. This company has one of those new telephone systems where if you want to talk about Asia, you push 1; if you want to talk about South America, you press 2, and so forth. For three days we kept trying to get through to someone who could talk to us about the area we wanted to visit. We'd get one tape and then another tape and then finally we'd get a human being who'd say, "I'm not in charge of that, someone else is." So you'd call the other person and their tape would say they're out to lunch.

Compare and contrast this nonpersonalized approach with that of the A. G. A. Correa Company of Wiscasset, Maine. Correa, which manufactures nautical jewelry, has made a point of providing the best service to its customers by *not* allowing the newfangled cyberphone systems to mess things up. "No operators standing by twenty-four hours a day and no voice mail," the Correa firm informs its callers. "Enormous effort is taken to provide unsurpassed telephone service; with this in mind, twenty-four-hour service is not available. Telephone hours are limited to our office hours, Monday–Friday, 9:00 A.M.–5:00 P.M. Thank you."

This is something that every organization will have to focus on in the new information age: making sure that the information you're getting and the technology you're using is a plus for your company, not a minus. Because it isn't technology that will give you a competitive advantage; it's the *use* of technology to allow you to find ways to do the "undoable."

Don't Be a Mainframe Thinker in a Personal Computer World.

We talked earlier about New Coke. What I'm saying is that progress just for the sake of progress isn't a plus. The progress has to actually improve you and your company and your products.

Not long ago, a friend of mine was asking me why companies like Procter & Gamble are constantly tinkering with his favorite products, like Crest and Prell, and putting "new improved formulas" on the market. He insisted that he'd prefer it if P&G just left everything alone and sold him the same products he was used to, probably the ones he has been buying for a hundred years, knowing this fellow.

He had a point, but what he overlooked was that product loyalty is nothing more than the absence of a better product. That's why companies keep trying to improve their products. If you stick with the same formula, you'll get passed by. In marketing, there is no status quo. Things are constantly changing, and if you don't change and keep up with the times, you'll be left behind. If you did a washload with the Tide that existed in 1953, when I joined the company, and a washload with today's Tide, you'd be absolutely amazed at the difference.

The shampoo that my friend used ten years ago didn't have hair conditioner in it. You don't want something that cleans your hair and does nothing else; you want nice-looking, shiny, soft, easy-to-manage hair. And that's what these improvements have made possible over the years. It's like an automobile. You wouldn't go into an automobile showroom today and buy 1926 technology, would you? Of course not!

Along the same lines, my best friend, Dr. A. C. Rolen, collects antique golf clubs down in Bristol, Tennessee. He'll go out and hit a ball with a club that dates back to the beginning of the century, and then hit the same ball with one of the new, state-of-the-art Ping clubs. Invariably, the new club drives the ball about twice as far as the old one. What is true with golf clubs is also the rule with business tools and business strategies: You can't use outmoded equipment or methods. They just don't work anymore.

To stay in business, continual improvement and continually making adjustments to the new realities are imperative. Anybody that says, "Hey, we've reached it!"—they're dead. In 1975, in a memo to W. E. Forbis, who was then my boss, I wrote, "We are still a young company with the curiosity to experiment." Yes, Procter & Gamble was a young company in 1975—a young company then 138 years old! Your company had better be young, no matter how long it has been in business.

"New" and "Improved" Is the Wave of the Future—as Long as It Truly Is an Improvement over the Past.

One of the current buzzwords for "new" and "improved" is the widely feared and loathed "downsizing"—a euphemism for companies and organizations reducing the number of workers they employ in a sometimes misguided attempt to cut costs. Without getting into a lengthy discussion of downsizing, which has been analyzed to death elsewhere, let me just offer a few thoughts.

During much of the nineteenth century, American farming was labor-intensive. Then along came mechanization, and the farm universe changed overnight. Tractors, bailers, reapers, combines, and the cotton gin could do work that once required hundreds of laborers and animals. All of which dramatically lowered the cost of farming and resulted in comparable increases in productivity.

A few years later, early in the twentieth century, the assembly line streamlined the manufacturing process. That, again, meant that fewer people were needed to do a particular job, and increased productivity. Now, in the late twentieth century, it's déjà vu all over again. With telephones, televisions, computers, and faxes all hooked up into a single network, the resulting information technology has irreversibly altered the workplace and reduced the number of human beings required to do most jobs at the same time it has raised productivity.

This phenomenon will almost certainly continue at an ever-increasing pace, as the microchip becomes the great enabler, allowing every advancement to be greater than the previous one. The power of information will beget even more power of information. As evidenced in the last century and at the beginning of the current one, technological breakthroughs always dislocate the status quo and create short-term shock waves throughout society. This in turn causes pain and suffering for many workers at the same time it moves humankind to a higher plane.

Unfortunately, much of the recent corporate downsizing has not been so much a result of technology as it has been a case of

CEOs' succumbing to the siren call of Wall Street and chopping the workforce—without chopping the work to be done. Corporate managers who take this helter-skelter approach will reap the whirlwind; they don't realize that their old industrial-era organization cannot compete in the new information age. In desperation, these managers tinker with the old in hopes of making the system operate properly. But short-term profit blips caused by the reduction of labor costs are by definition short term, and will not sustain organizations over the long term. The genius of management will be knowing what to do with what's left.

I'm all for streamlining the organization, as long as doing so truly helps drive costs out of the system. When you're living by your wits with a skinny little organization, it brings out the best in you and your people. But downsizing simply for the sake of downsizing—I'm adamantly opposed to that.

One of my underlying messages, if not my most important theme, is that everything we do must be grounded in common sense. If your employees are already giving you their all and you weed some of them out without reducing the workload for the people you retain, all you're doing is implementing a magic formula for failure.

It's a Small, Small, Small World—and Growing Smaller Every Day.

The world is a small place, and, thanks to technology, it's getting smaller by the month, the week, the day—even by the minute. So if you hope for success from now on and into the twenty-first century and beyond, you had better prepare yourself to deal with the rest of the world. Ugly Americans will be less and less and less in demand. In fact, the successful American CEO of the future will almost be required to have had some overseas experience and to be fluent in at least one foreign language, and preferably more.

During my four years in the Philippines, I gained a wealth of knowledge about dealing with strangers in strange lands. I hope that experiences like mine in the Philippines will become the norm rather than the exception for American business leaders.

Place the Emphasis on the "Us" Instead of the "Me."

In Japan—and, for that matter, throughout the Far East—the emphasis is on the total organization instead of on the individual, the way it is here. You don't hear people advocating "Looking Out for Number One" over there. In Japan and the rest of the East, the individual wins only when the team wins. We need to try to instill that attitude here. It's like an orchestra—if the members play together like a team, they make music. But if they play as eighty individuals, they just make noise.

This distinction was brought home to me firsthand several years ago when I gave a speech in southern Japan. I was using a translator, and I declared that the ten most important two-letter words are:

"If it is to be, it is up to me."

But what the translator told my audience was:

"If it is to be, it is up to *us.*"

What a marvelous mistake! I thought to myself. Right there, you have the entire contrast between Japanese culture and American culture summed up, simply by changing the word "me" to "us."

From what I have observed, most of the differences between the countries of Asia and the United States stem largely from two related characteristics that are common over there but lacking here: respect and discipline.

Yes, the Japanese truly respect one other. They respect their elders, they respect their fellows, they respect those younger than them or below them in the corporate hierarchy or in society. While here, we seem to respect no one.

I'm amazed by the amount of meanness and inhumanity in the world today—guys blowing up a federal building in Oklahoma. I think it's because there's so much frustration in our society. In our schools and homes we have gotten away from teaching respect for each other, that we are all alike, that we are all in this together. I happen to believe that the average, typical human being is basically a good person. I think that runs through everybody's veins. But I think a lot of people need to be left alone to do things for themselves. Also, I have found that people always perform better for themselves than they do when someone else is doing all their thinking for them and trying to solve their problems. Again, it's a case of freedom, empowerment, trust.

The second crucial difference between our culture and Japan's is that the Japanese are disciplined. This is not a discipline that's imposed from above—theirs is not an authoritarian society; it's a self-discipline, something that's definitely lacking in America today.

Of course, American people and society are much less disciplined in general, and life is much less structured today than it used to be. I doubt if the immortal Vince Lombardi would be a successful football coach today, unless he was able to adapt to the new conditions. One of his players made a statement to the effect that "Lombardi treats us all the same. Like dogs." But that was nearly thirty years ago. Imagine how out of place Lombardi and his system would be today! First of all, Lombardi himself would go crazy if he saw all these guys wearing earrings and celebrating each touchdown, each interception—hell, each tackle—as if they had just won the Super Bowl. (Silly me; I thought they were *paid* to score touchdowns, make interceptions, and tackle the guy with the ball. That's what they're supposed to be doing, yet they go through this big routine each time they do what they get paid to do. In my business, we don't start dancing and pointing and talking trash every time we sell a case of Tide; that's what we get paid to do.) And, second, today's players would rebel if Lombardi or any other coach tried to treat them "like dogs."

Why do these traits permeate Japanese society? As opposed to the situation here in the United States, in Japan these qualities are instilled by parents at home and by teachers at school. In Japan, as in most other Asian nations, the schools do a much better job of preparing their students to play a productive role in the workplace than ours do (in no small part because of the discipline throughout their society). We've all heard about the disparity in test scores, skill levels, and overall learning between American and Japanese students. Recently, I read a newspaper article that really captured the problems in American education. The story reported that although high-tech equipment can

quickly determine what's wrong with an automobile, U.S. automobile industry executives are having trouble finding qualified
mechanics to operate these new machines. "We've got a problem here, because the education system in this country is not
turning out people for the jobs of the future," commented the
CEO of GM, John F. Smith Jr. Smith went on to declare that
skilled technicians are in such short supply that American car
dealerships spend as much time and money stealing capable
mechanics from one another as they do training these people to
repair cars and trucks. If Smith's observations don't make us sit
up and take notice, I don't know what will.

I don't think we spend enough time—I know we don't in
corporate America—teaching the human and emotional side of
business. Up until about ten years ago there was no room in
corporate America for intuition. The practice was, and everybody was being taught, that all we dealt with was facts and hard
numbers. I think what we're going to find out in this new age is
that intuition, enthusiasm, the people part of the equation—all
of those are absolutely essential. And we're going to have to
redesign training programs to help people learn these lessons.
Part of it is the power of emotion—that is, the importance of
enthusiasm and how to instill enthusiasm. You've got to be
trained how to do that genuinely, not falsely.

What I propose is a twofold approach:

First, begin by going with the flow. As a result of major
social, educational, political and economic changes over the last
quarter century or so, the young people joining companies
today have different attitudes than the ones we used to hire.
Members of the generation that did not personally experience
the depression have been instilled with different values and a
different work ethic, different ideas of what they want out of
life. People in their thirties and forties can't even begin to com-
prehend how dedicated their predecessors were. So they're
playing by a whole new set of rules. Workers my age would say,
"Give me all the overtime you can. I'll work twenty-eight
hours a day." But the younger generation has a new attitude
and a new lifestyle, where freedom and leisure are so much
more important.

Moreover, episodes like the Vietnam War, Watergate, and

Iran-contra have eroded the younger generation's confidence in and respect for their leaders. Therefore, the most productive companies of the new era may be the ones that are able to capitalize on this irreversible trend in society by creating a less structured, top-down atmosphere. In those companies, employees will be happier and more productive. It's the whole idea of abolishing the pyramid structure—less organization, less control, more freedom for your employees.

Second, once you gain the confidence of your employees, that's when you might consider trying to impose some discipline. I think most people actually prefer discipline, prefer a structure, but no one imposes one on them anymore. In my opinion, that's one of the things that's wrong with American kids today— nobody disciplines them. Their parents and teachers throw up their hands and say, "Oh, well, they're incorrigible." Which isn't necessarily true. I think people demand discipline, and if you provide it to them, many of them will be grateful for it. Nature demands order; I think human beings demand order, too. When it's not there, that's when you start filling up the damn jails.

In spite of all that's happened in our society, human beings haven't changed all that much. I think a lot of things are changing around us, including the corporate structure—it must change; it should change. But, speaking as an experienced amateur archaeologist, I think that human beings have been basically the way they are now for at least ten thousand years, maybe longer. And I don't think there's going to be any great change in human nature in the foreseeable future, either.

I think people are still affected by some of the most basic things: The need to earn a living. The need to feel worthwhile while they're earning that living. The need to be treated well and respected. It really isn't all that complicated.

One Hundred Contests, One Hundred Successes.

Human beings require at least a flicker of hope. They have to have a candle burning somewhere, something to make them think that things are going to be better tomorrow than they are today. It's the job of the leader to give them that hope, and, in doing so, to help unleash the talent of each individual worker for the good of the employee and the enterprise as a whole. Increasing the productivity of the American worker is a task not for government but for private industry, and, ultimately, for the leader of each corporation.

It's also the job of the leader to recognize and admit that running a large company these days is too complicated a task for one person to be able to do it all. The new information age will require the decentralization of power. The older I get, the more I find myself, to the amazement of this conservative old rogue, quoting the icons and the words of the protesters and disrupters from America's fairly recent past. But the fact is that the decentralization of command means "Power to the people." Moreover, in the words of Bob Dylan, "The times, they are a-changing." And all of us must adapt.

In every corporate environment there is conflict. Conflict between doing what has always been done versus doing things differently. As we rush toward the twenty-first century, corporations must totally reinvent themselves and for most it will be painful and threatening. The rewards, however, for those who see the need to change and actually do it will be glorious indeed, for they will be positioned to play the new game on a very level playing field. Corporations are going to have to undergo a total metamorphosis. The transformation from caterpillar into butterfly will be painful for some. But the ones that are most receptive to change and understand the most about themselves and all the components of the world around them will enjoy the most success in this new era.

As the famous Chinese military leader Sun Tzu wrote in fourth century B.C. in one of my favorite books, *The Art of War,* "Know thyself. Know thy enemy. One hundred battles, one hundred victories."

I have appropriated Sun Tzu's message for today and the future: "Know thyself and thy competitors. Know thy customer and thy supplier and thy employee.

"One hundred contests, one hundred successes!"

Lou Pritchett's Twelve Questions for All Organizations.

In every speech I give, I wind up with the following twelve questions about organizations and their willingness and ability to adapt to the future. Usually, most members of my audience ask me for a copy of these questions. Until now, I haven't had them available in printed form, but here they are:

1. Is your current organizational structure designed to link with that of your customers at each key functional point?

2. Do your current information systems link seamlessly with those of your customers?

3. Are your products and services designed for better sameness, or for meaningful differences?

4. Is your company product focused or customer focused?

5. What do you want to do for your customers in three years that you cannot do for them today?

6. Are you viewing your human resources as costs to be reduced wherever and whenever possible, or as assets that require maintenance and investment?

7. Has success made you or your organization intolerant of opposing points of view, where criticism is resented and dissenters are isolated?

8. Does your organization's reward/recognition program encourage or discourage cross-functional teamwork and customer-supplier partnerships?

9. How badly would your business be affected if your key customer formed a partnership tomorrow with your key competitor?

10. When are you going to stop competing head-to-head with your rivals by doing what they do, and instead invent an entirely new game, leaving them to spend their time, energy, and money perfecting a game you and your major customers no longer play?

11. In your haste to fix, have you ever learned how to build?

12. Are you personally prepared to assume the role of *change agent* within your organization?

12
One Final Word

Live Every Day As If It's Your Last.

One final word, and, hey—this certainly is not original with me. In fact, over two thousand years ago, the Roman poet Horace wrote, "*Carpe diem! Quam minimum credula postero.*" Which means, "Seize the day! Trust as little as possible to the future." Or, in the words of the seventeenth-century English poet Robert Herrick, "Gather ye rose-buds while ye may, Old Time is still a-flying."

The point is, you really never *do* know which day might be your last. I remember the time in 1992 that Barbara and I were pursuing our interest in Mayan culture and archaeology in southern Mexico. After a stop at the Mayan archaeological site of Palenque, we drove over the mountains to the beautiful city of San Cristóbol de las Casas. We spent two days there and then headed for Mérida, where we would catch our flight home. There was a long and lonely road ahead of us to travel to Mérida, so I decided to gas up in a small village that had one large, clean service station attended by three young Mexicans.

I stopped in front of the correct pump and asked for a fill-up in my broken Spanish. Tremendously amused by my gringo Spanish, the young man working the pump held the gas-pump handle and waited for me to unlock the gasoline cap on our rental car. I removed the cap and went to stand directly behind the car, about three feet away from this young man. Suddenly, the hose discharged directly into his face, blinding him.

Shocked by the unexpected blast of gasoline and unable to see, he swung the hose wildly. The one-inch spray of gasoline hit me squarely under my chin. I quickly found myself covered from neck to shoes with about four liters of gasoline. In approximately five seconds I was thoroughly soaked and emitting a wavy cloud of gas fumes. Had anyone been smoking within a hundred feet, I would have gone up like a torch.

After what seemed like an eternity, the pump shut off and the other attendants rushed out to assist. By the time they reached me, I had removed my shirt and pants and was half way out of my underwear. They immediately hosed down the young attendant and me with fresh water, preventing permanent damage to our eyes or bodies. My only loss was a T-shirt and a pair of jeans.

In retrospect, I still get a chill when I think of what could have happened if someone had been smoking nearby. I also get a laugh when I think of all those Mexicans watching this crazy gringo stripping off his clothes and standing buck naked in the center of their town.

By the way, the station manager gave me a hundred-peso discount (the equivalent of about one dollar) for the amount of gasoline his employee had wasted while trying to fill my tank. One dollar—I could have died a horrible death for it! Sometime, in a strange land far from home, if not in your own neighborhood, you may unexpectedly learn both how cheap the price of life is and how precious life is.

So live life, every day of it, to the fullest. Live; live to the fullest; enjoy!

I have fought a good fight, I have finished my course, I have kept the faith.

II Timothy 4:7

BIBLIOGRAPHY

Albrecht, Karl, and Ron Zemke. *Service America!* Dow Jones-Irwin, 1985.

Barker, Joel Arthur. *Future Edge.* William Morrow & Company, Inc., 1992.

Beer, Michael, Russell A. Eisenstat, and Bert Spector. *The Critical Path to Corporate Renewal.* Harvard Business School Press, 1990.

Champy, James. *Reengineering Management.* HarperCollins, 1995.

Collins, James C., and Jerry I. Porras. *Built to Last.* HarperCollins, 1994.

Drucker, Peter. *Managing for the Future.* Truman Talley Books/Dutton, 1992.

Foster, Richard W. *Innovation: The Attacker's Advantage.* Summit Books, 1986.

Feather, Frank. *The Future Consumer.* Warwich Publishing Inc., 1993.

Garfield, Charles. *Second to None.* The Charles Garfield Group, 1992.

Gilder, George. *The Spirit of Enterprise.* Simon & Schuster, 1984.

Handy, Charles. *The Age of Unreason.* Harvard Business School Press, 1989.

Hickman, Craig R. *Mind of a Manager, Soul of a Leader.* John Wiley & Sons, Inc., 1990.

Kanter, Rosabeth Moss. *The Change Masters.* Simon & Schuster, 1983.

Katz, Donald R. *The Big Store.* Viking, 1987.

Miller, Danny. *The Icarus Paradox.* HarperCollins, 1990.

Miller, Lawrence M. *Barbarians to Bureaucrats.* Clarkson N. Potter, Inc., 1989.

Peters, Tom, and Nancy Austin. *A Passion For Excellence.* Random House, 1985.

Peters, Tom. *Thriving on Chaos.* Alfred A. Knopf, 1987.

Peters, Thomas J., and Robert H. Waterman Jr. *In Search of Excellence.* Harper & Row, 1982.

Peters, Tom. *Liberation Management.* Alfred A. Knopf, 1992.

Rapp, Stan, and Tom Collins. *The Great Marketing Turnaround.* Plume, 1992.

Sculley, John, with John A. Byrne. *Odyssey.* Harper & Row, 1987.

Senge, Peter M. *The Fifth Discipline.* Doubleday Currency, 1990.

Trimble, Vancel. *Sam Walton, the Inside Story of America's Richest Man.* Dutton, 1990.

Toffler, Alvin. *The Third Wave.* William Morrow & Company, Inc., 1980.

Walton, Sam, with John Huey. *Sam Walton: Made in America.* Doubleday, 1992.

Wilson, Larry, with Hersch Wilson. *Stop Selling, Start Partnering.* Oliver Wight Inc., 1994.

Wilson, Larry, with Hersch Wilson. *Changing the Game: The New Way to Sell.* Simon & Schuster, 1987.

Index

Louis A.Pritchett, after an exemplary career of thirty-six years with Procter & Gamble, is delighting audiences worldwide as a top rated speaker. Before he pioneered the partnership between P&G and Wal*Mart, he blazed trails in the Philippines during the Marcos regime, as President and General Manager of P&G's subsidiary in Manila. A lifelong Boy Scout and President of Pritchett Enterprises, Lou currently resides with his wife, Barbara, in Ponte Vedra Beach, Florida. Lou may be contacted at lou@loupritchett.com

978-0-595-44501-1
0-595-44501-2